James Lewis Farley

The resources of Turkey considered with especial reference to the profitable investment of capital in the Ottoman empire

James Lewis Farley

The resources of Turkey considered with especial reference to the profitable investment of capital in the Ottoman empire

ISBN/EAN: 9783337173869

Printed in Europe, USA, Canada, Australia, Japan

Cover: Foto ©Suzi / pixelio.de

More available books at **www.hansebooks.com**

THE
RESOURCES OF TURKEY

CONSIDERED WITH ESPECIAL REFERENCE TO THE

PROFITABLE INVESTMENT OF CAPITAL

IN THE OTTOMAN EMPIRE.

WITH STATISTICS OF THE TRADE AND COMMERCE OF
THE PRINCIPAL COMMERCIAL TOWNS, VIZ. CONSTANTINOPLE, SMYRNA, BROUSSA,
TREBIZOND, SAMSOUN, SALONICA, VOLO, MONASTIR, RHODES, MITYLENE, SCIO, CYPRUS, COS, CRETE,
IBRAILA, GALATZ, ISMAIL, RENI, BEYROUT, JERUSALEM, DAMASCUS, ALEPPO, AINTAB,
MARASH, ORFA, ALEXANDRETTA, TRIPOLI, AND LATAKIA.

By J. LEWIS FARLEY,

Author of 'Two Years in Syria' &c.

LONDON:
LONGMAN, GREEN, LONGMAN, AND ROBERTS.
1862.

TO

M. E. RODOCANACHI, ESQ.

MY DEAR SIR,

In the following pages I have endeavoured to trace the rise and progress of Turkish commerce, and, while engaged in making the necessary researches upon the subject, I have been more and more impressed with the fact that it is to the mercantile community, of which you are one of the principal members, that the extension of British trade in the Ottoman Empire is mainly indebted. In the year 1827 the value of our exports to Turkey amounted only to 531,704*l.*, whilst in 1860 it had increased to the sum of 5,457,839*l.*; and it is to the energy and perseverance of the Greeks, who now supply the connecting link so long wanting between Eastern and Western Europe, that this remarkable progress is to be attributed. The Greeks of the present day possess, in an eminent manner, a thirst for knowledge and improvement, and have carried commercial enterprise to a degree of perfection scarcely paralleled, under similar circumstances, in the history of the world. To that commercial enterprise it is owing that the consumption of our manufactures in Turkey is daily increasing; for our wares, exported chiefly by Greek merchants in the first instance to Alexandria, Beyrout, Smyrna, and Constantinople, are again shipped on board of Greek vessels and carried to

DEDICATION.

the various ports along the coasts of Asia Minor, &c., as well as to the numerous islands of the Ottoman Archipelago.

Under these circumstances, it is not unnatural that I should connect with a work devoted to the commerce of Turkey the name of a house which has so much contributed to the extension of British trade in that Empire. But, in dedicating my book to you, I am, at the same time, actuated by the desire of thus expressing my personal regard for yourself, and my estimation of those qualities, combining the thrift and energy of your race with the generosity and probity of the English merchant, which have obtained for you so universal a respect.

I am, my dear Sir,

Yours very faithfully,

J. LEWIS FARLEY.

PREFACE.

In a country like Turkey, where no statistics are published by the Government, it is exceedingly difficult to arrive at a correct estimate of its Trade and Commerce. An approximate valuation, however, is made, from time to time, by the various Foreign Consulates in the Levant; and, by comparing their official reports one with another, a result sufficiently accurate may be obtained. Of these reports I have freely availed myself in the following pages. My official position for nearly two years, 1857-1858, in Syria, and my residence during the years 1860 and 1861 in Constantinople, where I was appointed Accountant-General of the Bank of Turkey, afforded me many opportunities of obtaining much reliable information; and I am happy to have this opportunity of very sincerely thanking those gentlemen who so obligingly answered the several questions I addressed to them relative to the trade of the various places with which they were personally acquainted. To Mr. Whitaker, Her Britannic Majesty's Acting Vice-Consul at Gallipoli, I am particularly indebted; as also to Mr. Sandison, H. M. Consul, Brussa; Mr. Skene, H. M. Consul, Aleppo; Mr. Finn, H. M. Consul, Jerusalem; Mr. Campbell, H. M.

Consul, Rhodes; Mr. Wilkinson, H. M. Consul, Salonica; and Mr. R. J. Van Lennep, Dutch Consul-General at Smyrna.

At the present moment our capitalists are advancing a large sum of money to Turkey; and it may, therefore, be of some interest to know, as nearly as possible, what the resources of that country are, and to what extent British capital may safely aid in their development.

1 Southwick Crescent,
    Hyde Park, London.

CONTENTS.

CHAPTER		PAGE
I.	General Survey of Turkey	1
II.	Tenure of Land	7
III.	Finances	15
IV.	Agricultural Resources	35
V.	Mineral Resources	50
VI.	The Growth of Cotton	55
VII.	Banking in Turkey	63
VIII.	Constantinople	75
IX.	Smyrna	78
X.	Brussa	102
XI.	Trebizond	116
XII.	Samsoun	128
XIII.	Salonica	132
XIV.	Volo	140
XV.	Monastir	143
XVI.	Bosnia	151
XVII.	Rhodes	156
XVIII.	Mitylene	162
XIX.	Scio	165
XX.	Cyprus	174
XXI.	Cos	182
XXII.	Crete	185
XXIII.	Ibraila	191
XXIV.	Galatz	193
XXV.	Ismail and Reni	198
XXVI.	Syria	203
XXVII.	Beyrout	209
XXVIII.	Jerusalem	227

CHAPTER		PAGE
XXIX.	Damascus	229
XXX.	Aleppo	233
XXXI.	Aintab	243
XXXII.	Marash	248
XXXIII.	Orfa	251
XXXIV.	Alexandretta	253
XXXV.	Tripoli	257
XXXVI.	Latakia	262

APPENDICES.

		PAGE
I.	Treaty of Commerce between Great Britain and Turkey (August 16, 1838)	267
II.	Hatti-Humáyoun of February 18, 1856	272
III.	Treaty of Commerce between Great Britain and Turkey (April 29, 1861)	279

THE RESOURCES OF TURKEY.

CHAPTER I.

GENERAL SURVEY OF TURKEY.

As it is proposed in the following pages to examine the resources of Turkey, and to show what is the extent of the trade and commerce which English capital may develop, it may not be irrelevant or uninteresting to take, in the first place, a general survey of the Ottoman empire, on the subject of which it cannot be denied that much indifference, if not ignorance, exists. Indeed, I have met with persons—even among those whose position demands and should imply a perfect acquaintance with the matter—who possessed so little knowledge of the country as to imagine that all the inhabitants of Turkey are Turks, and that in Syria, an Arab must, necessarily, be a Mussulman. Now, Turkey, though an empire, is not a nation; it is rather an aggregate of nationalities or governments accidentally united by having been the subjects of a common conquest. It includes within its boundaries some of the fairest and most fertile portions of the world, and comprises some of the earliest and most celebrated seats of learning and civilization.*

EXTENT.

The total area of the empire, including the tributary provinces, is estimated at 1,836,478 square miles, and the extent and population of the several grand divisions in Europe, Asia, and Africa are as follow :—

Divisions.	Area. sq. m.	Population.	Popn. to sq. m.
Turkey in Europe	203,628	15,500,000	76·1
Turkey in Asia	673,746	16,050,000	23·8
Turkey in Africa	959,104	3,800,000	3·9
Total	1,836,478	35,350,000	19·2

POPULATION.

The total population, estimated according to the census taken in 1844 at 35,350,000, is distributed as follows, in the different divisions of the empire :—

Turkey in Europe.

Thrace	1,800,000
Bulgaria	3,000,000
Roumelia and Thessaly	2,700,000
	7,500,000

---

* Some objection may, perhaps, be taken to the introduction of the statistics contained in this chapter, but I think they are essential to a correct appreciation of the subject which is principally adverted to in the following pages. They are not inserted to increase the bulk of the work, nor are they in any manner intended as an irrelevant parade of topographical learning. Very few persons in England have any adequate knowledge of Turkish affairs, of the number of provinces, the population of the towns, the difference of races and religions; and this introductory chapter is therefore designed to supply information to my readers on these points,—to show them, in fact, what Turkey is, before they are invited to consider what Turkey may be.

Brought forward	7,500,000
Albania	1,200,000
Bosnia and the Herzegovina	1,100,000
The Islands	700,000
Moldavia	1,400,000
Wallachia	2,600,000
Servia	1,000,000
	15,500,000

Turkey in Asia.

Asia Minor, or Anatolia	10,700,000
Syria, Mesopotamia, and Kurdistan	4,450,000
Arabia	900,000
	16,050,000

Turkey in Africa.

Egypt	2,000,000
Tripoli, Fez, and Tunis	1,800,000
	3,800,000
Total	35,350,000

RACES.

The various races of which the population is composed may be thus classified:—

Races.	In Europe.	In Asia.	In Africa.	Total.
Ottomans	2,100,000	10,700,000	...	12,800,000
Greeks	1,000,000	1,000,000	...	2,000,000
Armenians	400,000	2,000,000	...	2,400,000
Jews	70,000	80,000	...	150,000
Slaves or Slavonians	6,200,000	...	...	6,200,000
Roumains	4,000,000	...	...	4,000,000
Albanians	1,500,000	...	...	1,500,000
Tartars	16,000	20,000	...	36,000
Arabs	...	885,000	3,800,000	4,685,000
Syrians and Chaldeans	...	200,000	...	200,000
Druses	...	80,000	...	80,000
Kurds	...	100,000	...	1,000,000
Turkomans	...	85,000	...	85,000
Gipsies	214,000	...	...	214,000
Total	15,500,000	16,050,000	3,800,000	35,350,000

RELIGIONS.

The classification according to religions is as follows:—

Religion.	In Europe.	In Asia.	In Africa.	Total.
Mussulmans	4,550,000	12,650,000	3,800,000	21,000,000
Greeks and Armenians	10,000,000	3,000,000	...	13,000,000
Catholics *	640,000	260,000	...	900,000
Jews	70,000	80,000	...	150,000
Other sects	240,000	60,000	...	300,000
Total	15,500,000	16,050,000	3,800,000	35,350,000

TERRITORIAL DIVISIONS.

The Turkish empire is divided into eyalets or governments-general, each of which is administered by a Pasha. These eyalets are divided into Sandjaks or provinces, governed by Kaïmakams or Lieutenant-governors. The Sandjaks are subdivided into Kazas or districts, and the Kazas again into Nahizéhs composed of villages or hamlets.

* The term Catholic is applied to the disciples of all the Eastern churches which acknowledge the authority of the See of Rome, although there are amongst them numerous differences in matters of discipline and ceremonial. Of these Eastern Catholics there are:—

1. Latins, or Catholics who use the Roman Liturgy, consisting of Greeks, Armenians, Bulgarians, Croats, &c., to the number of 640,000
2. United Greeks 25,000
3. United Armenians 75,000
4. Syrians and United Chaldeans . . 20,000
5. Maronites (with a Patriarch at Kanobin in Mount Lebanon) . . . . 140,000 — 260,000

Total 900,000

In Turkey in Europe there are 15 Eyalets, divided into 43 Sandjaks and 376 Kazas. In Turkey in Asia, 18 Eyalets, 78 Sandjaks, and 858 Kazas. In Turkey in Africa, 3 Eyalets, 17 Sandjaks, and 86 Kazas.

Turkey in Europe.

	Eyalets.	Chief Towns.	Population of Chief Towns.
1	Edirné (Thrace)	Adrianople	100,000
2	Silistria	Silistria	20,000
3	Boghdan or Moldavia	Jassy	50,000
4	Eflak or Wallachia	Bucharest	80,000
5	Widdin	Widdin	25,000
6	Nisch	Nissa	10,000
7	Uskup	Uskup	
8	Syrp (Servia)	Belgrade	50,000
9	The Fortress of Belgrade.		
10	Bosnia	Serajevo	60,000
11	Roumelia	Monastir	15,000
12	Yania	Janina	30,000
13	Selanik (Salonica)	Salonica	80,000
14	Djizäir (Islands)	Rhodes	30,000
15	Kyrt (Crete)	Candia	20,000

The Eyalets of Silistria, Widdin, and Nisch are formed from the ancient Kingdom of Bulgaria; those of Yania and Selanik (Salonica) comprise the ancient Epirus and Macedonia.

The Eyalets of Uskup and Roumelia are formed from Albania.

The Eyalet of Bosnia is composed of Bosnia, a part of Croatia and of the Herzegovina.

The Eyalet of Djizäir (The Islands) comprises all the islands of the Ottoman Archipelago, of which the principal are Rhodes, Cyprus, Cos, Tenedos, Lemnos, Mitylene, Scio, and Patmos.

Turkey in Asia.

	Eyalets.	Chief Towns.	Population of Chief Towns.
1	Kastamuni	Kastamun	
2	Khowdavendguiar	Brussa	100,000
3	Aïdin	Smyrna	160,000
4	Karaman	Koniyeh	30,000
5	Adana	Adana	6,000
6	Bozok	Angora	60,000
7	Sivas	Sivas	
8	Trabezoun	Trebizond	50,000
9	Erz-rum	Erz-rum	100,000
10	Kurdistan	Diarbekhr	60,000
11	Khabrout	Kharput	
12	Mossul	Mossul	65,000
13	Baghdad	Baghdad	105,000
14	Haleb (Aleppo)	Aleppo	100,000
15	Saïda	Beyrout	50,000
16	Scham	Damascus	180,000
17	Habesh	Djedda	18,000
18	Haremi-Nahevi	Medina	19,000

The Eyalet of Kastamuni comprises the ancient Paphlagonia; that of Khowdavendguiar part of the ancient Bythinia, Phrygia, and Mysia. The Eyalet of Aïdin is formed from part of Isauria, Lydia, Ionia, Caria, and Pisidia; the Eyalet of Karaman contains part of Isauria, Lydia, Pamphylia, Cilicia, Lycaonia, and Cappadocia. That of Adana comprises Cilicia Petræa; those of Bozok and Sivas, Cappadocia; while Trabezoun (Trebizond) is formed from the ancient provinces of Pontus and Colchis.

Turkey in Africa.

	Eyalets.	Chief Towns.	Population of Chief Towns.
1	Miar (Egypt)	Cairo	250,000
2	Tharablousi Garb (African Tripoli)	Tripoli	20,000
3	Tunis	Tunis	200,000

CHAPTER II.

TENURE OF LAND.

THE different classifications of land in Turkey, according to the tenures under which it is held, are four in number:—

1. Miri, or crown lands.
2. Vacouf, or pious foundations.
3. Malikaneh, or crown grants.
4. Mulkh, or freehold property.

1. The *miri*, or crown lands, forming by far the largest portion of the territory of the Sultan, are held direct from him; and his Government grants the right to cultivate an unoccupied tract on the payment of certain fees, which, of course, vary in proportion to its value. The deed which gives the applicant a title to the grant has the Sultan's cypher attached, and the possession of this document ensures the property to the holder and his heirs, while at the same time it forbids its alienation. The Sultan, however, still continues to exercise the rights of seigniory over the land in question, as is implied in the condition that if the owner neglects to cultivate it for a period of three years, it is forfeited to the crown. Although it is illegal to alienate this kind of property, the proprietor nevertheless reserves to himself the right of transferring the usufruct to another. This must be done in presence of the

municipal council, and the deed of transfer is sent to Constantinople to be ratified by the Government. The difficulties encountered in carrying out this operation, such as the loss of time, &c., tend materially to prevent land from changing hands, much to the detriment of agriculture, which thus often suffers from the want of capital.

The landlord seldom cultivates the soil himself, but lets it out to tenants, who, being poor villagers, look to the owner for the necessary supply of farming stock. The most common form of contract is that of *ortakgulik* or partnership. The proprietor, in addition to the use of his land and a cottage rent free, furnishes the seed; the labourer provides cattle and agricultural implements; and the annual produce, after the tithes are paid to the Government, is equally divided between landlord and cultivator. This equable division of capital and labour is apparently favourable to the peasant, and, were the conditions always faithfully observed, he ought undoubtedly to prosper. But the proprietor almost invariably contrives, through injustice and oppression, and sometimes the improvidence of the labourer himself, to involve him in debt; and such is the usurious rate of interest, that this is continually increasing, so that the labourers, as a class, are in a general state of comparative serfdom to the proprietor.

In other cases the farmer, instead of entering into a contract of partnership with the proprietor of the soil, prefers to borrow a sum of money sufficient to carry on a year's farming operations, the lender receiving either his money back with interest or an equivalent share of the produce. But once in the hands of a saraff,*

---

* A Saraff is a Native Banker.

the unfortunate farmer is quite certain to be victimized. I could give many instances of the manner in which the peasantry are plundered by the native bankers, but the following, that came under the personal observation of a gentleman resident for many years in Turkey, will sufficiently illustrate the importance of establishing institutions of credit which would in time relieve the agricultural classes from the burdens that oppress them. A farmer, who a few years ago had been reputed wealthy in his kaza, was peremptorily called upon by the saraff for repayment of a debt of 13,000 piastres. As he could not immediately raise the money, sundry farming and household necessaries were seized, and, being doubtless undervalued, passed into account for 4000 piastres: for the balance, the unfortunate debtor was compelled to transfer his right to 360 of the finest olive-trees in the district, for which, immediately on possession, his creditor refused sixty piastres per tree, or 21,600 piastres for what barely cost him 9000! The estimated value of these trees when in full bearing condition, to which they were again approximating, was from 100 to 120 piastres each, with the certain prospect of future enhancement, from the vast destruction of similar property during the previous winter. Another example will also illustrate what I have said. An industrious farmer in the neighbourhood of Smyrna was in sad perplexity about a debt of 21,000 piastres, that had been long accumulating: the more he paid, the more it appeared to increase. A casual visitor in the district, an European, was induced to look into the accounts, and with great difficulty elicited therefrom the following facts:—The original sum of 2700 piastres had been advanced seven years before; during the interval the debtor had paid in various shapes 16,000 piastres, and was still indebted in a balance of 21,000 piastres, which the party who undertook to investigate the accounts succeeded in reducing to 9000! The account, it appeared, had been made up and computed at monthly compound interest, repayable periodically in produce, at fixed rates; but as it was clearly never the intention of the creditor to lose such a customer, part of the produce was periodically received, and part allowed to remain over, the difference between contract price and market value being regularly added to the debt.

It is by no means an unusual circumstance for an usurer — banker or merchant may be the title he assumes — to enter into a stipulation with the elders of a village, whereby, for certain considerations, he engages to supply the villagers with funds and materials necessary for agricultural purposes. In thus constituting himself the village banker, he charges a monthly interest on his running account, and takes his reimbursement out of the produce raised, with the option, if the value of such produce exceeds the debt, of appropriating the whole at opening prices. Accordingly, he furnishes seed, provender, and all the materials for domestic and agricultural use, loaded with a premium of fifty to a hundred per cent. or more; he advances the money which may, from time to time, be requisite for the payment of taxes and other incidental claims, exacting the interest for each advance at rates varying from two to five and six per cent. per month. When the crops are matured, and the villagers assemble to fix the opening prices, if — as is usually the case, from the circumstance of such engagements being known — the usurer remains without a competitor, the produce passes into his hands at so low a valuation that it is impossible to discharge his claims; and thus a portion of his advances remains in the form of a permanent debt, which enables him to impose more onerous conditions for the ensuing season. If competitors should offer for the produce, and threaten to drive up the opening prices — a circumstance that rarely happens — he demands immediate restitution of his advances, with the alternative of arrest and imprisonment. Unless therefore his rivals are themselves prepared to acquit the debt, their superior offers are rejected, and they are compelled to retire from the field. This is the more easy to enforce, as the varied crops of Turkey being matured at different periods of the year, the value of ready produce, for which the casual buyer bids, will not cover the aggregate disbursements or cancel the claims of the local banker. Thus the village debt is never liquidated, and varies in amount according as good or bad harvests predominate; the inevitable result follows that the whole of the fixed property, such as vineyards and similar plantations, eventually changes hands. In some Sandjaks, whole districts, and in others detached villages, are in this deplorable condition. Once entangled in the meshes of these usurers, the independence of the peasantry is irrevocably lost. Debt and usury is the incubus which weighs most heavily on the agricultural resources of Turkey, and the proprietor who avails himself of these means to plunder the labourer is, in his turn, victimized by the capitalist, who profits by his sloth and prodigality to obtain possession of his property when payment can no longer be obtained from his revenue.

2. The tenure of *Vacouf* is more complete in its nature, and is of two kinds:—*Vacouf-el-Zaräi* and *Vacouf-el-Karamaïn*. The object of both is to pro-

vide for the religion of the State and the education of the people, by the erection of mosques and schools, besides eleemosynary institutions.

The *Vacouf-el-Zaräi* is land or other immovable property, originally obtained by grants from the crown, and entailed, not on the holder's natural heir, but on the eldest surviving member of his family. The grant is sometimes conceded for a limited period only, but generally in perpetuity. Analogous to this tenure is that which entails the property on all the descendants of the grantee in common, and as in such cases the inheritors in process of time become exceedingly numerous, those who are so disposed can, for an equivalent in money, alienate their right to the property.

The *Vacouf-el-Karamaïn* is property bequeathed by private individuals for the same pious purposes as enumerated above, more especially, however, for the erection of caravanseries, fountains, wells, and other accommodations for the convenience of those who make the pilgrimage to the holy cities; the object of the testators being to place it in the power of the poorest, by means of these pious legacies, to fulfil the great religious duty of visiting the tomb and birthplace of the Prophet. Property of this kind descends from father to son, and is inalienable, though means are found to evade the law by letting the land for such a length of time as to be tantamount to a sale. Through the operation of causes peculiar to the religion and government of the country, an examination of which would not, however, be within the scope of the present work, the tenure bearing the name of *Vacouf* now embraces a vast amount of property beyond the original grants for the purposes named.

The system of transfers called *âdet* (customary), which took its rise at a time when the ægis of "the church" was the most efficient, if not the only, protection *against* the rapacity of the Government, has continued and extended until at the present day the *Vacouf* class comprises a considerable portion of the whole house and landed property of the empire.*

3. The land called *Malikaneh* was chiefly held by Spahis, the old feudal troops to whom were awarded considerable grants in recompense for the military service required of them, and in particular for the safe conduct of the caravans of pilgrims on their way to Mecca. This property is hereditary, the payment of a fee by the heir being all that is required to make the succession valid, and, as it is exempt from tithe, the value of the tenure by *Malikaneh* is considerably enhanced. Of late years, however, when it has been found that the possessors died without direct heirs, these grants have been revoked; and it appears to be the intention, as it is plainly the interest of the Government, to annul grants the conditions attached to which have become obsolete, while at the same time they contribute nothing to the support of the State. The same laws forbidding the sale of land, and the same means for evading them, apply to this kind of property as to the preceding.

* As the *Vacoufs* are exempt from all taxation, the loss to the Treasury by this species of property is immense. Sultan Mahmoud II. meditated at one time their entire re-conversion into *miri* or crown lands, intending to provide for the religious institutions out of the general revenue; but pious scruples, or considerations of State policy, interfered to preserve the *Vacoufs* as a rich source of wealth to their administrators, and of costly embarrassment to the Government. It is said, however, that the subject is again under consideration by the present Sultan Abdul-Aziz.

4. *Mulkh*, or freehold property, is naturally the tenure most advantageous to occupiers. A great proportion of house property in the towns and of the land in the neighbourhood of villages is *mulkh*, which the peasants purchase from time to time from the Government, on very moderate terms. As it is freehold, they can of course dispose of it at their pleasure, and they are interested in its being improved, as Government has no right over it beyond that of claiming the tithe of the produce. To have a valid claim to land held by this tenure, the estate must be registered in books kept for that purpose by the municipal council. The prosperity of the last few years has created a competition for this species of property, and in many places the value of land has consequently increased fifty or sixty per cent. In the same proportion as freehold property is acquired by agricultural labourers, we may reasonably look for improvement in their social condition; though from their ignorance of the uses of capital, natural to a primitive people, they find at present few fields for profitable investment, and, from the want of institutions in which their money could be safely deposited, are too frequently tempted to bury, or otherwise conceal their superfluous wealth.

CHAPTER III.

FINANCES.

The system of raising the revenue in Turkey differs very much from ours, as, instead of imposing unequal burdens by indirect taxation, the Ottoman government follows the systems of all the great empires of antiquity, the Assyrian, Babylonian, the Roman, the Persian under Cyrus, the Macedonian under Alexander, and the French under Charlemagne, in raising their revenue chiefly by direct taxation. But the ruinous system which has prevailed since the reign of Mohammed II., of permitting the taxes to be farmed, causes the finances of the country to be in a comparatively low condition. "The best and most frugal way of levying a tax," says Adam Smith, " can never be by farm. Over and above what is necessary for paying the stipulated rent, the salaries of the officers, and the whole expense of administration, the farmer must always draw from the produce of the tax a certain profit, proportioned at least to the advance which he makes, to the risk which he runs, to the trouble which he is at, and to the knowledge and skill which it requires to manage so very complicated a concern. Government, by establishing an administration under their own immediate inspection, of the same kind with that which the farmer establishes, might at least save this profit, which is almost always exorbitant. To farm any considerable branch of the public revenue requires either a great capital or a great credit; circumstances which would alone restrict the competition for such an undertaking to a very small number of people. Of the few who have this capital or credit, a still smaller number have the necessary knowledge or experience; another circumstance which restricts the competition still further. The very few who are in a condition to become competitors find it more for their interests to combine together, to become co-partners instead of competitors, and, where the farm is set up to auction, to offer no rent but what is much below the real value. In countries where the public revenues are in farm, the farmers are generally the most opulent people." . .

. . "They (the farmers) have no bowels for the contributors, who are not their subjects, and whose universal bankruptcy, if it should happen the day after their farm is expired, would not much affect their interest. Even a bad sovereign feels more compassion for his people than can ever be expected from the farmers of his revenue. He knows that the permanent grandeur of his family depends upon the prosperity of his people, and he will never knowingly ruin that prosperity for the sake of any momentary interest of his own. It is otherwise with the farmers of his revenue, whose grandeur may frequently be the effect of his ruin and not of the prosperity of his people."

In France, in 1775, the greater part of the actual revenue of the Crown was derived from eight different sources, five of which were under farm, and three levied by an administration under the immediate inspection and direction of government, and it was

CHAPTER III.

FINANCES.

THE system of raising the revenue in Turkey differs very much from ours, as, instead of imposing unequal burdens by indirect taxation, the Ottoman government follows the systems of all the great empires of antiquity, the Assyrian, Babylonian, the Roman, the Persian under Cyrus, the Macedonian under Alexander, and the French under Charlemagne, in raising their revenue chiefly by direct taxation. But the ruinous system which has prevailed since the reign of Mohammed II., of permitting the taxes to be farmed, causes the finances of the country to be in a comparatively low condition. "The best and most frugal way of levying a tax," says Adam Smith, "can never be by farm. Over and above what is necessary for paying the stipulated rent, the salaries of the officers, and the whole expense of administration, the farmer must always draw from the produce of the tax a certain profit, proportioned at least to the advance which he makes, to the risk which he runs, to the trouble which he is at, and to the knowledge and skill which it requires to manage so very complicated a concern. Government, by establishing an administration under their own immediate inspection, of the same kind with that which the farmer establishes, might at least save this profit, which is almost always exorbitant. To farm any considerable branch of the public revenue requires either a great capital or a great credit; circumstances which would alone restrict the competition for such an undertaking to a very small number of people. Of the few who have this capital or credit, a still smaller number have the necessary knowledge or experience; another circumstance which restricts the competition still further. The very few who are in a condition to become competitors find it more for their interests to combine together, to become co-partners instead of competitors, and, where the farm is set up to auction, to offer no rent but what is much below the real value. In countries where the public revenues are in farm, the farmers are generally the most opulent people." . .

. . "They (the farmers) have no bowels for the contributors, who are not their subjects, and whose universal bankruptcy, if it should happen the day after their farm is expired, would not much affect their interest. Even a bad sovereign feels more compassion for his people than can ever be expected from the farmers of his revenue. He knows that the permanent grandeur of his family depends upon the prosperity of his people, and he will never knowingly ruin that prosperity for the sake of any momentary interest of his own. It is otherwise with the farmers of his revenue, whose grandeur may frequently be the effect of his ruin and not of the prosperity of his people."

In France, in 1775, the greater part of the actual revenue of the Crown was derived from eight different sources, five of which were under farm, and three levied by an administration under the immediate inspection and direction of government, and it was universally acknowledged that in proportion to what the latter took out of the pockets of the people, they brought more into the treasury than the other five, of which the administration was much more wasteful and expensive.

With regard to Turkey, I have not the least doubt that if direct collection of the taxes were substituted for the present system of farms, the revenue would, in a very short time, be doubled. As an example of what might be done if the taxes were levied by an administration under the immediate inspection of government, I may instance the fact that the Customs of Bosnia and the Herzegovina, from the 13th of March, 1852, to the 13th of March, 1853, were sold by auction to a native company for 705,000 piastres, and the company made 80,000 piastres by the speculation. This would give the sum of 6776$l.$ for the Customs of the year 1852. In the year 1853 the Turkish Government resolved to take them on its own account; and the result of good management was that in that year they realised 23,980$l.$, and in 1854, 24,182$l.$

The revenue of Turkey is chiefly derived from taxes of three denominations — the Verghi, the Aashr, and the Roussoumiat.

The Verghi, which corresponds to our *income tax*, is a tax on the whole population of about fifty dollars for each house or family. When the last census was taken in 1844, a certain number of families of each religious denomination were ascertained to belong to a particular village or town; the sum to be required was calculated and the collection left to the heads of the different communities, who are supposed to tax the rich according to their means, so as to supply what cannot be paid by families too poor to afford their share of the burden. As may be imagined, the collection of this tax is often a means of oppression in the hands of those entrusted with it, particularly as, notwithstanding any changes in circumstances or population among the different towns or villages, the sum originally fixed when the census was taken is generally required. Thus it happens that some villages, the population of which has decreased, are very heavily taxed, until at last the burden becomes such that the inhabitants desert their homes altogether. Other villages which were formerly small have, on the other hand, greatly increased, and still only pay the small amount originally fixed upon. About ten years ago, an endeavour was made to rectify this inequality by an imperfect re-adjustment of the taxation, in certain districts, but Government interests will continue to suffer until a more effective remedial measure be taken, in the shape of a new census.

The Aashr or tithe is a tax of ten per cent. upon the produce of cultivation, and is farmed out in districts or villages to the highest bidder. The farmer of the tax does not permit the crops to be cut until it suits his convenience to attend in person, or, at all events, till he sends some one to see that he is not defrauded. Thus, it is not at all unusual to see crops standing for three weeks after they are fully ripe, so that in the process of reaping they must shed at least half the produce.

It is not the fiscal dues imposed by the State which are burdensome to the people; on the contrary, taxation in Turkey is much lighter than in most other countries. It is the abuses of collection, the extortion of the revenue farmers or their agents, and the usurious rates of interest charged by the Saraffs that oppress the agriculturist, and by retarding the development of the vast natural resources of the empire, prevent her from taking that position, among the commercial nations of Europe, to which by nature she is eminently entitled.

The Roussoumiat is revenue derived from the sale of the customs, stamps, the sale of animals, taxes on shops, bakeries, butcheries, mills, &c., &c., and from the rent of lands belonging to the crown. The receipts of the customs are derived from a duty of 5 per cent. *ad valorem* on all descriptions of foreign goods imported, whether raw or manufactured; 3 per cent. being charged on landing the said goods, and 2 per cent. being due on their sale in the port of disembarkation, or on conveyance into the interior. This charge is moderate; but the interference of the Legislature with the exportation of the produce or manufactures, by means of an export duty of 12 per cent., systematically violates the best understood and acknowledged principles of economical law, for, as compared with the 5 per cent. charged on foreign imported merchandise, Turkish goods, on exportation, are saddled with an additional burden of 7 per cent., an inequality which, of course, acts as a direct obstruction to a reciprocity of trade. This tax, although prejudicial, is, however, much less so than the system which it replaced. Before the time of Reschid Pasha, individuals and firms bought from the Government the exclusive right to purchase the produce of a district or of a province. One man had the monopoly of wheat, another of barley, another of tobacco, and so on. The monopolist fixed his own price, and, of course, resold, either to the retailers or to the exporters, at a large profit. Reschid abolished this practice, and every one now does as he likes with what he produces. But the sale of these monopolies gave an important revenue, and an export duty of 12 per cent.

was therefore substituted, viz., 9 per cent. on all commodities transported from one province to another, and 3 per cent. additional if exported by sea.

A new treaty of commerce, however, has been concluded between Great Britain and Turkey, by which the duty on imports will be raised from 5 to 8 per cent. *ad valorem*, while the duty on exports will be reduced from 12 to 8 per cent. This export duty of 8 per cent. will be annually reduced by 1 per cent. until it shall in this manner be finally reduced to a fixed duty of 1 per cent., *ad valorem*, destined to cover the general expenses of administration and control. Similar conventions have been concluded between the Porte and France, as well as with the Italian Government.*

Of the above-mentioned sources of revenue, the Verghi remains pretty nearly the same each year, but the Aashr and Roussoumiat are continually varying according to the state of the crops, harvests, and other circumstances.

It is not within the scope of the present volume to enter upon the important question of financial reform, but, nevertheless, I think it will not be out of place if, relying upon a personal and practical acquaintance with the condition and resources of the country obtained during a long residence in Constantinople and other portions of the empire, I take this opportunity of stating that there is nothing in the financial condition of Turkey which need create alarm or distrust. When a country is overwhelmed with debt, with an enormous deficit in its budget, without power of retrenchment, and with its resources exhausted, then, indeed, the statesman and financier, however great their ability and skill,

* See Appendix No. 3.

may well despair of being able to retrieve the public credit. But in a country whose debts do not exceed some three years' revenue, where large retrenchments may be made without injury to the public service, where taxation is only oppressive by its unequal distribution, and where immense resources abound on every side, a temporary deficit in the budget, although it may be for the moment a source of considerable embarrassment to the Government, cannot afford a legitimate ground for anxiety or fear.

The able report just presented to His Imperial Majesty the Sultan Abdul-Aziz by his Highness Fuad Pasha, the Grand Vizier, enters very fully into the past situation of the country, and gives a clear and straightforward analysis of the present financial position of the empire.* According to this document the receipts and expenditure for the year 1861 were as follow :—

* The following is a translation of the report of His Highness the Grand Vizier, Fuad Pasha, to His Imperial Majesty the Sultan Abdul-Aziz, upon the financial situation of the empire, and the means to be taken in order to re-establish an equilibrium between the revenue and expenditure of the country.

IMPERIAL EDICT.

I fully approve all the measures contained in this report, and I hereby order that the same be carried out, and without delay.

Sire,—The Imperial Hatt, issued on the 18 Redjeb, 1278 (1862), advising the adoption of prompt and efficacious measures, in order to improve the financial state of the empire, proclaimed at the same time the principle of credit, the basis of every system of finance, and pointed out to the Government of your Imperial Majesty the means of insuring a favourable solution.

In fact, public credit is the lever of all the wonders of our age, and the terms on which kingdoms obtain it are, first, economy in their administration—that is to say, the employment of the public money in matters useful to the State; and, secondly, the faithful fulfilment of all obligations entered into.

The Imperial Hatt is being carried out; special budgets are being prepared in all the Ministerial departments, and the efforts of Government will be devoted to arranging the accounts, under due control, of every

General total of the revenues	£11,164,552
General total of the expenses	12,739,088
Leaving a deficit of	£1,574,536

department, so that they may be published at the beginning of the next financial year.

The Government need not go far back in its financial annals to trace the first insufficiency of the ordinary resources of the Treasury. The very recent date of Turkey's first appeal to public credit in Europe proves this, and the small amount of its deficit, in comparison with the public debt of other countries, shows the moderate extent of the need which has arisen. It was only in 1270 (1854) and 1271 (1855) that the balance between the revenues and the expenses of the empire was disturbed. This was the result of a most expensive war, and, later, of considerable expenses caused by precautionary measures, which the general state of the world rendered necessary.

Moreover, a rigid economy has not always been practised in the internal expenses; and it cannot be denied that this circumstance has also tended to keep up and increase the derangement of the finances. Owing to these circumstances, the Treasury not being able to meet punctually all its engagements, the Government was obliged, on the one hand, to have recourse to the dangerous system of paper money, and on the other to collecting the taxes in advance, to onerous loans, as well as to other measures equally ruinous, which have led to the present embarrassments of the country.

None of these events are to be ascribed to the reign of your Imperial Majesty, who has only inherited the difficulties of the past. Your firm determination is to put an end to them, and the happy effects of the commands of your Majesty, who requires that every one shall submit to the principle of economy which your Majesty has personally adopted since your accession, are daily becoming more and more manifest.

The prompt and satisfactory improvement which, with Divine aid, is about to be effected in our finances, does not admit of the least doubt. I hasten therefore to obey the orders of your Imperial Majesty, who has commanded me, as the first of my duties, to lay before you the state of the finances of your empire, and to submit at the same time the measures likely to effect the amelioration desired.

The total of the floating debt of the Treasury, constituting a deficiency which the ordinary and extraordinary resources of the empire have been insufficient to meet, amounts to 4,000,000 purses (18,284,800*l.*), of which one-half is represented by the paper money in circulation, and the other half by special debts contracted under various heads. The paper money is one of the most evident causes—indeed, the real cause—of our present difficulties and of the discredit of our finances. The date of the introduction of paper money coincides with that of administrative reform.

The outlay for the year 1862 will be further increased by the interest and sinking fund on the new English

It was used as a temporary means to remedy the delays in collecting the revenue, caused by important changes introduced at that period in the civil and financial administration of the empire.

Later, the causes mentioned above having rendered it necessary to persevere in this measure, the paper money (the quantity of which has varied at different periods) has at length attained its present amount.

Your Imperial Majesty is well aware that paper money, which has no real equivalent value, is but a ficticious means of credit. It is equal to the depreciation in the value of the exchange, and incessantly disturbs all commercial affairs. This, reacting on the credit of the State, never fails to insure the most distressing results.

The circulation of the Caïmé (paper money) has always been confined to the capital; but Constantinople, being neither an agricultural district nor a manufacturing town, is obliged to draw its supplies from Europe, or else from the interior of the empire. Constantinople is therefore additionally compelled to provide itself with specie, as the Caïmé could not be sent to Europe, and is not current in the provinces. In proportion as the demand for specie, while raising the price of coin, naturally reduced the value of the paper money, the burden of which depreciation Constantinople alone was unable to bear, it was intended, from the necessity of leaving the Caïmé in circulation, to extend this system to the provinces, in order to modify the effects of a circulation which weighed exclusively on the capital. On the presumption that this necessity would be prolonged, it seemed that no other measure could be adopted; but it is evident that, if Constantinople has suffered in its commercial intercourse with Europe in consequence of the depreciation of the paper money, the empire in all parts would suffer from the same causes in its relations with the rest of the world.

Numerous instances in history confirm these remarks. Paper money has been current in different States of Europe; England, France, the United States of America, Sweden, and Denmark cannot but remember it. Russia and Austria suffer to this day from their dearly-bought experience.

Even if it were possible to fix the limit to which these issues might be reduced without much danger, still it would not prevent the value of paper money undergoing frequent fluctuations, whether from the effect of commercial movement or from alarm to public confidence.

It is therefore undoubted that the issue of paper money is not a wise financial measure on the part of the Government of your Majesty, but evidently a dangerous expedient to be adopted only in cases of emergency.

It would be impossible to estimate accurately the losses on exchange and home loans, as well as on the new stock of consolidated floating debt; while, on the other hand, the re-

which the currency of the paper money at Constantinople causes to commerce and to the Imperial Treasury. But, as regards the Treasury alone, it would not be far from truth to estimate them at 500,000 to 600,000 purses annually (2,000,000*l.* to 3,000,000*l.*) These losses were well known, and the Government of your Imperial Majesty has submitted to many sacrifices in the hope of getting rid of the cause. Indeed, at one time there remained but a small quantity of paper money in circulation, and yet the difficulties caused by other liabilities obliged the Government to annul the measures which had been adopted; and not only were they an obstacle to the final withdrawal of the paper money, but entailed the necessity of again having recourse to it.

The Caïmés are a sort of debt on the part of the Government, who should make every effort to discharge it, for more than one reason. But under the pressure of the extraordinary circumstances related above, and in presence of liabilities of some importance (to which must also be added the losses in exchange caused by the depreciation of the paper money), the Imperial Treasury, to meet these liabilities, was obliged to make use of revenue assigned to the urgent requirements of the army and navy, and of the other departments of the Administration. Moreover, in order to meet other indispensable expenses the Government was obliged, on the one hand, to contract onerous loans, and on the other to guarantee them by making over in advance its ordinary revenues, so that the losses which were entailed on the Treasury, and the amount of its liabilities, were continually increasing.

Nevertheless, since the accession of your Imperial Majesty, the measures of economy adopted in conformity with your commands, and the sacrifices which have been made, have considerably reduced the amount of these liabilities, and according to recent investigations, they now form a floating debt of about 2,000,000 purses (9,142,400*l.*) Add the debt resulting from the Caïmés in circulation, and these are the only obstacles to the regular discharge of the public service.

Before submitting to your Majesty the ways and means which appear to me best adapted for regulating the liabilities resulting from the floating debt, including the Caïmés, so as to get rid of them for the future, it is necessary to inquire what are the wants of the public service, and what resources the Imperial Treasury has at its disposal to meet them.

The general budget of the ensuing year is in course of preparation; but, as it has not been possible to complete it in time, the budget of the year 1277 (1860-61) will, for the moment, serve as a basis for the estimates. It will be seen by the tabular statement annexed, which I have the honour to submit to your Imperial Majesty, that the budget of the expenditure of this last year comprises four great divisions, under the

ceipts will be augmented by the proceeds of new taxes and by various proposed economies in the different following heads:—1. External debt; 2. Internal debt; 3. Civil list and pensions; 4. the sums allowed to the department of each Minister.

The external debt resulting from the four Loans contracted in 1271 (1854), 1272 (1855), 1275 (1858), and 1277 (1860–1861), represents a redeemable capital of 3,300,000 purses (15,084,960*l*.) entailing a charge on the budget of 1277 (1860-61) for interest and sinking fund of

	Purses.	£
The external debt ... interest and sinking fund of	209,498	957,657
The internal debt comprises a portion of the floating debt and of the consolidated debt; these, under the names of Tahvilati Mumtazés, and of Eshami Djedides, require annually	125,000	571,400
The total of the consolidated debts, or one-eighth of the expenditure	334,498	£1,529,057
Add the consolidated Eshamis, the Serghis of 10 years, &c.	319,514	£1,460,562
	654,012	£2,989,619
The third division comprises the civil list, divers pensions granted to retired functionaries, presents sent to Mecca, &c.	398,851 399	£1,823,231
Finally, the fourth division is intended to meet the sums required for paying the public services dependent on each Ministerial department	1,733,951 145	£7,926,238
General total of expenditure	2,786,815 044	£12,739,088

The budget of receipts is subdivided into six heads, under the following denominations:—1. Direct taxes; 2. Indirect taxes; 3. Public establishments; 4. Special products and divers duties; 5. Tributes; 6. Special revenues accruing to some of the Ministerial departments.

	Purses Psts.	
The whole of these revenues amount to	2,442,368 169	£11,164,552
The expenses as stated above being	2,786,815 044	£12,739,088
There would be a deficit of	344,446 375	£1,574,536

It is necessary to observe here that the revenues of 1277 (1860–61) were naturally influenced by the critical circumstances which the Trea-

departments of the State. Thus by a reduction of expenditure on the one hand, and the imposition of new sury had to encounter, and also that the expenditure was increased by the same causes.

As already stated above, the total of the Caïmés in circulation, and of the floating debt, is estimated at about four millions of purses (18,284,800*l.*); but this sum, which exceeds the amount put down in the official registers, includes also the deficit of the budget of last year, estimated at about 300,000 purses (1,371,360*l.*), and it has been set down at 4,000,000 in order to insure the greatest possible accuracy when the expenditure shall be definitively settled.

The summary of the actual state of the Treasury shows a deficiency of—

	Purses.	£
1. In Caïmés	2,000,000	9,142,400
2. In floating debt	2,000,000	9,142,400
And an ordinary deficit of 344,446 purses	4,000,000	£18,284,800

Compared with other countries, it is only very recently that Turkey has experienced a deficiency of revenue and has been obliged to have recourse to loans. No doubt it would have been much better if both could have been avoided, but the amount need not cause the slightest apprehension, either for the present or the future.

In comparing the budget of the Ottoman empire with that of some of other States which were long ago obliged to consolidate their debts in arrear, and continue periodically the same course, it should be stated that the amount of the Ottoman public debt which it is intended to consolidate is relatively very small.

For example, in England, on a total expenditure in 1850 of 12,636,800 purses (1,436 millions francs), a sum of 6,292,000 purses (715 millions francs) was required to pay the interest on the public debt.

In France, in 1850, the budget amounted to 12,584,000 purses (1,434 millions francs), and from this a third had to be deducted to meet the interest on the public debt.

In the United States, in 1848 to 1849, the Federal budget amounted to 2,701,600 purses (307 millions francs), and more than one-fourth was required for the interest on the public debt.

In Austria the budget amounts to about 6,456,400 purses (738 millions francs), one-fifth of which is required to pay the interest on the national debt.

In Turkey, where the budget amounts to 2,786,815 purses (12,739,088*l.*), 334,498 purses (1,529,057*l.*) are required for the payment of the interest on the consolidated debt, or only about one-eighth.

taxes on the other, an excess of revenue may be anticipated of 898,483*l.* for the current year. The probable

The measures taken by some of the Governments of Europe at certain periods of their history to meet the insufficiency of their resources are well known. The state of the Imperial Treasury is not such as would justify the exceptional measures adopted by those Governments for the safety of the State.

In order to meet the existing deficit and redeem the public debt, there are two sources to which the Government may legitimately have recourse—viz., taxes and loans.

In Turkey the amount of taxation paid by each individual is forty-five piastres; in England it is probably more than 300 piastres, and in France it exceeds 250.

This portion of taxation paid by each individual shows the wealth of nations. It is not meant to affirm that in countries where the amount of taxation per head is small it can be raised to a level with those most heavily taxed; but as far as Turkey is concerned, in spite of the imperfection of her system of taxation, which, however, has been much improved in several parts of the empire, it is evident that the taxes per head are too low. It may, therefore, be reasonably concluded that the public taxes might be increased on many articles for which its population at present is too lightly taxed.

The collecting of the tithes is in a great measure withdrawn from the hands of the contractors (*fermiers*), and intrusted directly to those of the people, who derive the same benefits therefrom as were accorded to the former. The laws relating to stamps, licences, and other taxes, which produce such large revenues in all other countries, are put in force again and made more perfect; an important increase in revenue from these sources may therefore be expected. Further, conformably with the new treaties of commerce entered into with the allied Powers, salt and tobacco become a Government monopoly. Tobacco, so far from being an article of absolute necessity, is simply one of luxury, and all States derive therefrom considerable revenues. In subjecting the tobacco consumed in the interior of the empire to a tax which will not in any way affect its cultivation, and which will be proportioned to the means of the population, a revenue will be obtained which, although at first not so considerable as that derived from it in some other countries, will still be very large.

As regards salt, it is true that it constitutes one of the urgent wants of the people, but its consumption, per head, is insignificant. This article is in other countries heavily taxed. In Turkey, the salt-pits belonging exclusively to the State, the sale of salt will also be very productive, although it might be much less than the quantity made.

The 30,000 purses (137,136*l.*), or thereabouts, required for the working

receipts and expenditure for the year 1862 may, therefore, be summed up as follows :—

and proper administration of the mines and forests may be taken from the capital required for the extinction of the debt, and it may be predicted that this measure will produce at once large returns from these two sources, which cannot fail to increase considerably in future.

Besides the resources which have been enumerated, the duties of the Custom-house, which were formerly so low, have been altered and fixed in conformity with the real value of the merchandise. These new duties will alone produce an increase of 30 per cent., and, notwithstanding the annual diminution which is to take place in the duties on the exports in conformity with the new treaties, and which will be balanced by other revenues, it is proved by investigations made, that the surplus which will be obtained by the increase of duties on imports will add largely to the revenue.

It may, therefore, be fairly presumed that the resources above stated, exclusive of the budget of 1277 (1860-61), will produce a total increase in the receipts of 715,000 purses (3,268,408$l.$) Moreover, if the paper money be withdrawn, thereby avoiding the loss now caused in the exchange, and the different Ministerial departments receive their allowances in time to enable them to pay for their purchases regularly and in ready money, the Treasury would further save 150,000 purses (685,680$l.$)

Such are the measures which cannot fail to increase the resources of the Treasury.

With regard to a loan, the proposals which have been made to us respecting this matter by an eminent banking firm in Europe have been accepted. The produce of this loan, added to the resources which the Government is receiving from the interior, and of which a portion has been already paid, will suffice for insuring the settlement of the various debts of the Imperial Treasury.

The basis for the consolidation of these debts has not yet been definitively fixed, but a portion of these liabilities will be paid in specie; salaries and pensions will not form part of the consolidation, but will also be paid in full and in specie. To sum up, the consolidated debts of the empire with the interest as well as the floating debt, to be arranged, and the money required for the purpose—in short, the interest which the Treasury will have to pay for these sums, will not really be of any considerable amount. On the other hand, the measures to be adopted are far from onerous, compared with those which have been taken by other countries under pressure of circumstances; but in this country it will be necessary to put into practice these measures so as to meet the liabilities contracted in the interior of the empire as well as those contracted abroad. This result can only be attained by establishing an equilibrium

FINANCES.

RECEIPTS.

Receipts of the Budget of 1861		£11,164,552
Proceeds of proposed new taxes in 1862, viz. :—		
Tobacco	£457,120	
Salt	548,544	
Stamps	182,848	
Licenses and excise duties on spirits	182,848	
Surplus from revenues of Vacouf	137,136	
Direct taxes at Constantinople	91,424	
Forests and mines	45,712	
Increase in Customs' dues under new Treaty of Commerce	914,240	
Increase on the *Verghi* tax	228,560	
,, tithes	342,840	
From horse-shoes (tax on horses)	45,712	
,, *Tapous* (transfers of landed property)	91,424	3,268,408
Total of the receipts		£14,432,960

---

between the expenditure and the receipts, so soon as we shall have received the funds required for the payment of these debts.

Should your Imperial Majesty deign to sanction these measures, the estimates for the receipts and expenditure of the year 1278 (1862) may be summed up as follows :—

	Purses.	
Receipts of 1278 (1862)	3,307,368	£15,118,640
Expenses of 1278 (1862)	3,110,815	£14,220,157
Excess of revenue	196,553	£898,483

It must, however, be remembered that, though the receipts may be equal to the estimates, it is also possible that certain miscalculations may arise both in the ordinary revenues of the country as well as in those of the new receipts; or it may happen that the projected reductions in the expenditure may not be fully realised. Therefore, the excess of receipts over expenditure, cited above, is intended to meet every possible deficiency in the estimates.

Competent counsellors are at this moment engaged in drawing up the projects of laws relative to the details for realising regularly the full amount of the revenues to be created. These laws will be duly carried out when the taxes are collected.

The Government has decided to establish at the same time a committee (syndicate), empowered to receive directly the revenues which are assigned as guarantees for payment of the internal debt, the foreign

Expenditure.

Expenses of the Budget of 1861	£12,739,088
Interest and sinking fund on the New English loan	685,680
Interest on the 400,000 purses to be borrowed in the Empire	109,709
Interest on the stock to be created for the consolidation of the floating debt	685,680
	£14,220,157

Deduct.

Estimated decrease to be carried out in the expenses of the various departments	685,680
Total of the expenses	£13,534,477

debt, as well as the loan about to be contracted, and to pay over the same as they become due. A commission, composed of competent persons, is now engaged in devising the best measures for carrying out this project. The result of their deliberations will be submitted to the gracious approval of your Majesty.

The accounts of the years preceding that which is now about to commence will be kept separate; that is to say, a department will be specially appointed to re-examine all former accounts, and, considering the advantages which the new system secures, so far as regularity and greater facility are concerned, this method will be adopted in all the accounts connected with the receipts and expenses of the State. These measures have been fully discussed, as well as the means best calculated to prevent the various departments from contracting separate debts, and to centralize all financial operations.

All these projects will be laid before your Imperial Majesty as soon as they shall be drawn up.

As the accession of your Imperial Majesty has inaugurated a new era of prosperity for the empire and the nation, and as the welfare of the country is the sole object of your Majesty's solicitude, I am convinced that the temporary embarrassments of our finances will speedily disappear, thanks to the efforts which will be made, I am persuaded, by all the functionaries of the empire, to carry out the measures stated above, in obedience to the commands of your Imperial Majesty, whose reign will be distinguished by glory and prosperity.

Translation of the original.

The Drogoman of the Imperial Divan.

A. AARIFY.

Sublime Porte, Feb. 19.

Receipts of 1862.

General total of the receipts of 1862   £14,432,960
General total of the expenses of 1862   13,534,477

Excess of revenue .   £898,483

The total of the Caïmés (paper money) in circulation, and of the floating debt, is estimated at 18,284,800*l*. Of this sum 6,000,000*l*. will be at once paid off with the proceeds of the new foreign and home loans, leaving a balance of 12,284,800*l*. to be converted into a consolidated stock. Of the new taxes above referred to, a special sum has been assigned for the payment of the interests and sinking funds; but a very important question here arises — how shall these revenues be assigned so as to inspire the public with perfect confidence? Local commissions appointed by Government, or any other imperial institution, would not give this confidence to the public; the reason is evident, they have been tried and they have failed. But it would be very different if such an institution as a National Bank could be established. Such operations would come precisely within its legitimate province, as being based on recognised statutes, directed by an independent body, and bound to periodical publicity of accounts. The direct assignment to such bank of special revenues for the payment of the interest and sinking fund of some particular government stock would fully maintain its value and satisfy the public, whilst the appointment of the governor, sub-governor, and auditor to the bank, would afford a sufficient security and guarantee to the Government itself. There can be no doubt that the service which such a banking institution might render to the Government and the country are incalculable, by preventing the various fluctuations in the exchanges, by economising, through its branches and agencies, the collection of the revenues, and by transacting the daily negotiations of the Treasury in the purchase and sale of the precious metals and bills, without subjecting the Government to the snares and machinations of all the jobbers in the market. In virtue of its national character the bank would naturally be in account current with all the local authorities wherever a branch was established. It would by this means absorb a large proportion of the specie now in circulation, and, by continuing to receive in metallic and pay in paper, the notes of the bank would be disseminated widely throughout the empire; thus money would be rendered more abundant, vast sums would be saved to the public annually which are now paid for the transport of coin, and a stop would be put to the illicit practices of the "Sweaters" who at present carry on so successful a trade. With the establishment of branches in each town of importance, a certain amount of regularity in money transactions would be diffused over the whole empire. The bank would enter immediately into competition with the usurers who oppress and plunder the hapless agriculturists; the moral influence of the bank would hold in check extortion on the part of the collectors of revenue, and as this influence became gradually perceptible, and the native population discovered that the high sanction under which the bank was operating was a guarantee for its integrity and not a cloak for iniquitous exactions, the immense sums which are now hoarded, especially in Asia Minor and Syria, would come to light and flow into its coffers. A National Bank then would clearly exercise a very great and very beneficial influence throughout the entire empire. It would be within reach of all classes: it would facilitate the undertakings of the agricultural and industrial portion of the inhabitants; it would aid by judicious assistance the legitimate operations of the commercial community, and, by thus encouraging all that tends to the development of the vast natural resources of the country, and by propagating those tastes for industry and enterprise which have so largely contributed to our own national wealth, give to Turkey the helping hand she needs to take a first step towards the attainment of that position for which nature destined her among the civilized nations of the world.*

Turkey is the last country in the world to contend against European enterprise, if it once get rooted in the soil. As soon as the higher classes, naturally easy and indolent, see that wealth is flowing in from sources which to them were valueless, and that their savings can be invested without risk or exertion and realize to them an increasing income, the vast hoards of treasure accumulated and carefully hidden in the nooks and corners of the interior will be allowed to see the light of day, and native capital will itself assist in converting the wilderness of waste into productive fields. The Turkish peasant is a hardworking and patient being; and, even under difficulties of no ordinary description,

---

* It is no exaggeration whatever, but a melancholy truth, that at the period of the establishment of the Bank of Scotland (1695), that country, partly owing to such a succession of disasters as cannot be paralleled in the history of any independent nation, and partly owing to its position on the outskirts of the civilized world, and far removed from the humanising influence of commerce, was the most utterly barbarous, savage, and lawless kingdom in Europe. And it is equally undeniable that the two great causes of her rapid rise in civilization and wealth, were her systems of national education and banking!—*Macleod's Theory and Practice of Banking.*

he exhibits all the characteristics of a good labourer and a peaceful subject. With untold wealth, then, lying actually within a few feet of the surface of the ground, with a soil that lacks but the kindly process of the sower to repay a thousandfold the seed that is dropped on its bosom, and with a people who want but the shadow of protection against those whom custom and ignorance have permitted to ruin and oppress them, the regeneration of Turkey ceases to be a hopeless task. The principle of reform, moreover, has been acknowledged and approved by the Sovereign power. The will of the Sultan has been published from one end of Turkey to the other, according to Mussulman law. It has, or ought to have, the weight of a sacred ordinance. It has besides been accepted as the initiation of a better state of things by the comity of European nations in solemn conference assembled, and, judging from the sound and statesmanlike measures already adopted by his Highness Fuad Pasha, there can be no doubt that it will soon become an immediate and practical reality.

CHAPTER IV.

AGRICULTURAL RESOURCES.

Few countries in the world possess, to the same extent, those natural advantages enjoyed by Turkey. Throughout the greater part of the empire, the soil and climate permit of the almost inexhaustible production, in excess of the wants of the inhabitants, of those ordinary raw materials which form everywhere the great staples of food and manufacture. Grain, wool, cotton, hemp, hides, tallow, timber, are everywhere produced in abundance; while, in addition to these ordinary products, Turkey yields in profusion those rarer articles of merchandise, such as drugs, dyes, gums, fruit, vegetable oils, silk, sugar, and tobacco, which can only be abundantly and profitably produced under conditions of special advantage of climate and geographical position.

GRAIN.

From the earliest times the fertility of the soil has been remarkable. In the days of Herodotus, it was so admirably adapted for corn that it never produced less than two-hundredfold, and in seasons particularly favourable, it sometimes amounted to three hundred. "The ear of the wheat as well as the barley," he says, "is four digits broad. But the immense height

In the years 1858, 1859, and 1860, Turkey exported:*

To Great Britain.

	1858		1859		1860	
	Quarters.	Value in Pounds sterling.	Quarters.	Value in Pounds sterling.	Quarters.	Value in Pounds sterling.
Wheat	208,484	405,979	74,448	137,641	163,999	435,268
Barley	420,661	454,043	187,756	190,644	669,218	955,889
Maize	594,195	878,650	742,063	1,064,716	916,673	1,580,997
Other kinds	23,223	33,159	13,966	21,707	28,098	39,123
		£1,771,831		£1,414,708		£3,011,277

To France.

	1858		1859		1860	
	Quantities.	Value in Francs.	Quantities.	Value in Francs.	Quantities.	Value in Francs.
Wheat	1,070,808 hectol.	18,203,736	436,178 h.	7,240,555	470,189 h.	11,566,649
Barley, Rye, and Oats	334,595 ,,	3,586,757				
Maize	152,894 ,,	2,216,963	484,066 ,,	5,839,003	198,684 ,,	2,753,767
Millet	458,258 kilog.	178,690				
Other kinds	8,255,187 ,,	1,286,971	1,168,143 k.	443,904	1,203,695 k.	458,544
		Fr.25,423,117		Fr.13,523,462		Fr.14,778,960

* These figures do not comprise the exports from Egypt, Tripoli, or Tunis. The commerce of those dependencies is not included in the following pages.

to which the cenchrus and sesamum stalks grow, although I have witnessed it myself, I dare not mention, lest those who have not visited the country should disbelieve my report." At the present day the soil is not less fruitful, for according to Beaujour, the yield of corn in some parts of Macedonia amounts to three-hundredfold.* In 1847, the value of the agricultural produce exported from Macedonia by Salonica alone amounted to upwards of 800,000*l.*, of which cereal productions formed an item of 600,000*l.* In 1848, the quantity of corn exported from Bulgaria and Roumelia exceeded 4,440,000 bushels. In 1855, Galatz and Ibraila exported upwards of 2,000,000 imperial quarters of grain, while the annual produce of corn in Asia Minor is estimated at 25,000,000 Turkish kilos, or 705,100,000 kilogrammes, equal to 25,473,250 bushels.

WOOL.

The wools of Roumelia (Turkey in Europe) are held in very high estimation. They usually contain sixty parts of white, twenty of fine black, first quality, and twenty of gray, second quality. Macedonia, Thessaly, and Albania produce about 6,500,000 lbs. of wool, of which 2,200,000 lbs. are exported by Salonica, and 1,000,000 lbs. by the port of Volo, in Thessaly. That part of Bulgaria, bordering on the Danube, called the Dobrutscha, contains abundant pasturage, and produces annually about 4,125,000 lbs. Thrace does not

---

* There are some places in European Turkey where the land is so fruitful that two crops are obtained from it in the year. For example, at the village of Velvendos, in the district of Charshumba, about eighteen hours distant from Monastir, barley is sown in September and cut in May. Indian corn is then planted, which is gathered in the September following.

possess pasturages as rich as those of Bulgaria and Macedonia; nevertheless, the production of that province is estimated at 6,000,000 lbs., of which two-thirds are exported, and one-third used for home consumption.

It is impossible to arrive at a satisfactory valuation of the amount of wool produced in Asia Minor. The most important market, however, for that article is Smyrna, from whence is exported 7,150,000 lbs., of which one-half goes to the United States, and the other to France and England. The province of Konieh furnishes about 7,000,000 lbs.; and Caramania, which extends along the coast from the Gulf of Satalia to the Gulf of Alexandretta, and inland to the neighbourhood of Angora and Sivas, produces 600,000 lbs., containing one part of white, and three parts of black and gray.

Syria produces a considerable quantity of wool, but it is difficult to obtain any reliable statistics upon the subject. In 1855, however, Aleppo exported 1500 tons, value 108,000*l*. In 1857, Tripoli exported to the value of 5360*l*., and in the same year Beyrout exported to the value of 51,029*l*.; while, in 1858, 4181 bales were shipped from the port of Alexandretta.

The wools of Upper Asia, comprising those of Kurdistan and the provinces bordering on the Black Sea, are shipped at the ports of Trebizond and Samsoun, but no returns are available.

The province of Angora, famous for the silky fleeces of its goats, exports about 6,875,000 lbs. of wool or hair by the ports of Smyrna, Samsoun, and Constantinople.

AGRICULTURAL RESOURCES.

Turkey exported in 1858, 1859, and 1860:

To Great Britain.

	1858		1859		1860	
	Lbs.	Value in Pounds sterling.	Lbs.	Value in Pounds sterling.	Lbs.	Value in Pounds sterling.
Wool, sheep and lambs'	387,588	14,256	693,644	30,674	1,165,100	49,458
" or hair, goats'	3,703,618	560,362	2,252,566	341,949	2,512,447	378,071
		£574,618		£372,623		£427,529

To France.

	1858		1859		1860	
	Kil.	Francs.	Kil.	Francs.	Kil.	Francs.
Wool	2,801,127	3,997,691	4,357,868	7,808,771	5,866,703	17,053,687
" or hair, goats'	55,052	239,476	117,886	511,934	123,153	535,716
		Fr. 4,237,167		Fr. 8,320,705		Fr. 17,589,403

In 1858, 1859, and 1860, Turkey exported:

To Great Britain.

	1858		1859		1860	
	Quantity.	Value in Pounds sterling.	Quantity.	Value in Pounds sterling.	Quantity.	Value in Pounds sterling.
Silk, raw	99,024 lbs.	78,632	136,305 lbs.	138,653	164,194 lbs.	119,961
,, cocoons, &c.	441 cwts.	5,998	930 cwts.	13,997	1,623 cwts.	28,550
		£84,630		£152,650		£148,511

To France.

	1858		1859		1860	
	Kil.	France.	Kil.	France.	Kil.	France.
Silk, raw	582,889	30,886,447	559,844	31,871,815	615,807	36,948,420
,, (bourre de soie)	79,924	639,392	78,913	710,217	109,243	1,037,808
,, cocoons	747,019	13,446,342	1,100,498	24,210,966	1,894,243	30,073,346
,, eggs of silk-worm	14,251	2,137,650	37,272	7,454,400	42,432	8,486,400
		Fr. 47,109,831		Fr. 64,247,398		Fr. 76,545,974

SILK.

The rearing of the silk-worm forms one of the most profitable resources of Turkey. In 1852, the production of silk in the province of Adrianople was valued at 184,250 lbs., of which 154,750 lbs. were exported to France. In the same year the district of Volo, in Thessaly, produced 138,875 lbs., of which 116,875 lbs. were exported. The yield of silk at Brussa, in 1855, amounted to 1,120,000 lbs., of the value of 1,500,000*l*. In 1857, Beyrout exported to the value of 308,715*l*.; Tripoli, 88,200*l*.; and Smyrna, 121,833*l*.

TOBACCO.

This plant is cultivated in every part of Turkey where the elevation of the temperature admits of its production. In Macedonia there are two species, known under the name of *nicotiana latifolia* and *nicotiana rustica*, which occupy an eighth part of the ploughed lands, and by the cultivation of which twenty thousand families are supported. The annual harvest, or gathering, of tobacco in Macedonia is estimated at 100,000 bales; of which 40,000 bales are consumed in European Turkey, 30,000 are exported to Egypt, 10,000 to Barbary, and 20,000 to Italy.

The increased exports from the district of Cavalla will be apparent from the following table.

Quantities of Tobacco annually Shipped from Cavalla District to different Home and Foreign Markets from the Year 1848 to 1859 inclusive.

Years.	Great Britain.	Austria.	France.	Destination. Greece.	Russia.	Sardinia.	Turkish Empire.	Total.
	lbs.	lbs.	lbs.	lbs.	lbs.	lbs.	lbs.	lbs.
1848	.	650,000	878,000	35,000	150,000	.	6,500,000	8,213,000
1849	6,440	167,200	1,493,000	55,000	150,000	.	6,432,000	8,303,640
1850	489,440	572,000	1,072,500	11,000	200,000	385,000	6,503,000	9,232,940
1851	502,320	770,000	1,304,000	24,750	230,000	302,500	6,360,000	9,493,570
1852	722,568	572,000	.	171,000	280,000	125,400	7,140,000	9,010,968
1853	1,306,200	.	1,255,000	646,000	300,000	.	8,300,000	11,807,200
1854	2,758,756	460,000	244,300	215,000	330,000	195,700	10,400,000	14,603,756
1855	167,120	1,200,000	604,900	134,000	370,000	155,000	14,000,000	16,631,020
1856	1,155,465	1,410,000	1,129,200	150,000	400,000	.	13,500,000	17,744,665
1857	2,164,708	1,150,000	.	325,000	420,000	.	14,200,000	18,259,708
1858	679,980	1,453,200	1,238,800	390,314	450,000	130,480	17,200,000	21,542,774
1859	297,040	448,000	2,691,228	457,408	450,000	224,000	14,100,000	18,667,676

The following calculation shows the profit arising from the cultivation of tobacco in Macedonia. Assuming that a plot of five acres can be cultivated by two families, numbering from four to six adult males and females, and a proportionate number of non-adults, the outlay and return would be as follow:—

Outlay.

	£	s.	d.
By the landlord —			
Tilling the land, at 12s. per acre	3	0	0
Manure, 400 horse-loads, at 2d. per load	3	6	0
Folding flocks on the field	2	0	0
Indian-corn flour, rice, oil, and other food, in part maintenance of the two labourers' families	5	0	0
Deterioration of implements, buildings, and other charges	3	14	0
	£17	0	0
By the peasant —			
Quota of outlay for the maintenance of the two families	15	0	0
Total outlay	£32	0	0

Return.

Average yield of crop (500 lbs. per acre) —
2,500 lbs. of tobacco
 250 ,, less tithes

	£	s.	d.
2,250 ,, worth, at average price, 1s.	112	10	0
Net profit	£80	10	0

Profit per acre £16 2s. 0d.

	£	s.	d.
Landlord's share	40	5	0
Peasant's share	40	5	0
	£80	10	0

Magnesia, Pergamos, and Samsoun, in Asia Minor, produce tobacco of excellent quality; but that cultivated in the district of Latakia (Syria), is the most esteemed. The consumption of tobacco by the native population is enormous; nevertheless, the exportation continues annually to increase. In 1856,

Samsoun exported by British ships alone 13,662 bales, equal to 2049 tons weight; and in 1857, Beyrout exported to the value of 112,442*l.*

In 1858, 1859, and 1860, Turkey exported:—

	1858	
	Quantity.	Value in Pounds sterling.
To Great Britain	1,546,359 lbs.	£51,471
To France	507,158 kil.	£21,098
	1859	
To Great Britain	211,329 lbs.	£5,060
To France	1,165,563 kil.	£67,603
	1860	
To Great Britain	1,197,834 lbs.	£26,569
To France	384,479 kil.	£22,761

MADDER.

This root is principally cultivated in Asia Minor and Syria. In 1857 Smyrna exported 117,383 kintals, value 301,065*l.**, and in the same year Beyrout exported to the value of 30,580*l.*

The total exports to Great Britain and France were:—

	1858	
	Quantity.	Value in Pounds sterling.
To Great Britain	157,987 cwt.	£411,972
To France	90,125 kil.	£2,884
	1859	
To Great Britain	171,920 cwt.	£432,916
To France	182,447 kil.	£6,641
	1860	
To Great Britain	170,947 cwt.	£433,856
To France	856,095 kil.	£29,450

* In 1858 Smyrna exported 187,603 kintals of madder root. 1 kintal = 125 lbs. English.

VALONIA.

Valonia, so extensively used for tanning, is the fruit of a species of oak (*quercus ægylops*), and is found in European Turkey, the isles of the Archipelago, and Asia Minor. With due attention to its cultivation, Turkey is capable of producing valonia to almost any extent. In 1857, Smyrna exported 476,288 kintals, value 325,682*l*.

In 1858, 1859, and 1860, Turkey exported:—

	Quantity.	Value in Pounds sterling.
1858		
To Great Britain	19,176 tons	£264,876
To France	267,736 kil.	£23,560
1859		
To Great Britain	26,242 tons	£382,347
To France	555,665 kil.	£51,121
1860		
To Great Britain	17,868 tons	£261,501
To France	508,549 kil.	£46,786

OPIUM.

Smyrna is the principal market for the sale of opium. In 1857, there were shipped from that port, chiefly to England, the United States, and China, 3271 cases of 80 to 90 tchékis, value 266,382*l*.*

---

* Opium is much used by the Turks as a soporific, or as an incentive. Those Turks who are in the habit of constantly eating it are called *Theriakis*. They take it in order to procure a kind of sweet lethargy which seems to place them between life and death. That state, which lulls all thought asleep without excluding the sensations, has such charms that it is by no means uncommon to meet with *Theriakis* who spend their life in drinking coffee, smoking their pipe, and swallowing opium. I have heard of an *effendi* who took every day thirty cups of coffee, smoked sixty pipes, swallowed three drachms of opium, and whose sole food was four ounces of rice.

Turkey exported in 1858, 1859, and 1860:—

1858

	Quantity.	Value in Pounds sterling.
To Great Britain	90,397 lbs.	£89,449
To France	5,734 kil.	£12,615

1859

	Quantity.	Value in Pounds sterling.
To Great Britain	136,695 lbs.	£133,149
To France	7,188 kil.	£14,376

1860

	Quantity.	Value in Pounds sterling.
To Great Britain	195,366 lbs.	£187,643
To France	10,561 kil.	£23,236

YELLOW BERRIES.

This seed, made use of in dyeing, is the berry of the small buckthorn, or *rhamnus minor;* it is of the size of a pepper-corn, of an astringent, bitter taste, and of a green colour, bordering upon yellow. The shrub was known to the ancients under the name of *pixacantha*, or prickly box; the French call it *graine d'Avignon*. In 1857, Smyrna exported 10,911 kintals, value 24,549*l.*

In 1858, 1859, and 1860, Turkey exported:—

1858

	Quantity.	Value in Pounds sterling.
To Great Britain	2,863 cwt.	£5,964
To France	105,221 kil.	£5,051

1859

	Quantity.	Value in Pounds sterling.
To Great Britain	8,795 cwt.	£17,089
To France	.	.

1860

	Quantity.	Value in Pounds sterling.
To Great Britain	2,844 cwt.	£5,262
To France	158,387 kil.	£7,603

The following tables of the exports from Turkey to Great Britain and France, during the year 1860, will give a definite idea of the various products of the Ottoman empire:—

Specification of the Exports from Turkey to Great Britain in the year 1860.

Names of Articles.		Quantities.	Value in Pounds sterling.
Berries, yellow	cwts.	2,844	5,262
Boxwood	tons	4,133	45,647
Corn: wheat	qrs.	163,999	435,268
barley	,,	669,218	955,889
maize	,,	916,673	1,580,997
other kinds	,,	28,098	39,123
Figs	cwts.	43,463	90,922
Galls	,,	7,153	34,529
Gum, tragacanth	,,	767	7,406
Iron, chromate of	tons	135	2,160
Madder root	cwts.	170,947	433,856
Nuts, small	bushels	6,110	4,530
Oil, olive	tuns	439	24,021
or otto of roses	lbs.	1,143	15,828
Opium	,,	195,366	187,643
Raisins	cwts.	76,896	126,513
Scammony	lbs.	26,262	35,758
Seed: flax and linseed	qrs.	266	674
millet	,,	53,425	11,519
rape	,,	15,976	47,444
Silk, raw	lbs.	164,194	119,961
cocoons, &c.	cwts.	1,623	28,550
Skins, lamb, undressed	no.	272,603	17,037
Sponges	lbs.	369,358	238,383
Stone, in lumps, not in any manner hewn	tons	2,093	28,957
Tallow	cwts.	4,118	11,494
Terra umbra	,,	394	79
Tobacco, unmanufactured	lbs.	1,197,834	26,569
Valonia	tons	17,868	261,501
Wool, or hair, goats'	lbs.	2,512,447	378,071
sheep and lambs'	,,	1,165,100	49,458
Woollen manufactures: carpets and rugs	sq. yds.	37,316	15,293
unenumerated	value	. .	574
All other articles		. .	244,576
		Total	£5,505,492

Specification of the Exports from Turkey to France in 1860.

Rang d' Importance.	Désignation des Marchandises.		Quantités.	Francs.
		Unités.		
1	Soies écrues grége	kilog.	615,807	36,948,420
2	Œufs de vers à soie	,,	42,432	8,486,400
3	Graines oléagineuses	,,	14,751,021	7,504,967
4	Laines en masse	,,	5,366,706	17,053,687
5	Froment (grain)	hectol.	470,189	11,566,649
6	Poils de chevreau bruts	kilog.	123,153	535,716
7	Soies en cocons	,,	1,394,243	30,073,346
8	Huile d'olive	,,	3,240,746	3,388,895
9	Peaux brutes	,,	1,267,866	3,965,625
10	Coton en laine	,,	1,815,156	2,995,007
11	Raisins secs	,,	2,508,520	2,884,798
12	Bourre de soie en masse écrue	,,	109,243	1,037,808
13	Seigle, maïs, orge, avoine (grain)	hectol.	198,684	2,753,767
14	Noix de galle et avelanèdes	kilog.	508,549	1,169,663
15	Racines de réglisse	,,	2,148,490	1,074,245
16	Cuivre pur de 1re fusion	,,	475,032	1,282,586
17	Tabac en feuilles ou en côtes	,,	384,479	569,029
18	Viandes salées	,,	1,123,014	914,222
19	Garance en racines sèches	,,	856,095	736,242
20	Cuivre allié d'etain de 1re fusion	,,	203,060	609,180
21	Peaux de lièvre brutes	,,	35,261	176,305
22	Essence de roses	,,	590	619,500
23	Bois d'ébénisterie	,,	1,121,352	280,927
24	Opium	,,	10,561	580,855
25	Os et cornes de bétail brutes	,,	628,442	356,608
26	Perles fines	gram.	16,537	281,129
27	Légumes secs et leur farines	kilog.	1,206,695	458,544
28	Cire jaune ou brune	,,	150,117	750,585
29	Eponges	,,	27,928	467,476
30	Tissus, passementerie, et rubans de laine	,,	7,998	113,870
31	Bijouterie	gram.	32,557	199,379
32	Nattes et tresses de paille grossières	kilog.	12,520	12,520

Rang d'Import-ance.	Désignation des Marchandises.		Quantités.	Francs.
		Unités.		
33	Fruits secs autres que les raisins	kilog.	168,293	118,768
34	Gommes pures exotiques	,,	71,995	61,196
35	Bois de teinture en bûches	,,	423,349	42,335
36	Vins	litre	69,070	65,332
37	Noir minéral naturel	kilog.	124,000	24,800
38	Sangsues	le mille	1,990	129,350
39	Nerprun et rocou	kilog.	158,387	190,065
40	Pierres à aiguiser	,,	91,750	45,875
41	Acide oléique	,,	90,989	77,341
42	Merrains de chêne	pièce	122,230	85,561
43	Son	kilog.	521,468	52,147
	Autres articles		. . .	1,614,333
	Totaux	.	Francs	143,455,053 or £5,738,202

CHAPTER V.

MINERAL RESOURCES.

Of the various natural resources of Turkey which remain comparatively undeveloped, the most important, perhaps, are her Mines and Forests. Of the former it would be quite impossible to calculate the value, for the soil teems with mineral wealth ready to enrich those who have the energy to seek for it. Pliny tells us that in his time the riches of ancient Cyprus arose to a considerable extent from its copper mines, the most productive of which were those of Tamasus in the centre of the island, Soli on the north coast, and Amathos and Cyrium on the south. Gold and silver were found in these mines; while the precious stones of Cyprus—the emerald, agate, malachite, jaspar, opal—and the minerals asbestos and rock-crystal, were valued and held in high estimation by the luxurious Romans. Mount Atabyros in Rhodes, and the island of Lemnos—the fabled abode of Vulcan—were also famous for their copper mines. The mountains of Thrace were remarkable for their mines of precious metals. The island of Thassos was enriched by the possession of her gold mines; and the forests of Mount Ida, in Crete, supplied wood for the forging and smelting of iron. But the ancient Greeks and Romans, with all their power and grandeur, could not buy up the future, and were compelled to leave the soil with all its hidden treasures to the descendants of those who followed the fortunes of the son of Amurath.

The magic power, however, which in old days was supposed to lay open the secrets of the earth, has long since been dispelled; but there exists in the nineteenth century a greater power than was ever ascribed to magic or to genii,— the power of industry and labour, supported by capital, and backed by those grand discoveries in science of which our ancestors were ignorant. The application of that moving power—industry and labour, supported by capital—to the undeveloped mineral resources of Turkey would prove of incalculable advantage to the government of the Sultan, and open up a wide and remunerative field for commercial enterprise.

Of the numerous mines discovered some years ago in Asia Minor, there are but ten at present in operation, and these yield scarcely two-thirds of what they are capable of producing. The average annual produce of these mines is as follows :—

Silver Mines : —
Dénék-Madène	156,436 okes.	
Gamuch-Hané	17,520 „	
Hadjikoi	134,976 „	
Akdagh-Madène	119,520 „	
Guéban-Madène	142,350 „	
		570,796
Lead Mines		175,000

Copper Mines : —
Argana-Madène	720,000 „	
Esséli	156,888 „	
Kuré-Madène	27,612 „	
Helvali	61,020 „	
		965,520
		1,711,316 okes.

The copper mine of Cuné, whose produce received the designation of Tokat, Trebizond, or Diarbekhr, according to the place at which it was wrought, is perhaps the richest in the world, the hills all around appearing to be one mass of carbonate of copper; but it is, I believe, very nearly if not altogether abandoned. The silver, lead, and copper mines in the neighbourhood of Trebizond are seriously neglected, although that of Triboly is known to have produced, even under bad management, six to eight thousand hundred weight of copper annually. The rich mines of Bosnia and Servia*, of Wallachia and Macedonia, remain, comparatively, unproductive; while the silver and lead mines of Thessaly, which were, a iew years ago, very profitably worked, are now no longer in full operation.

The lead and silver mines in the district of Volo, in Thessaly, yield, on an average, about thirty-five per cent. of mixed metal,—consisting of lead, silver, and gold. They were first discovered in 1848, by an Ionian named Cazotti, and a firman was granted by the Sultan to Izett Pasha, the then Minister of Police, for a term of eleven years. Izett Pasha, after working a few of the mines on his own account for three years, gave up the enterprise as unsuccessful; and in 1856, a second firman was obtained extending the privileges of the first for a term of thirty-one years. The Provinces of Tricalla and Joannina, mentioned in the Sultan's concession, include the entire of Thessaly, a considerable portion of Lower Albania, and a section of Macedonia,—the whole embracing a superficial area of great extent, and many ranges of mountains rich in mineral deposits of gold, silver, lead, copper, iron, antimony, arsenic, and coal,—

---

* See Bosnia.

all of which the proprietor of the firman has the exclusive privilege of working, upon the annual payment of 70,000 piastres (about 650*l.*), in lieu of all royalties, customs' dues, and other taxes.

The district possesses unusual advantages for the export of minerals, having a great extent of sea-board, both in the Adriatic Sea and in the Grecian Archipelago. The boundary in the Adriatic Sea comprises a length of 200 miles, extending northwards along the sea-coast from the Gulf of Arta, past the island of Corfu, to within a short distance of the town and harbour of Durazzo, in Albania. The boundary in the Grecian Archipelago embraces about one hundred miles of sea-coast from the Gulf of Volo to Katterina, in the Gulf of Salonica. Along the latter coast, on the eastern slopes of Mount Pelion, and about three-quarters of a mile from the sea, the present proprietor of the firman has expended upwards of 50,000*l.* on the completion of extensive works which have been profitably employed in dressing and smelting the rich ores of Galena, numerous veins having been discovered in Mount Pelion, from which considerable quantities of lead, silver, and gold are extracted.

Some of the ores of Galena, in the mountain, are very rich—yielding as much as 82 per cent. of metal. The mineral veins vary in breadth from two to ten feet, and, on an average, yield about 35 per cent. of mixed metal, consisting of lead, silver, and gold. The gold and silver are refined at the works to such a high degree, that not more than two parts in a thousand of any foreign matter can be detected, and the lead is admitted to be of the softest and best quality. The Pelion works, when in full operation, are capable of smelting from nine to ten tons of mixed metal daily, and of separating the silver and gold from the lead. There are generally from sixty to eighty, and sometimes as much as 150 ounces of silver, and from six to eight dwts. of gold, in a ton of metal, and its average worth for gold, silver, and lead, is from 28*l.* to 30*l.* per ton. Thus, the value of the metals which can be produced from only a very small portion of Mount Pelion, amounts to 280*l.* or 300*l.* a day.

From the works, the lead, silver, and gold are carried down on mules—about three-quarters of a mile—to Khorefto, the roadstead of Zaghora, and then shipped on board Greek vessels for Salonica, from whence it is re-shipped to Constantinople. House rent and living are exceedingly cheap in the neighbourhood, the climate is good, and the locality in which the works are situated is very healthy. "It is a delightful spot," says Dodwell, in his *Travels in Greece*, " and exhibits in all their rich mixture of foliage and diversity of form, the luxuriantly spreading platanus, the majestically robust chesnut, the waving poplar, the aspiring cypress, which are happily intermingled with the vine, pomegranate, almond, and fig. Here the weary may repose, and those who hunger and thirst may be satisfied. The nightingale and other birds are heard even in the most frequented streets, and plenty and security are everywhere diffused."

CHAPTER VI.

THE GROWTH OF COTTON.

COTTON was formerly one of the chief staples of Turkish commerce, but, during the past fifty years, its cultivation has considerably declined. As very great anxiety, however, is felt at the present moment with regard to the future supply of this important article, it will not be out of place if I here direct the attention of those interested in the matter to the facilities which exist for the growth and improvement of that plant in the Ottoman empire. The natural advantages possessed by Turkey, in her soil, climate, and geographical position, offer every inducement to the capitalist, and few enterprises would, perhaps, be more profitable at the present time than one having for its object the improved cultivation of cotton in that country.

In the department of Salonica, cotton is grown to a considerable extent, but it is principally gathered in the district of Sérés, a city of Macedonia, well-known in European Turkey for the richness of its market, and situated fifteen leagues to the north-west of Salonica, in the centre of the great valley through which flows the river Strymon. The annual harvest of cotton in the valley of Sérés has lately very much decreased, but fifty years ago it was estimated at 70,000 bales, of which 30,000 were exported to Germany, 12,000 to France, 4000 to Trieste, 1500 to Leghorn, and as many more to Genoa. At present, however, nearly all the cotton goes to Germany, whence Sérés takes jewellery, ironmongery, cotton, woollen and silk manufactured goods, &c. At the annual fair of Sérés, held from the 20th of February to the 30th of March, 1860, imported goods were sold as follow :—

	£
From Austria and Germany	64,425
Great Britain	17,500
Turkey	8,827
France	4,916
Holland	648
Total	£96,316

From the above figures it will be seen that the Germans have nearly a monopoly of the trade, in consequence of the preference which they give to the cotton of Sérés. It has been estimated that Macedonia produces 800,000 imperial quarters of corn, 100,000 bales of tobacco, and 80,000 bales of cotton; yet only one-fourth part of the land is under cultivation, and even that part does not yield one-third of what it is capable of doing.

Cyprus produces annually about 1,375,000 lbs. of cotton, but its growth in that island is capable of very great extension. In the southern and western parts of the island of Rhodes, there are plains containing about 4000 acres of land belonging to the government, in every way adapted for the cultivation of cotton. In the neighbourhood of Brussa, experiments have been made from New Orleans seed, and the samples were, a short time ago, very favourably reported upon, and give promise of the valuable addition being made of superior cotton to the products of that quarter.

In the Province of Diarbekhr, and in fact all over Asiatic Turkey, particularly in Mesopotamia, cotton could be grown to almost any extent; and when it is considered that Turkey in Asia possesses an area of 673,746 square miles, with a population of but 16,050,000, giving only 23·8 to the square mile, it may be imagined what vast tracts of fertile land are there lying unproductive. Enormous areas where water is plentiful and the soil most fruitful could be readily obtained upon the easy terms of paying to the government ten per cent. on the value of the produce in lieu of rent, and the cultivation of cotton for the English market would not only be a remunerative enterprise for those engaged in it, but, while benefiting to a very great extent the condition of the native population, would at the same time increase considerably the revenues of the Turkish Government.

Towards the end of the last and the beginning of the present century, when the production of cotton in America and in Egypt was still very limited, large shipments of cotton were made from the port of Smyrna (Asia Minor) to Europe, chiefly to Venice, Genoa, France, Holland, and a small portion to England. In the mercantile books of the few European firms then existing in Smyrna, the annual export of cotton is often mentioned as attaining a quantity varying from 150,000 to 200,000 bales. Mr. R. J. Van Lennep, the present Dutch Consul-General at Smyrna, has mentioned to me that the old Dutch house of David Van Lennep and Co. alone used to ship at that time, to the Netherlands and to Venice, about 50,000 to 60,000 bales per annum. When the war broke out, however, towards the end of the last century, shipments of cotton from Smyrna became a hazardous speculation, as during the French occupation of Egypt many cargoes sent from Smyrna to Europe were seized by privateers and sold in Malta. This state of things continued, with intermittent facilities and difficulties, until the years 1814 and 1815, and must have been very prejudicial to the growth of cotton in Asia Minor, for I find from copies of letters written in Smyrna during these two years that the annual exportation is mentioned as having been only about 70,000 bales. In 1820, just before the Greek revolution, the yearly exports of cotton from Smyrna were estimated at 40,000 to 45,000 bales, but since the year 1840 the crop of cotton has never exceeded 8000 bales a year, of which not more than 2000 to 3000 bales were exported, the balance being required for home consumption. Recently, however, prices have increased, and the peasants appear to pay more attention to its cultivation. During the year 1860, 7000 bales of cotton were exported from the port of Smyrna, while during the past year the exports amounted to nearly 20,000 bales. The localities in the neighbourhood of Smyrna producing cotton, at present, are Souboudja, Kirek-Agadjé, Canaba, Kinck, and Baindir. Formerly cotton was also grown in Magnesia, Menemen, Aidin, and in almost all the flat and level parts of the country. In Tarsus and the vicinity of Satalia, as well as the island of Cyprus, cotton was largely produced.

In Syria the cotton plant has been grown for ages, but owing to the defective mode of cultivation, and to the want of new seed, the quality has degenerated. An experiment has, however, recently been made with seed from America, and the sample of the quality produced has been pronounced fully equal to the cotton of

New Orleans. Vast tracts of fertile land are lying waste in Syria where cotton could be advantageously grown. The waste lands on both sides of the Euphrates, the valleys of the Bekaa and Baalbek, the plains watered by the Orontes and the Jordan, as well as those beyond Damascus, and in the neighbourhood of Tarsus and Alexandretta, are capable of producing cotton to an almost unlimited extent. Damascus, Nablous, St. Jean d'Acre, and Tarsus produce at present about 24,750,000 lbs. of cotton annually.

There can be no doubt, therefore, entertained as to the possibility of an immense increase of the quantity of cotton grown in Turkey. The two great desiderata are, the introduction of new seed and the substitution of a better mode of cultivation than that now pursued; but complete success can only be achieved by means of European enterprise and European capital.

No country in the world can surpass Turkey in its capability of supplying all those various productions required by man, and the seas which wash her shores afford every advantage to her maritime commerce. The Black Sea receives the trade of Bulgaria, of Roumelia, and Armenia; the Archipelago that of Anatolia, Macedonia, and Thessaly; the Adriatic Sea that of Albania; the Persian Gulf that of Irak, while the Bosphorus and Dardanelles give her the absolute command of the Sea of Marmora, which bathes the walls of Constantinople. It is, in fact, this capability of supplying raw material at a low price and of excellent quality which gives to Turkish commerce that importance and consideration in which it is held by the European Powers. Turkey is no longer a manufacturing country. The numerous and varied manufactures which formerly sufficed, not only for the consumption of the empire, but which also stocked the markets of the Levant, as well as those of several countries in Europe, have, in some instances, rapidly declined, and in others become altogether extinct. The soap manufactories in Crete have, it is true, considerably increased: the manufactures of light silks and gold and silk embroidery from Cyprus are highly esteemed; the camlets of Angora, the sandals of Scio, the printed calicoes of Tokat, the crapes and gauzes of Salonica, the carpets of Smyrna, still form a considerable portion of the home trade; but on the other hand, the manufactures in steel for which Damascus was so long famous no longer exist; the muslin-looms of Scutari and Tirnova, which in 1812 numbered 2000, were reduced in 1841 to 200; the silk-looms of Salonica, numbering from twenty-five to twenty-eight in 1847, have now fallen to eighteen; while Brussa and Diarbekhr, which were so renowned for their velvets, satins, and silk stuffs, do not now produce a tenth part of what they yielded thirty or forty years ago. Baghdad was once the centre of very flourishing trades, especially those of calico-printing, tanning and preparing leather, pottery, jewellery, &c. Aleppo was still more famous; for its manufactures of gold thread, of cotton tissues, cotton, and silk, silk and gold, and pure cotton called nankeens, gave occupation to more than 40,000 looms, of which, in the year 1856, there remained only 5560. Formerly, there was no person who did not wear some article of silk; the embroidery of men's and women's dresses, the belts of the peasantry, the inner garments and the shirting of the whole population above the condition of a labourer, were of that material. But now taste has changed: Sheffield steel supplies the place of that of Damascus, cloths and every variety of cottons have supplanted silk; English muslins are preferred to those of India, and Cashmere shawls have given place to the Zebras of Glasgow and Manchester. In the year 1827, the exports of cotton manufactured goods from Great Britain to Turkey amounted only to 464,873*l.*; in the year 1857, they had increased to the sum of 2,847,386*l.*, and during the year 1860, to 4,225,395*l.* In the year 1827, the value of our total exports to Turkey was 531,704*l.*, but in 1860, our total exports amounted to 5,457,839*l.* The following tables will give an idea of the increased consumption of our manufactures by Turkey since the year 1846, and it will be apparent that in proportion as increased facilities are afforded for the production of raw material—either by the introduction of foreign capital, by improved means of transit from the interior to the coast, or by a less vexatious mode of collecting revenue—the purchasing power of the people will be to the same extent augmented, and we will continue to find in Turkey an increasing and profitable market for our merchandise.

Value of the Exports (the produce and manufacture of the United Kingdom) from Great Britain to Turkey.

	1846	1851	1853	1857	1860
To Turkey Proper	1,749,125	1,937,011	2,029,305	3,107,401	4,408,910
Wallachia and Moldavia	195,154	284,348	179,510	201,466	172,872
Syria and Palestine	267,618	359,871	306,580	703,375	655,323
	2,211,897	2,581,230	2,515,395	4,012,242	5,237,105

Specification of the Exports (the produce and manufacture of the United Kingdom) from Great Britain to Turkey, in the year 1860.

Names of Articles.		Quantities.	Value in Pounds sterling.
Apparel, slops, and haberdashery	value		£28,975
Beer and ale	barrels	1,067	4,559
Bread and biscuit	cwts.	22	102
Butter	,,	321	1,265
Coals, cinders and culm	tons	223,472	105,053
Copper, wrought and unwrought	cwts.	13,413	77,568
Cottons, entered by the yard	yards	229,201,826	3,324,492
,, ,, at value	value		22,122
Cotton yarn	lbs.	22,824,004	878,781
Earthenware and porcelain	value		24,558
Furniture, cabinet and upholstery ware	,,		3,261
Glass manufactures	,,		11,458
Gunpowder	lbs.	65,795	1,930
Hardwares and cutlery	cwts.	10,053	40,092
Iron, wrought and unwrought, including unwrought steel	tons	20,864	172,345
Linens, entered by the yard	yards	927,549	21,817
,, ,, at value	value		2,400
Linen yarn	lbs.	41,933	2,336
Machinery and millwork, including steam engines	value		62,097
Painters' colours	,,		3,558
Plate, plated ware, jewellery and watches	,,		10,718
Provisions	,,		321
Silk manufactures	,,		14,482
Soap	cwts.	328	461
Stationery	value		29,862
Sugar, refined	cwts.	18,410	51,636
Telegraphic wire, &c.	value		7,325
Tin, unwrought	cwts.	6,599	44,711
Tin plates	value		38,193
Woollens, entered by the piece	pieces	33,227	74,399
,, ,, ,, yard	yards	661,097	34,966
,, ,, at value	value		9,440
Of all other articles			131,222
		Total	£5,237,105

CHAPTER VII.

BANKING IN TURKEY.

THE attention of the public has been directed for some time past to the subject of "Banking in Turkey." Every one knows that the establishment of banks must naturally lead to a very great increase in the trade and commerce of the Ottoman empire; but few, perhaps, are aware to what extent their success will be advantageous to ourselves. The commerce of Turkey may be extended, her resources may be more fully developed, but the question is,—"Of what importance will that be to us?" We are fully alive to the necessity of drawing closer the ties that connect us with France, and we are highly pleased with the prospect that, at some future time, our manufactures will be admitted into her ports, freed from the prohibitory duties which at present exist; but we appear altogether to overlook the fact, that in Turkey there exists a mart for our manufactures still more extensive than that of France, and that, while the French ports have been in some respects closed against us, the ports of the Ottoman empire have been always open, not alone to our manufactures, but to the commerce of the world. Since the throne of the Sultans has been established at Constantinople, commercial restraints have been unknown, and unlimited free trade has prevailed in the most extended sense imaginable.

Never has the Divan dreamt, under any pretext of national interest, or even of reprisals, of restricting this advantage, which is still in force, in its most unlimited acceptation, in the case of all nations who wish to furnish matters for the consumption of that vast empire, and to take their share of its produce in return. In Turkey, every object exchanged is admitted, and circulates without encountering any other obstacle than the payment of an infinitely small part of its value in passing the custom-house. Accordingly, the Turkish markets, supplied by all countries, do not reject any of the produce that commercial spirit may send into circulation; they do not impose any tax on the ships that bring this produce; they are seldom, or rather never, the theatre of those disordered movements occasioned by the unforeseen rarity of certain articles, which sometimes cause the prices to rise to an exorbitant extent, and convert commerce into a system of perpetual alarm and danger. In fact, as I have said, liberty of commerce reigns without limit, and free trade exists in its most extended form.*

Previous to the time of Reschid Pasha, the only recognised duty on imports from Great Britain was three per cent. *ad valorem;* but other imposts were levied by the authorities at and after the sale of the goods imported, and often in a manner even more oppressive than the amount itself. By the commercial treaty, however, with England, of the 16th of August, 1838, and subsequently by similar treaties with other European States, as also with America, all these imposts and exactions were abolished; the duty on foreign goods, whether raw or manufactured, being fixed at the same

---

* See "*Le Moniteur Ottoman.*" 1832.

rate of three per cent.; and, in lieu of all other and interior duties, one fixed duty of two per cent. was established, on payment of which all goods could be sold and re-sold without further duty or restriction.*

The impetus given to trade by this treaty was very great. For example, the number of British vessels that entered the port of Constantinople in the year 1837 was 432, tonnage 86,253; in the year 1838 there were 419, tonnage 120,860; in the year 1848 the number had increased to 1,397, tonnage 358,422; and in the year 1856 to 2,504, tonnage 898,753.

The imports into Turkey from Great Britain in 1827 amounted only to 531,704*l.*; in the year 1830 they had increased to 1,139,616*l.*; but in 1850 the value of British merchandise imported at the port of Constantinople alone amounted to 2,512,594*l.*, viz.:—Cotton and woollen manufactures, and some iron and zinc plates, in sailing vessels from Liverpool, 753,031*l.*; East and West India produce, and various kinds of British manufactures, in sailing vessels from London, 223,425*l.*; fine cotton and woollen manufactures, cochineal, indigo, &c., in steamers from Southampton, 833,670*l.*; fine cotton and woollen manufactures, &c., in screw-steamers from Liverpool, 612,000*l.*; ditto, in steamers from London, 16,300*l.*; iron, 27,000*l.*; coals, 8,763*l.*; coals and sundry goods from England in foreign vessels, 38,405*l.*; total, 2,512,594*l.*

The war in the Crimea, which was followed by the peace of Paris, brought us into still closer connexion with Turkey; and the Hatti-Humáyoun, or imperial order, issued in Constantinople on the 18th of February,

---

* By the recent commercial treaty between Great Britain and Turkey, the import duty on foreign goods has been raised to 8 per cent. *ad valorem.* See Appendices Nos. 1 and 3.

1856, gave not alone confidence to Europe, but also security to the subjects of the Sultan.*

The principal provisions of this imperial order are as follow:—

'3. Full liberty of worship is guaranteed to every religious profession. No one can be forced to change his religion.

'4. No legal documents shall acknowledge any inferiority of one class of Ottoman subjects to another, in consequence of difference in religion, race, or language.

'17. All foreigners may possess landed property, obeying the laws, and paying the taxes; for this purpose arrangements shall be made with foreign Powers.

'24. Banks and similar institutions shall be created as means to reform the monetary and financial systems of the empire, and to create capital and wealth.

'25. Roads and canals shall be made. All restrictions on commerce and on agriculture shall be abolished.'

In every portion of Turkey this confidence and security was followed by an almost unparalleled augmentation of commercial prosperity. The total number of vessels that entered and cleared at the port of Constantinople in the year 1837 was 7,342; in 1838 the number was 11,250; in 1848, 13,839; and in 1852, 15,770; but during the year 1856 there entered and cleared 36,274; tonnage, 7,378,769.

At Smyrna the number of vessels that entered and cleared in 1852 was 2,733, tonnage 538,904; in the year 1856 the number was 3,522, tonnage 879,228. The value of the imports and exports at Samsoun, in

---

* The ordinances of the Sultan are called Hatti-Humáyoun (the august writing) or *Hatti-Schérif* (the illustrious writing), because every document sent to the official department bears at the top, besides the ordinary signature (*touhra*), a short line of His Majesty's writing, such as—*Moudji-bindje 'amel olouna.* Let this accordingly be performed.— See Appendix No. 2.

1853, was 836,871*l.*; in 1856, 1,429,285*l*. At Alexandretta, in 1853, imports and exports 451,634*l.*; in 1856, 1,068,313*l*. At Crete, the imports and exports in 1837 amounted to 192,244*l.*; in 1854, to 436,943*l.*; and in 1856, to 839,072*l*. At Trebizond, the imports in 1848 amounted to 1,726,052*l.*; in 1853, to 1,742,693*l.*; and in 1856, to 2,816,304*l*. At Beyrout, in 1848, the imports and exports were only 799,914*l.*; and in 1853, 1,347,408*l.*; but in the year 1856 they increased to 1,958,333*l.*

The total value of imports into, and exports from, Turkey in the year 1852 was about 20,000,000*l.*; and if we may form an opinion from the increased trade with Great Britain and France, that amount must now be doubled.*

The increase of the imports and exports from the years 1851 to 1860 may be seen from the following table:—

Years.	Imports and Exports between Turkey and Great Britain.	Imports and Exports between Turkey and France.	TOTAL.
	£	£	£
1851	7,000,398	2,899,254	9,899,652
1852	6,864,741	3,476,915	10,341,656
1854	6,251,131	4,031,939	10,283,070
1858	9,535,239	6,235,181	15,770,420
1859	9,629,536	6,900,531	16,530,067
1860	10,963,329	8,385,156	19,348,585

The above figures are evidence of the immense growth of the trade and commerce of Turkey; but the question, perhaps, still remains—" Of what importance is that to us?" The answer is very simple, namely, that Turkey is one of the best customers we have for our produce and manufactures. In 1858 the value of our

* It is estimated that the annual trade of Turkey with Foreign countries amounts at present to 48,000,000*l.*, and that between the provinces to 20,000,000*l.*; giving a total of 68,000,000*l.* per annum.

exports (the produce and manufacture of the United Kingdom) was:—

To Turkey	£5,192,095
,, France	4,863,131

In the year 1860, however, the exportations of British and Irish produce and manufactures to the principal foreign countries were as follow:—

To Hamburg, Bremen, and Lübeck	£10,364,237
,, Holland	6,114,862
,, France	5,249,980
,, Turkey	5,237,105
,, Russia	3,268,479
,, Egypt	2,479,737
,, Spain	2,471,447
,, Prussia	1,884,403
,, Sardinia	1,864,338
,, Portugal	1,698,931
,, Belgium	1,610,144
,, Two Sicilies	1,321,339
,, Hanover	1,107,570
,, Sweden and Norway	1,044,717
,, Tuscany	1,034,435
,, Austria	993,669
,, Denmark	731,162
,, Greece	343,500
,, Papal States	294,175

Of our exports to Turkey, our cotton manufactures form the most important item. In 1860, the total exports were 5,457,839l., in which cotton goods entered as 4,225,395l., viz., 22,824,004 lbs. of cotton twist, value 878,781l.; 229,201,826 yards of plain and printed calicoes, value 3,324,492l.; muslins, lace, and patent net, &c., 22,122l.

When we bear in mind that the consumption of our produce and manufactures by Turkey has increased from 464,873l. in 1827, to 5,237,105l. in 1860, and that too under circumstances in every way adverse to the extension of commerce, with banking little better understood there than it was 2000 years ago, and with interest on money ruling as high as in the time of Bocheris the Wise (800 B.C.), who passed a law by which it was forbidden to allow the interest to increase beyond double the principal sum, it is but a natural consequence that, with the general commerce of Turkey extended, and her resources more fully developed, as they must be, by the establishment of banks, our commercial relations with the Ottoman empire will still further increase, and the inhabitants of Turkey will still continue to be amongst the best customers for our produce and manufactures.

Nor is it at all likely that new banking enterprises will in any way injure the older one, as in a commercial community one bank always prepares the ground for other similar establishments. This has been proved over and over again in England, Scotland, Ireland, India, and Australia, and so it will be in Turkey. It is, however, of the greatest importance that their operations should not be confined to Constantinople, Smyrna, and a few of the larger towns in the Sultan's dominions, but that branches and agencies should be extended throughout the length and breadth of the land, wherever a field for commerce already exists or may be created. To establish banks with any more limited view, would be to only half test the resources of the country. At Salonica, Adrianople, Brussa, Diarbekhr, Tarsus, Jaffa, Damascus, and Baghdad, there is a large return to be had for money, with quite as safe investment, as at Constantinople, Smyrna, Aleppo, and Beyrout. Moreover, at the present day, every town of any size—especially any seaport—is in such constant communication with the capital, that remittances of money to and fro become a matter of every-day necessity. Nor should it be forgotten that if banking in Turkey, nay, if Turkey itself, is to flourish, the trading community must be rescued from the fangs of the native Saraff, who makes his enormous but unholy gains by a fictitious raising and lowering of the exchange, by elsewhere unheard-of usury, and, in cases not a few, by "sweating" the coins which pass through his hands. From these—and from others like them, who have grown rich on their plunder of the government itself—English banking in Turkey, conducted by Englishmen, and on English principles, is destined to redeem the country, at the same time legitimately increasing English influence, and making no inconsiderable profits for those whose capital is thus invested. Were the natural resources of the empire less abundant it might be otherwise; but in every province, from Lake Van to the Adriatic, mines of undeveloped wealth lie buried in the soil, needing only capital and industrial activity to multiply, manifold, the public revenues, and enrich both capitalist and cultivator.

It is, however, a good deal the fashion in England to talk largely of the "risk" of investing money in Turkey. But most of those who speak thus know nothing whatever of the country, while many do it with the positive intention of deterring others from shooting over the manor on which they themselves have such profitable sport. Where were—where are—the vast majority of fortunes amassed by Trieste, Leghorn, Marseilles, and Genoa merchants made, if not in the Levant? If it be so dangerous to invest money in trade with Constantinople, Smyrna, Aleppo, Beyrout, or Damascus, why do so many French and Italian firms—even wealthy houses —establish branches in all these places; and how is it that they, almost without exception, realize such large and speedy profits? Or how is it, if—as these interested prophets of evil would have everybody believe — nothing but loss attends transactions with Turkey, that, year by year, more and more continental capital is employed in trade with the Levant? Galata, indeed, is perhaps less commercially exact than Lombard Street; Smyrna, in the same respect, will not bear comparison with Liverpool; nor is a Lebanon silk-grower at all times as ready as a Yorkshire wool-stapler to "meet his little bill." But, nevertheless, there are throughout the Levant very few ultimate losses in trade, and exceedingly little of that deliberate and systematized fraud which in these days is to be met with, more or less, in every European city. Nor should a very important fact be lost sight of, namely, that if commerce in the East has its special evils, it has also its special and more than counterbalancing advantages. Twelve, fourteen, and sixteen per cent., net profit, are not to be made every day in Europe; whilst, in Turkey, with proper care and management, no banking or trading establishment should return less; and that, too, without more risk than legitimate speculation will authorise. In all countries losses will and do occur in business; but with ordinary foresight, common prudence, and knowledge of the people, they need certainly not be greater in Turkey than in any other place where men buy, sell, and discount in the common and legitimate way of trade.

STATISTICS

OF

THE RESOURCES OF TURKEY.

TURKEY PROPER.

CHAPTER VIII.

CONSTANTINOPLE.

Constantinople is situated between the Black Sea and the Sea of Marmora, at the entrance of the Bosphorus, which separates Europe from Asia. In commercial importance it ranks immediately after Liverpool and London, and before Marseilles. Its harbour, capable of containing twelve hundred ships, is considered one of the finest in the world.

The population of Constantinople was estimated in 1852 at 891,000, divided as follows:—

Mussulmans	475,000
Armenians	205,000
United Armenians	17,000
Greeks	132,000
Jews	37,000
Foreigners	25,000
Total	891,000

In the year 1850, the value of British merchandise imported into Constantinople amounted, as per the following table, to 2,512,594*l*.

	Value.
In Sailing Vessels from Liverpool:—	
Cotton and woollen manufactures, and some iron and zinc plates	£753,031
In Sailing Vessels from London:—	
East and West India produce, and various kinds of British manufactures	223,425
Carried forward	£976,456

Brought forward	£976,456
In Steamers from Southampton:—	
Fine cotton and woollen manufactures, cochineal, indigo, &c.	833,670
In Screw Steamers from Liverpool:—	
Same kind of cargoes as from Southampton	612,000
In a Steamer from London	16,300
From England, iron	27,000
„ „ coals	8,763
In Foreign Vessels from England:—	
Coals and sundry goods	38,405
	£2,512,594

The immense increase which has taken place in the trade of Constantinople will be at once evident from the fact that in the above year, 1850, when the importations from Great Britain amounted to 2,512,594*l.*, only 796 British vessels, tonnage 208,136, entered the port, whereas in 1856 there entered 2504, tonnage 898,753. The total number of British vessels that entered and cleared at the port of Constantinople in the year 1838 was only 838, tonnage 241,720. In 1848 the number had increased to 2,761, tonnage 708,883; and in 1856 the number still further increased to 5,341, tonnage 1,763,207. The total number of vessels of all nations that entered and cleared in the year 1850 was 10,956, tonnage 1,943,347. In 1851 the number was 13,069, tonnage 2,397,316; in 1856, the total number increased to 36,274, tonnage 7,378,769; while in the year 1859 the number of sailing vessels alone amounted to 27,029, tonnage 5,060,526.

The following tabular statement gives the number and tonnage of the vessels of each nation, exclusive of steam vessels, that entered and cleared at the port of Constantinople in the year 1859:—

Nationality of Vessels.		Entered.		Cleared.		Total number of ships.	Total of Tonnage.
		Number of ships.	Tonnage.	Number of ships.	Tonnage.		
Turkish flag.	Turkey	4,845	559,862	4,389	497,012	9,234	1,056,874
	Wallachia	420	39,095	437	43,502	857	82,597
	Moldavia	170	16,060	164	15,131	334	31,191
	Servia	41	9,808	44	5,548	85	13,356
	Samos	216	20,090	217	19,795	433	39,885
		5,692	642,915	5,251	580,988	10,938	1,223,903
Greece		3,354	557,703	3,376	558,703	6,730	1,116,406
Great Britain		1,563	460,166	1,612	474,915	3,175	935,081
Austria		965	349,236	983	354,292	1,948	703,522
Russia		406	165,796	417	167,970	823	333,766
Naples		351	106,251	364	102,502	715	208,753
Sweden and Norway		338	87,216	332	85,868	670	173,084
Ionian Islands		467	80,065	452	77,593	919	157,558
Prussia		109	24,618	112	25,947	221	50,565
France		113	24,357	113	24,357	226	48,714
Holland		136	20,973	133	20,569	269	41,542
Mecklenburg		119	12,152	115	11,812	234	23,964
America		26	9,201	26	9,201	52	18,402
Denmark		31	5,579	31	5,579	62	11,158
Belgium		10	3,997	10	3,997	20	7,994
Bremen		8	1,933	8	1,933	16	3,866
Spain		2	1,030	2	1,030	4	2,060
Lubeck		1	91	1	91	2	182
		13,691	2,553,279	13,338	2,507,247	27,029	5,060,526

CHAPTER IX.

SMYRNA.

Resolutions relative to the establishment of a Branch Bank at Smyrna.

1. THAT Smyrna is one of the most important commercial cities in the Ottoman empire, and that its trade is rapidly increasing, as the following tabular statement will testify:—

IMPORTS AND EXPORTS AT THE PORT OF SMYRNA.

Years.	Imports.	Exports.	Total.
	£	£	£
1852	1,131,117	1,472,211	2,603,328
1853	1,093,074	1,705,748	2,798,822
1854	1,134,926	1,329,599	2,464,525
1855	2,141,681	2,367,142	4,508,823
1857*	2,549,472	2,497,232	5,046,704
1859	2,320,417	2,213,235	4,533,652
1860†	2,485,991	1,923,319	4,409,310

2. That the exigencies of this increasing commerce require increased banking facilities.

3. That the establishment of a Bank, which would confine itself to the legitimate operations of banking and afford aid in assisting commerce—avoiding on its own part all direct or indirect interference with or competition in trade—would be a great boon to the commercial community of Smyrna, and would at the same time be a safe and profitable medium for the investment of capital.

* See Specification of Imports and Exports for the year 1857, page 92.
† See General Statement of the Commerce of Smyrna in the year 1860, page 91.

4. That a Bank founded on such principles, and conducted by gentlemen in whom the commercial community of Smyrna could repose confidence, would undoubtedly realize considerable profits, and return ample dividends to its shareholders.

5. That the above resolutions be forwarded to Mr. J. Lewis Farley, and that he be requested to take such measures as may be conducive to the establishment of a Bank at Smyrna as speedily as possible.

Smyrna, the 21st of August, 1861.

[Here follow the Signatures.*]

The town and commerce of Smyrna are so well known that it would be superfluous to say more than that it has an essentially commercial population of about 160,000 persons of all nations†, transacting busi-

* The original resolutions, &c., are in my possession.

† Mr. Blunt (her Britannic Majesty's Consul), in his report to the Foreign Office, estimates the population of Smyrna at 160,000, and states that "the Turkish population of Smyrna, which in 1830 was 80,000 souls, is at present only 41,000, while the Greek population of Smyrna, which in 1830 was 20,000 souls, is to-day 75,000 souls." The local journal *L'Impartial*, however, disputes the accuracy of this statement, and reckons the population of Smyrna as follows:—

Mussulmans		42,000
Greeks		28,000
Armenians		7,000
Jews		14,000
Latins		4,500
Total Ottoman subjects		95,500
Foreigners:—		
French subjects	546	
do. protected	314	
		860
Austrian subjects	3,150	
do. protected	60	
		3,210
Italian subjects	3,000	
do. protected	60	
		3,060
Carried forward	7,130	95,500

ness with foreign countries to the annual amount (aggregating imports and exports) of six to seven millions sterling*; in addition to which there is a local and inland trade of considerable importance, now rendered susceptible of further development through the facilities for transport afforded by the recently-opened railway.

Some years ago, a local Joint Stock Bank existed in Smyrna, which prospered well for a time; but the managers having fallen into the error (not unfrequent among bankers in the East when tempted by a high rate of interest) of locking up a large portion of their capital in mortgages, the bank was unable to meet the extraordinary demands upon its coffers created by the crisis of 1847, and accordingly came to a standstill.

Subsequently, a number of small firms, *soi-disant* bankers, started up with little capital, but with a minute practical experience in the banking affairs of the place, acquired in following the occupation of bill-brokers during the existence of the bank. On its failure, these firms added to their brokerage business a species of bill-jobbing—buying foreign bills and paying for them in three or four weekly instalments—

Brought forward		7,130	95,500
English subjects	1,200		
Maltese	750		
Ionians	3,500		
Protected	1		
		5,451	
Dutch		336	
Russians		50	
Americans, Danes, Belgians, Prussians, Spaniards, Swedes, &c.		200	
Persians		120	
Greeks		15,000	
			28,287
			123,787

* This amount includes the trade carried on by the Smyrna merchants at several of the outports on the coast. See Report, page 96.

re-selling them with their endorsement (on the place) at a profit, and getting a quarter per cent. brokerage besides on the transaction. For several years all the banking business of Smyrna was carried on by these houses, chiefly Chiotes, who, with their proverbial adroitness in monetary transactions, for the most part amassed considerable fortunes; and the Ottoman Bank would have found in them formidable rivals but for the truly Levantine mania, which affected one and all, for converting their gains, as soon as realised, into bricks and mortar, thus rendering them incapable of coping with an establishment possessing a large disposable capital. It was, therefore, a natural consequence, that when in September 1856 the Ottoman Bank opened a branch in Smyrna, the wings of the small bankers were materially clipped, and most of them were forced to fall back upon their old trade of bill-brokers.

I must not omit to mention another class of houses which exists in Smyrna in limited number, and to which—for want of a better—custom has assigned the title of bankers, on the *lucus a non lucendo* principle, I presume, for no one banks with them, nor do they bank with anybody. These houses are offshoots of Constantinople firms, their province being generally to create funds for the parent establishment. It is through the operations of these firms that the commercial tranquillity of Smyrna is from time to time disturbed by sudden unmeaning fluctuations in exchanges, of which the local commerce furnishes no explanation, but which are the echoes of some Galata Bourse agitation. These fluctuations are supposed to portend some great event— a war, a loan, a bank, a revolution in the Danubian provinces, &c.; but the simple truth is, that some large house or other at Constantinople has to draw or to remit a heavy amount—as the case may be—and the agitation is got up to give the exchange a turn in the right direction. A bank at Smyrna would protect the traders from these harassing influences.

The nature, therefore, of the business which offers to a banking house in Smyrna, and of the system which appears best adapted to meet the requirements of that place, will deserve a little consideration. In order, however, to appreciate the only system applicable to the country, it is necessary to divest one's mind of prejudice in favour of Lombard Street practice. It is impossible to transplant the English system in its integrity into Turkey, and, even were it possible, no satisfactory result would be obtained. The banker must therefore be content to take the practice of the country for his basis of operations, and to engraft upon it such English customs as may not too much clash with local prejudices, bearing in mind that, although the Lombard Street system is admirably adapted to the elaborately finished commercial machinery of which it forms a part, it is not necessarily so perfect in itself as to be able to stand the test of isolation—its perfection consisting only in its applicability to surrounding circumstances. At Smyrna, the circumstances being different, the banker must modify his system accordingly, and, laying down a few general principles for his guidance, must seek to conciliate the many conflicting prejudices and interests by which his clientèle, composed of all creeds and nationalities, are influenced.

One item of business to which every possible encouragement should be given, is that of Drawing Accounts, not only for the profit which it yields, but for the insight which it gives into the affairs of the bank's customers. Among the merchants, however, very few will keep a balance; on the contrary, the bank would be called upon to grant to the majority of its trading customers a cash credit proportioned to the standing, means, and character of each*. I think that the directors of the local Bank fell into an error in the rules they laid down regarding the rates of interest to be charged and paid to customers. From twelve to fifteen per cent. was charged upon credits, while only six per cent. was allowed upon balances and deposits, in consequence of which these last were almost prohibited. It would seem more rational to proportion the rate allowed to that which the local commerce is willing to pay, and two-thirds appear to me to be a proper proportion. Legal interest in Turkey is twelve per cent., and taking this as a minimum, there is always a demand for money for commercial purposes; but, on the other hand, for private individuals who wish to place their money at interest without entering into the intricacies of commerce, or the delusions and snares of a Turkish mortgage, there exists no facility whatever. Therefore it is my conviction that were twelve per cent. and eight per cent. established as the rates in prosperous times, subject to increase in seasons of scarcity, a large amount of deposits at the lower

---

* "There is one part of their system, which is stated by all the witnesses (and, in the opinion of the committee, very justly stated) to have had the best effects upon the people of Scotland, and particularly upon the middle and poorer classes of society, in producing and encouraging habits of frugality and industry. The practice referred to is that of cash credits * * * From the facility which these cash credits give to all the small transactions of the country, and from the opportunities which they afford to persons who begin business with little or no capital but their character, to employ profitably the minutest products of their industry, it cannot be doubted that the most important advantages are derived to the whole community."—*Report of the Committee of the House of Lords to inquire into the Irish and Scotch Circulations*, 1826, p. 4.

rate would flow into the bank, and these could be employed at the higher rate among its commercial customers; while at the same time greater inducement would be offered to constituents to keep a permanent balance to their credit. In addition to the interest charged to customers, a commission not exceeding one-eighth per cent. should be levied on the debit side of every account; and this item will form an important feature in the profits of the bank. It is evident that, in order to carry out the system of cash credits here recommended, the manager will have to exercise a great amount of vigilance and discretion, and to consider:— *First*, the nationality of his customer. *Second*, the nature of his business, whether import, export, local, or governmental. *Third*, His individual character. *Fourth*, His means. It would be out of place here to enlarge upon these points: it will suffice to state that import houses are for this species of credit more reliable than those doing an export trade, due regard being had to nationality; that but little dependence can, at present, be placed upon houses doing business with Government; and that the strictly local trader—who buys the goods which arrive from the interior, and sells to export houses, giving often in payment imported goods which he buys on the spot—is, of all, the safest and surest.

Smyrna draws annually upon Europe for about 3,000,000*l.* sterling, against shipments; and, probably, another million of credit or accommodation paper. Smyrna remits about 4,000,000*l.* per annum for imported goods, and the credit bills have also to be covered. Hence, the balance of trade being against the country, the supply of trade bills is inadequate to the wants of remitters, and this disparity is the more sensibly felt from the fact that a large proportion of the drafts are given off in the month of September against fruit, thus creating a glut of paper for a few weeks and leaving an insufficient provision for the rest of the year. The consequence of this is, that during the month of September a great decline takes place in exchanges, while, for the rest of the year, the rate for three-months bills is invariably $\frac{1}{2}$ to 1 per cent. in favour of the sellers, the difference representing the cost of shipping specie. But this difference is frequently in excess of the charges on shipments of gold, for the fact is that the circulation is maintained by all the abusive coinages, such as the beshlik and copper of Turkey, the swanzig of Austria, and the carbovanz of Russia : gold being generally scarce, and at a premium. It is evident, however, that the import houses, whose trade requires regular remittances, can profit but to a very limited extent by the low rate of exchange which rules during the fruit season, and that they are necessarily put to much inconvenience for the rest of the year to find paper suited to their wants. Here, then, is an opening of which the banker alone can take advantage.

The course which the manager will have to pursue, with regard to his transactions in foreign bills, will be as follows :—He will take bills within certain limits from all his exporting customers, and furnish all his importing constituents with the paper they require for their remittances. The countervalue of the bills bought, passing through the drawing account of each, will be chargeable with the $\frac{1}{8}$ per cent. commission ; and since for transactions between the banker and his own customers the intervention of a broker is avoided, the seller, on whom would otherwise fall the $\frac{1}{4}$ per cent. brokerage, is glad to accept from the banker a somewhat lower rate of exchange than he would out of doors, and the more so that the proceeds of bills sold to the bank are immediately available, while, if sold elsewhere, the custom of the place is to extend the payment over a period of three or four weeks. In buying his customers' bills the banker will naturally regulate the rate of exchange according to the quality of the paper. There are bills which it will suit him to buy at $\frac{1}{4}$ per cent. lower than his own selling rate, and others on which he will make 2 per cent. or more; on an average, his list of drafts and remittances should show 1 per cent. clear profit on exchange, and it will frequently be more. The importing customers of the bank will also look to that establishment to supply them with the periodical remittances which they have to make to Europe; and it will be in the interest of the banker to follow to some extent the custom of the place, and allow those who buy their drafts to pay for them in two, three, or four weekly instalments, as a better rate of exchange can always be thus obtained, and the credit thus afforded being passed in the drawing account, the $\frac{1}{8}$ per cent. becomes chargeable upon it. A brief experience, combined with the personal acquaintance which a banker must cultivate among his constituents, will very shortly show who may or who may not be trusted; and, by firmly insisting on punctuality, and steadily withholding facilities of this nature from those who once make default, the banker will readily bring his clients into order, while, if he follow up a uniformly firm but, at the same time, loyal and obliging mode of dealing, they will become as manageable a body as if they were all amenable to British law.

I shall not enter here into the discussion of arbitrations of exchange, because I consider that operations of this kind involve an amount of risk which a manager of a joint-stock bank should not incur. It will be necessary merely to watch the exchanges on the Continent and profit by any evident advantage which may present itself, but only in so far as the regular business of the bank may be thereby facilitated or benefited.

The applications for short loans would, at some seasons of the year, be numerous. Importing firms demand accommodation of this kind on shipping documents of goods arriving, or on goods already warehoused. Exporting firms, more especially those who deal in opium, as well as local traders, frequently require advances on goods waiting an opportunity for shipment in the one case, or held for a rise in the local market in the other. From 12 to 18 per cent., with a small commission, is paid for loans of this nature, which should only be for sixty days at the outside.

It will appear strange to the English banker that the item of bill discounting should not appear in the operations of a bank in Smyrna. The fact is that there are no bills to discount. The balance of trade being against Smyrna, there is no demand in foreign markets for bills on that place, and the local trade is conducted by means of "Bons," or acknowledgements given by the debtor to the creditor; sometimes payable at a fixed date, sometimes with no specific maturity. In the latter case, the debtor pays a portion every Saturday, the payments being endorsed upon the Bon. The greater number of these Bons are given by the retail dealers in the bazaars to the importers, through whom their shops are supplied, but they can only be available to the merchant as a collateral security for advances; the instances are very rare where they can be discounted by a banker, although they pass from hand to hand among merchants, especially native Armenians and Jews, without endorsement.

Thus it will be seen that the business falling to the lot of a bank established in Smyrna will consist of the following items, viz. :—

1. Keeping current accounts on commission.
2. Receiving deposits at interest.
3. Granting cash credits, or advancing money on bills of lading or warehoused goods.
4. Dealing in foreign exchanges.

It now remains to be considered what amount the bank should have at its disposal in order to take up and maintain a position of first-rate importance; and, with this view, I am of opinion that a capital of not less than 120,000*l.* would be requisite, or, at all events, desirable; very extensive transactions could be conducted with less, but I am inclined to think that it would be found insufficient after a short period. In addition to the above effective capital, the bank should have the faculty of drawing on the principal towns of Europe for about double the amount of the capital, covering the drafts at or before maturity. These credits should be distributed in about the following proportions :—

London	£120,000
Paris {and/or} Marseilles	60,000
Trieste {and/or} Vienna	50,000
Genoa, Leghorn, and other places	10,000
	£240,000

It is not difficult to calculate the returns which might

and should be derived from the above capital, supported and assisted by the credits indicated. Of the 120,000*l.* capital, 20,000*l.* would suffice for a reserve; leaving 100,000*l.* to be employed among the customers of the bank and others. The credits would be employed in furnishing remittances to the importing customers, and would be covered by bills purchased from exporting customers at a lower rate. Taking, then, 12 per cent. interest, and ⅛ per cent. commission, as the terms of the bank—

£100,000, at 12 per cent., would yield	£12,000
⅛ per cent. commission on four times that amount, as the investments would never exceed three months	500
£2,000,000, drawn and remitted, yielding net ½ per cent.	10,000
⅛ per cent. commission on twice this amount	5,000
The whole giving a certain revenue of at least	£27,500

— to which must be added commissions on accounts current, difference of interest on money received upon deposit and employed at an advanced rate, as well as the profit made during the fruit season, which may be calculated as a certainty.

Considering the manner in which the banking business of Smyrna is carried on, it will be apparent that the establishment of another bank in that town would be regarded as a great boon by the commercial classes, and the representations which have been very recently made to me on the subject lead to the same conclusion. I have, therefore, no hesitation in saying that there is an excellent opening for such an undertaking: all success, however, would depend upon the manner in which the management turned that opening to account. It must be borne in mind that the commercial body of

Smyrna is made up of a variety of nationalities, each of which has different habits, different ideas, and transacts business in a different way; and it must be the care of the manager to study the requirements of each, and the nature of his business, in order to determine what is the legitimate course for the bank to pursue under circumstances (to English ideas) of an exceptional nature, rather than to lay down a set of arbitrary rules, based upon English practice, in enforcing which offence would be perpetually given to some national prejudice, and thereby cause the loss of many valuable clients. It is worthy of remark, that few commercial towns support a crisis so well as Smyrna. In 1857, when produce had depreciated in England 60 per cent., and money was in demand in Smyrna at 2 and 3 per cent. per week, there was but one failure; and, in the late terrible crisis of 1860, but one firm engaged in regular trade suffered. Yet it must not be argued from this that Smyrna is a wealthy place; as a body, I should say that the means of the commercial classes of Smyrna were extremely limited; but I think that no one can fail to be struck with the economy and industry which are there practised. The Smyrna merchant is at his work from sunrise to sundown, and then adjourns from his office to his casino, to combine business for the morrow: a desk, a chair, and a sofa compose his office furniture; anything in excess of this provokes ridicule, and brings the innovator into discredit. At home, the strictest economy is observed; domestic wants are frugally provided for; and there is a total absence of luxury or display. This I consider to be the secret of the stability of Smyrna firms.

General Statement of the Commerce of Smyrna for the year 1860.

	Importations. Value in Pounds sterling.	Exportations. Value in Pounds sterling.
Great Britain	£805,875	£769,133
Turkey	624,964	186,578
France	387,794	285,770
Austria	292,840	276,913
America	131,754	204,323
Russia	48,622	44,778
East Indies (opium)	—	36,425
Sardinia	36,253 }	81,460
Tuscany	31,224 }	
Belgium	33,605	—
Greece	33,554	10,360
Holland	27,400	12,183
Malta	12,607	—
Sundry places, viz.:— Two Sicilies, Roman States, Ionian Islands, Rio Janeiro, &c.	19,499	15,396
Total	£2,485,091	£1,923,319

In 1859, the imports amounted to 2,320,417*l.*, which gives an increase of 165,574*l.* for the year 1860. The exports, which in 1859 were 2,213,235*l.*, exhibit in 1860 a decrease of 289,916*l.*

General Statement of the Navigation of Smyrna in the year 1860.

Entered.	No.	Tonnage.	Cleared.	No.	Tonnage.
Sailing vessels	872	122,600	Sailing vessels	871	118,449
Steamers	622	295,167	Steamers	622	294,220
Total	1494	417,767	Total	1493	412,669

Specification and Value of Imports at the Port of Smyrna, in the year 1857.

Names of Articles.	Quantities.	Value in Piastres. Ex. 120 Ps., £1.
Alum	189 barrels	85,050
Bottles	5090 crates	173,000
Butter	1231 barrels	2,285,920
Bricks and tiles	494,100 pieces	225,520
Canvas	501 bales	570,300
Caps (Fezes)	1292 cases	7,836,900
Caviar	143 hogsheads	2,224,700
Chairs and other furniture.	1887 packages	1,018,700
Cheese	4008 cases	2,559,660
Cinnamon	393 "	262,900
Cloths	2222 bales	16,968,300
Cloves	239 bags	107,540
Cochineal	188 barrels	876,150
Coals	28,670 tons	6,425,050
Coffee	16,984 bags	7,642,560
Copper	332 cases, &c.	1,560,300
Cordage	2789 bales	1,112,100
Cotton and woollen manufactures	16,331 "	82,152,500
Cotton twist	6682 "	16,048,900
Dates	1697 barrels	908,500
Drugs and medicines	2839 packages	3,345,200
Earthenware	1560 barrels	1,622,200
Firearms	549 cases	2,460,500
Fish (salted)	4831 barrels	1,424,140
Flour	4498 barrels and bags	967,700
Frankincense	207 barrels	140,320
	Carried forward—Piastres	161,004,610

Specification and Value of Imports at the Port of Smyrna, in the year 1857.—(Continued.)

Names of Articles.	Quantities.	Value in Piastres. Ex. 120 Ps., £1.
	Brought forward	161,004,610
Glassware and window glass	9512 cases	4,009,700
Gold thread	167 packages	2,620,500
Gunpowder	7654 barrels	995,020
Henna	2584 bags	808,000
Indigo	260 cases	2,884,000
Iron, in bars	5136 tons	8,304,070
Ironmongery, &c.	7893 packages	24,559,600
Logwood	21,542 pieces	468,870
Marble and stone	269,175 cases and pieces.	1,000,520
Nails, &c.	6381 barrels, &c.	2,579,370
Paints (prepared)	2482 ,,	165,940
Paper, &c.	2875 cases, &c.	4,407,200
Pepper and allspice	1275 sacks	567,260
Pewter	349 barrels	621,000
Pipe sticks	752,000 pieces	1,131,500
Porcelain	523 cases	1,064,500
Potatoes	3974 barrels and sacks	331,140
Rice	31,399 bags	13,192,600
Rum and brandy	8185 barrels	4,868,900
Sal-ammoniac	85 ,,	137,520
Shot, &c.	2027 ,,	952,220
Silk goods	1224 cases	11,181,000
Skins (tanned, &c.)	7312 bales, &c.	7,065,460
Soap	7877 cases, &c.	3,962,400
Steel	2094 ,,	650,000
Sugar	11,032 barrels	10,998,400
Sulphur and matches	2544 barrels and cases	1,164,800
Tar and resin	3558 barrels	302,940
Timber	2,795,228 pieces	9,315,270
Tin	2223 cases	533,520
Tobacco	17,868 bales, &c.	13,989,950
Vitriol	533 barrels	132,400
Watches and jewellery	226 cases	4,436,000
White lead	2196 ,,	383,320
Wines and liqueurs	2538 casks and cases	863,560
Wire and scrap iron	2058 barrels	4,047,500
Zinc	215 ,,	209,150
	Total . Piastres	305,936,710

Specification and Value of Exports at the Port of Smyrna, in the year 1857.

Names of Articles.	Quantities.	Value in Piastres. Ex. 120 Ps., £1.
Almonds	564 kintals	338,400
Aniseed	365 ,,	172,980
Attar, otto of roses	47 cases	622,000
Barley	529,122 kilos	7,936,820
Bees'-wax	1971 kintals	2,523,080
Bones	13,554 ,,	474,390
Boxwood	2680 ,,	120,600
Carpets	1096 bales	5,727,000
Cocoons (silk)	679 kintals	4,074,000
Copper (old)	142 ,,	156,200
Cotton	10,497 ,,	3,202,290
Cotton thread (of Anatolia)	2683 ,,	1,873,100
Figs (dried)	100,805 ,,	25,473,250
Flax seed	618 ,,	74,380
Flour	4800 ,,	475,000
Fruits (dried)	13,438 ,,	1,182,780
Gall nuts	4598 ,,	1,785,600
Goats'-hair	1185 ,,	1,892,300
Gum	3226 ,,	3,517,100
Hemp seed	19,160 kilos	459,840
Hides	7578 kintals	4,226,130
Horse-hair	168 ,,	95,400
Leeches	475 cases, &c.	287,000
Liquorice juice	4284 kintals	1,285,200
Maize	17,500 kilos	332,500
Madder	117,383 kintals	36,127,830
Nuts and walnuts	1100 ,,	165,600
Olive oil	2180 ,,	763,000
Opium	3271 cases of 80 to 90 ch6q.	31,965,900
Poppy seed	170 kintals	20,400
Rags	34,750 ,,	2,753,750
Raisins	196,482 ,,	41,285,360
Salt	460,250 kilos	1,956,260
Scammony	3604 okes	1,361,820
Sesame seed	31,633 kilos	1,771,450
Skins (lambs' and goats')	780 bales	1,089,600
,, (hares')	432 ,,	1,728,000
Silk	3602 kintals and okes.	14,620,000
	Carried forward—Piastres	203,916,310

Specification and Value of Exports at the Port of Smyrna, in the year 1857.—(Continued.)

Names of Articles.	Quantities.	Value in Piastres. Ex. 120 Ps., £1.
	Brought forward .	203,916,310
Spirits of wine	3380 kintals and okes.	965,100
Sponges	2745 cases	4,105,600
Valonia	476,288 kintals	39,081,840
Wheat	257,621 kilos	9,787,140
Wines of the country	21,626 kintals	3,072,580
Wool	57,320 ,,	33,589,470
Yellow berries	10,911 ,,	2,945,970
Sundries	{ 103,996 kilos 1129 kintals }	2,203,780
	Total . Piastres	299,667,700

Kintal	. . . . .	125 lbs. English.
Kilo	. . . . .	1 bushel.
Oke	. . . . .	2¾ lbs.

Report on the Trade of Smyrna in connection with the Establishment of a Branch Bank.*

The increasing importance of the trade of Smyrna is clearly shown from the statement contained in the resolutions which have been forwarded to you relative to the establishment, in this town, of a branch bank. This statement shows an aggregate amount of imports and exports, for the year 1852, of 2,603,328*l.*, and, by a constant progress, it reaches, in the year 1860, the amount of 4,409,310*l.* Considerable improvement has

* This report has been kindly forwarded to me by a member of one of the oldest mercantile firms in Smyrna. It strengthens, to a considerable extent, the observations which I have already made upon the subject.

been taking place, during the past few years, in the means of transporting goods from the interior of the country to Smyrna; amongst which the most important is that of the railroad from Smyrna to Aidin, one of the richest agricultural districts in Asia Minor. More civil and personal liberty is, perhaps, enjoyed by the rural population of this part of Turkey than in any other part of the empire, and its immediate consequence has been an increasing production of the soil. The general population of Asia Minor, especially the Christian portion, is also decidedly on the increase. The facts lead to the conclusion that the actual amount of trade in Smyrna will, in the course of a few years, be doubled or trebled.

The natural position of Smyrna is such that the greater part of Asia Minor depends upon it for the sale of the country's produce, as well as for the importation of the manufactures of Europe, and the colonial products of the East and West Indies.

The export trade of Smyrna consists principally of the raw produce of Asia Minor, and the import trade of manufactured goods and colonial produce from England, America, France, Holland, Germany, Austria, Italy, &c. The most important productions of Asia Minor exported from Smyrna come to market in the following order:— Silk cocoons, silk cocoon seed, raw silk, sheep's wool, kid, lamb, and goats' skins, opium, grain of all kinds, such as barley, wheat, Indian corn, dried fruits of different qualities, madder roots, cotton, oil seeds, yellow berries, yellow wax, flax, many kinds of gums and drugs, valonia, olive oil, &c. The imports consist chiefly of manufactured cotton, woollen and silk goods, from England, France, Italy, and Switzerland; cotton yarn, coffee, refined sugar, pepper, arms, gunpowder, iron bars, nails, many kinds of iron wares, tin, coals, &c.

The above enumeration shows the great variety of goods on which the Smyrna trade is based, and banking operations connected with this trade, provided they be properly understood and conducted, are in every way safe and profitable.

Besides the trade carried on in Smyrna itself, almost all the trade along the coast of Asia Minor, from the Dardanelles to the South as far as Tarsus, the islands of Mitylene, Scio, and Rhodes included, is conducted for account of Smyrna houses, by whom the funds are furnished. Vessels are sent to many outports along the coast and to the islands, in order to load direct for Europe, such goods as valonia, grain, seeds, fruits, &c., to a yearly amount varying from three to four millions sterling.

The amount of money required to carry on the whole trade connected with Smyrna may be estimated yearly at an approximate sum of seven or eight millions sterling, and this offers a large scope for banking operations. The banking business carried on in Smyrna, by banking houses and such establishments, has never been adequate to the actual necessities of the trade, either from a want of sufficient capital, or from the impossibility of embracing the whole range of business doing in Smyrna. This accounts for the large profits made by such establishments, as also for the great fluctuation in exchanges — varying from 1 to 5 per cent. according to circumstances — and the necessity in which merchants are often placed to have gold or silver money brought from Europe, in order to pay for their purchases.

The import trade begins in the months of March,

April, and June; importers are then in want of paper to remit to Europe, and, as export trade at that moment is small, a considerable demand for paper takes place in the first six months of the year, with a corresponding rise in the exchanges. Importers then very often take paper on England and France, to be paid for at thirty or forty days, with interest usually reckoned on the Exchange at 1 to 1½ per cent. per month. During that period the country merchants also require funds to send into the interior, for the purchase of produce, and money can be lent to them at a high rate of interest.

Then, again, when produce begins to come to market in July, and is being bought for exportation, paper is more abundant; exchanges lower and continue lowering as late as the month of November, when they begin to rise once more. Banking operations managed so as to sell drafts in the first part of the year, and purchase drafts for remittance in the latter, always leave a regular and constant profit.

It very often occurs that importers, exporters, and country merchants have goods on hand, which they cannot dispose of, on account of the temporary state of the market, and require to make advances to their friends on the same. Money can be advanced on such goods without any risk.

There are in Smyrna three courses for money :—The *exchange rate*, in which bills and the produce of the country are paid, the Turkish pound being reckoned at 113½ piastres; the *tarif rate*, in which import goods from Europe are paid, reckoning the Turkish pound at 120 piastres; and the *current rate*, at which all the retail dealers' trade is carried on, the Turkish pound reckoning at 140 piastres. All the merchants' accounts are kept at the *exchange rate*. Although these various courses of money may give some gain to a bank, they have been abusively introduced in Smyrna; and a bank, by contributing to bring all money transactions to one uniform rate, would confer a great boon to the mercantile community of the country.

In connection with a National bank, there are many other operations which would bring very regular profits to a branch, if it should be established in Smyrna.

The revenues of the Customs, of the tithes, and of all the other duties levied in the provinces of Asia Minor, are sent to Constantinople to the central Government, by way of Smyrna, in groups of money. They amount to about one and a-half to two millions sterling per annum. Such mode of making remittances is very expensive to Government, and attended with no small risk. Arrangements might be made advantageous to the Government and the bank, so as to have all that money cashed in Smyrna, and either paid by the notes of the bank, or remitted in good mercantile paper on Constantinople with a gain of $\frac{3}{4}$ or $\frac{1}{2}$ per cent., and thus spare unnecessary expenses and risk.

It could also be arranged that merchants who have to send money into the interior for the purchase of produce, could get orders from the Bank of Smyrna to be paid to their agents in the interior. The Turkish Government would then be spared the expense and risk of sending funds from the interior to Smyrna, and merchants in the same manner, from Smyrna to the interior, in which case a commission of 1 per cent. on both sides would be readily allowed to the branch bank for such operations.

Many other transactions of smaller importance, but all of them leaving handsome profits, can be occasionally met with, such as drafts at short dates on Constantinople, and good remittances at 20 or 30 days' credit, on which a profit of 2 to 3 per cent. is a very common thing. Advances can also be made on deposits of jewellery, &c., and on landed or house property, with high rates of interest, but the latter is out of the range of a regular banking business, and should be avoided.

From all that has been stated above, the whole amount circulating in the trade of Smyrna, adding the Government revenues, may be estimated, on an average, at from nine to ten millions sterling per annum.

The aim of a bank should be naturally to have as much of this circulation pass through its medium as possible, by offering such facilities and security to the mercantile community as would prove advantageous and beneficial to all parties. On the supposition of such an establishment doing, after some time, business to the amount of three or four millions sterling only, it would require a capital of from 200,000*l.* to 300,000*l.*, say 250,000*l.*, to carry it on properly, with convenience and good chances of profits to those interested. A capital is naturally required to inspire confidence to the mercantile community.

The kind of business to which a bank in Smyrna should devote itself, should be, in the opinion of the undersigned, the following:—

1st. To open accounts with merchants of Smyrna enjoying a regular mercantile credit, at conditions to be drawn up in the form of rules by the managers, the bank acting as cashier to the merchants for all their monied transactions.

2nd. To discount good bills on Europe either to be re-sold in Smyrna or sent for encashment.

3rd. To draw bills on England, France, and other parts of Europe or Asia, to suit the convenience of the clients of the bank. To this end, the bank should be provided with sufficient credits on Europe, Constantinople, and other places, which could be made use of when necessary.

It is not customary in the Levant for merchants to draw bills on other merchants in the country for the purpose of discount, as done in England and on the Continent. For goods sold, obligations are given by the buyer to be paid after a certain time, and it would be the bank's business to encash such obligations for account of the merchants.

Before closing this report, it is necessary to remark that no banking establishment has as yet been conducted in Smyrna on the principles and the system as drawn up under the above heads.

There are some four or five private banks, with a capital varying from 1,000*l.* to 3,000*l.*, established by a few merchants for the sake of aiding their own transactions, which shows the want felt for an establishment that would embrace and concentrate money operations. There are also good houses doing occasionally banking business in the way of drafts and remittances, when profits are so large that they are induced to enter into such transactions.

But, in their full extent, the advantages of a banking establishment, confined to the legitimate operations of banking, and avoiding on its own part all direct or indirect interference with, or competition in trade, have never been tested in Smyrna, nor has capital ever been solely invested in such a kind of business, so as to show its safety, and the profits to be derived therefrom.

CHAPTER X.

BRUSSA.

Report by Mr. Sandison, Her Britannic Majesty's Consul, on the Inducements for forming a Branch Bank at Brussa.

FROM the importance of Brussa, by its position and trade, the establishment of a bank here could not fail to be welcome. The merchants and other men of business have accordingly signed resolutions, as transmitted to you, in approbation, coinciding with the sentiments of the public generally. By his Excellency, our Governor, and other Ottoman authorities with whom I have communicated, the project has been received with cordial satisfaction, as calculated, if carried out, to confer invaluable benefits on the place and country connected, and they gave me the assurance that it should meet with every countenance and support on their part which might be requisite.

By none has it been received with disfavour, save possibly by some habitual lenders at exorbitant usury, whose exactions render a bank the more called for, enabling it also to compete with and supersede them to greater advantage, on terms which, though high indeed for the use of money as compared with those customary in advanced countries like England, would here be considered reasonable and eligible.

The common lowest rate of interest being 15 to 20

per cent. per annum, even on security, and up to double that and more frequently paid, it may be conceived what are the wants here of monied capital, and how willingly applicants of the first class would present for it at 9 to 10 per cent. interest. Besides, money being most wanted during the busy season of cocoon and silk purchases (from the end of June to October), it then happens that buyers, before they can receive fresh funds from their connections at Constantinople, may often be in need of 500*l*. to 2,000*l*. or 3,000*l*. or more, to meet engagements, or extend their purchases when the market is advantageous. In such case, they could not, if at all, obtain cash for their drafts on Constantinople at five to eleven days' sight, under 2, or more likely 3 per cent. of discount agio, and such is the state of things at the present moment. In consequence, merchants, who from regard to their credit will not submit to such sacrifice, must defer payments or forego intended operations, seldom finding other resources for their purpose. At other times, when there is not the same pressure for money, bills on the capital at short sight may be at par to 1 per cent. discount, or at a premium, when demanded. It would be part of the business of a bank to regularize the course of such operations, so as to accommodate drawers and remitters alike for a suitable moderate commission, and the bank would further necessarily be resorted to for the negotiation at times of bills on foreign countries, the course to be regulated by that at Constantinople, there being no direct exchange here on any other country.

Although Brussa had formerly considerable manufactures of silk, and silk and cotton stuffs, these, for many years, have become insignificant, being superseded by the use of British cotton goods, and the great staple trade of the place is now that in raw silk and cocoons. It was greatly feared that the disease, which was some time ago destructive among the worms, might continue, as identical with the epidemy in Europe; but, happily, this season there has been on the whole a fair product, and even copious beyond wont in various places of importance where sound eggs were employed. There also the insects have renewed their larvæ in the most prolific and healthy state, to furnish provision for a fresh, sound brood over all the silk region, which extends from the peninsula of Cyzicus on the west, at variable distances inland from the coast, to the valley of the Sangarius eastwards.

The largest yield of cocoons ever known was in 1855, of which the equivalent in silk reached near 400,000 okes of 2 4-5 lbs. (1,120,000 lbs.), of the value of 1,500,000*l*. What this last may amount to is yet not perfectly known, but when the product comes to 300,000 okes (840,000 lbs.) of silk, it is still accounted very favourable. The prices being, however, highly remunerative, and the fears of the silk-worm disease, it is to be hoped, truly removed, the culture of the mulberry and production of silk are likely to receive from next year a developement never yet attained.

So late as sixteen years back all the silk was wound off from the cocoons on single reels turned by hand, according to the rude old routine of the country. This is fast going out, and very nearly superseded already by regular filatures worked by steam, or in some cases by water, where adapted; and each year, by successive practice, the silk is being made more uniform and perfect, so that our best marks sell in England and France much on a par with French and Italian silk of the same numbers distinguished by deniers.

There are forty-six of those filatures in the town and villages close adjoining, and thirty-six in other places under the Brussa jurisdiction, furnished with 3,700 reels in all, of which 2,100 are at Brussa; but from want of capital to lay in sufficient stocks of cocoons in time, an adverse state of the market, or other contingencies, few filatures have been worked throughout the whole year. Were they kept constantly employed, those of Brussa might yield annually 350,000 lbs. of silk, of the actual value of 500,000*l.* on the spot, and the remaining filatures 270,000 lbs., of the value of 380,000*l.* From this, however, some deduction is to be made for stoppages to repair machinery and other casualties, still leaving a total to the amount of 800,000*l.* to 840,000*l.*

With almost all the other filatures besides its own the trade of Brussa is by partnership, or purchases of their silk, in some way connected; and the owners or workers of nearly all of them have large need of capital to assist them, as the money which they can borrow here or from saraffs at Constantinople must be on very costly terms; it is therefore usual for the principal "fileurs," who export on their own account, to get advances, through agents at Constantinople, from houses at Marseilles and Lyons for the purchase of cocoons to a limited extent at a time, consigning the silk as ready to those houses which exercise the power of realising at any time they may think fit in order to cover their advances. The interest charged on these advances is 6 per cent., but with extra commissions in receiving the money here, the accommodation costs 2 to 3 per cent. more, and the shippers, as observable, have little or no control over the sale in the French market. They would therefore prefer, as suiting them far better, to pay 9 to

10 per cent. interest to a bank for the loan of capital needed, particularly for the purpose of enabling them to lay in their full stock of cocoons in the early part of the season when most abundant, and when brought to market in the fresh state. The filature owners, being thus free from foreign engagements, would have the option of shipping to England or France, or selling their silk here, as found most eligible; and others who work expressly for local sale, having the same wants, would be willing customers of the bank for the same advantages in providing stock, and being less pressed to sell merely to get in their money.

Formerly three-fourths, at least, of the Brussa raw silk went to England, and the rest of what was exported chiefly to France. Now the case is reversed, only one house sending all its filature silk to the London market, and some of the others occasional parcels, as they find prices at Marseilles or Lyons suit better. This is partly ascribed to the English throwsters requiring extreme nicety in the uniformity of the tissue according to the numbers. Those usually reeled here are 11 to 12 (deniers), but 9-10, being finer, can also easily be produced when more advantageous. The Brussa silk has the property, much looked to in England, of being elastic; and from what I could collect from a broker in the silk line at home, who was lately here, there seems no reason why the Brussa article should not again be extensively imported into England.

The general purchases of cocoons and silk of every kind for export might also be facilitated by the agency of the bank, and this is further needful from the want so much felt for the means of discounting bills, the rate being most excessive when such a thing does occur, but no doubt the introduction of the practice would follow from the existence of a bank. In the course of transactions between this and contiguous places, good bills at eleven days, or other short dates, are sometimes drawn on Brussa, and large sums remitted from hence against orders for cocoons and silk, all which business there is reason to expect might be more conveniently and safely regulated through a bank; for it is almost incredible what parties perfectly safe, and of first solidity, are at times, and that very lately, under the necessity of paying for the use of sums for but a few days, the interest actually being as much as one-fourth to one-third per cent. per day.

The amount is probably not great of loans or advances made on jewellery or the like valuables deposited in pledge against repayment at a fixed term; but individuals and families have often to pay enormous rates, when in extreme need, to raise money on them, as only to be had from unconscientious usurers. Many persons might avail themselves of the advantages of procuring it on such securities, easily valued, at the moderate rate for the country of 9 to 10 or even 12 per cent. With respect to the secreting of such precious ornaments, that is no longer usual or necessary, the subject being now secure from arbitrary spoliation by those in power, unless perhaps in the more remote and lawless parts of Turkey not yet brought under regular rule.

As the bank chest would necessarily be in fire-proof premises, this would offer the more inducement for deposits being lodged there of money, and sometimes jewellery, when not wanted for immediate use; and, though everything new must start from a commencement, it is most likely that merchants and residents generally having any cash of consequence passing through their hands would ere long keep an account with the bank, and place their funds there for greater convenience and security. The director of the Mizan office, where the tithe on silk is collected, told me he was quite ready to place a large sum now on hand in such desirable custody until orders for its disposal.

It frequently happens that the superintendent of the revenue of the province has large calls upon him to make remittances to the Porte, or for some local disburse on the public service, with an empty chest and taxes probably in arrear, and on such occasions there is but one individual to depend upon who can supply him to any extent, and who has consequently a virtual monopoly of the business, by which his gains for a disburse of even a few months are known to come to 20 and 30 per cent. The bank, however, could lend on a moderate scale, and under formal guarantee for being refunded from local taxes, consisting of fixed assessments, which are ascertainable from the registers; therefore no sort of instrument could be more safe. Such contingencies can only be noticed as merely casual and of indeterminate amount, but the resort to those anticipations of the provincial revenue might become more important, and with convenience to the service, when their cost is reduced to fair proportions.

In addition to those fixed contributions collected direct by the authorities, there are the Government tithes farmed out annually in gross for each large district to contractors at the capital, who sub-let them in parcels at a profit. The corn tithe of Brussa was for this year, but not until the nature of the harvest was known, so farmed for a sum equivalent to 33,000*l.*, to be again subdivided into lots usually bought by local parties. The tithe on olives, a crop incessantly liable to failure every second or third year, is let apart. That on silk, the most important of all, is united with the customs on it, which have just been taken conjointly at 120,000*l.* Merchants and other inhabitants here, who have always an eye to the purchase of those tithes for gain, would wish to have facilities for participation in the farming of them more largely in gross or detail, to the exclusion of strangers; and for this reason, amongst others, they are desirous of a bank being established, to which they might have recourse for the requisite advances, secured for reimbursement on the successive receipts of the tax.

Were the bank to extend its operations to the aid of the agricultural classes, there is no sort of industry to which the application of capital, could it be adapted, is more copiously wanted. This forms the business of the Armenian saraffs and other of the monied men of the city, among the Turks particularly, who all of them charge at least 18 to 24 per cent. per annum of interest, and it is quite usual for them to get this much on loans for five to eight months, when the peasant is much straitened to pay his taxes, engaging to refund from his next returns in grain or silk, and transferring over as security the title-deeds of his property. One never hears of the lenders failing to get paid in full, though the peasant may be distressed by a debt accumulating at compound interest, from crops falling short, or other adverse circumstances. Exact payment to a day is not to be counted upon, perhaps from delay in realising produce; but care is taken to have ample value to meet all contingencies, and the chiefs or community of the village often become collectively or severally substantial guarantees for such loans.

Could a satisfactory system be brought to work for

affording assistance to the rural classes, the extensive scope for it would be found in the improvement which would follow in the better stocking and culture of their farms, to the increase of production, and that of silk in the foremost rank, from the encouragement for it previously stated. Further, it appears that cotton from New Orleans seed ought to succeed well in this quarter, from experiments made last year close in our vicinity, though on a small scale, and too late in the planting to allow all the pods to come to maturity. The specimens sent home were very favourably reported upon by the Manchester Supply Association, and give promise of the valuable addition being made of superior cotton to our products.

The bulk of the opium sold at Smyrna is raised in this province, and the culture of the poppy commences at no great distance from Brussa, though not hitherto a market for the article. Considerable quantities of maize are in some years exported from our coast, and the territory also yields a large surplus of wheat, part of it as fine as anywhere grown, for shipment in plenteous seasons; but the rugged roads and heavy expense of carriage from the interior, as usual in Turkey, are the great drawbacks to that trade. Wool in small quantity, valonia occasionally, salted olives to the amount of 40,000,000 lbs., when the crop is good; Olympus wine of merit on a limited scale, and common wines and spirits largely from our seaboard, are the other exports. The chief import trade is in British cotton stuffs and yarns to the extent of 200,000*l.*; other articles to the value of 100,000*l.* annually.

Our usual scala or port of communication with the capital is Ghio or Ghemlek, 20 miles from hence, at the head of the Gulf of Mundania. It has safe anchorage and depth of water for ships of every draught; steamers run regularly between it and Constantinople twice, sometimes three or four times a week, and there is as often an intermediate post. It has some direct trade with the Danube and Odessa, but vessels very seldom load there for foreign ports to the westward. The silks of Brussa pass through it to be forwarded by the steamers to the capital, and thence exported.

Ghio is a thriving and rising place for trade, and before its destruction by fire a few years ago contained 640 houses, the rebuilding of which has been stopped until the completion of surveys, as shortly expected, for the reconstruction on a regular plan. Ground and buildings there are very valuable alike for residence and stores, and there would be large and safe scope for making advances, if only to the extent of the worth of the ground, to assist in rebuilding the town. The inhabitants, lodged in temporary sheds or huts, are in general possessed of means to rebuild, but it would be so much taken for the time from their ordinary trading capital.

There is no sort of regular banking business carried on here, nor anything approaching nearer to it than that of the saraffs already noticed, and which is chiefly with the surrounding country in loans and farming of tithes. Their common rate of interest received is 20 per cent. per annum, but may be often more.

(Signed)   D. SANDISON,
Her Britannic Majesty's Consul, Brussa.
To J. LEWIS FARLEY.

The undersigned merchants and others concerned in trade and money transactions at Brussa, being desirous of expressing their opinion on the expediency of a branch bank in that city, have agreed to the following resolutions :—

1. That Brussa is the seat and centre of a great trade in silk, the raising of which product is on the increase, and the value of which, in favourable years, may amount to 1,200,000*l.* sterling or more; and that the town of Brussa alone now contains 43 filatures of all sizes, furnished with 1,800 reels, each reel capable of yielding 60 okes (168 lbs.) of silk in the year, making a total of 108,000 okes (302,400 lbs.), of the actual value of about 400,000*l.* sterling; whilst other neighbouring places in connection with Brussa contain filatures of more than the like power in all, which would make the entire product of the filatures, if worked complete, amount to 800,000*l.*

2. That the requisite facilities in cash are wanting for the stocking with cocoons and working those filatures, and for other exigencies of the silk and local trade in general, as well as for other operations customary in the country.

3. That the agio or discount on bills on Constantinople for the short term of eleven days has latterly, on any urgency, scarcely ever been below $1\frac{1}{2}$ to 2 per cent. for the first signatures, when any sum of consequence is to be had, as rarely, against paper, and that this agio is sometimes 3 to 4 per cent. for eleven to thirty days' bills.

4. That there are no means of negotiating here bills on foreign countries direct, but solely through the medium of Constantinople, which is a great disadvantage to trade.

5. That the ordinary rate of interest in the country is at least 15 to 18 per cent. per annum, even against pledges in jewels or other precious articles; and oftener loans either on open credit or with any security whatever are only made at the rate of 2 to 3 per cent. per month, likewise frequently enough at 18 to 20 per cent. for a term of five or six months.

6. That this enormous rate of interest weighs heavily on the peasantry and other country people, and fetters agriculture.

7. That, from what precedes, the establishment of a branch

bank here is desirable and necessary in the highest degree, at the same time that an advantageous field offers for the employment of its funds.

8. That the merchants and public in general would willingly and conveniently agree to the rate of 9 to 10 per cent. per annum interest on advances or loans in gold coin, repayable in coin of the same denomination; whilst, according to circumstances, a bank might likewise make loans or advances at 12 up to 15 per cent. on the same basis.

9. That a bank would alike be of great convenience for placing there, in sure deposit, disposable cash which persons may have in hand, and for the greater facility of payments and receipts.

10. That although it may be very difficult to fix the total sum which the bank might employ on extending its operations to neighbouring places, such as those containing filatures, and according to the sort of business which its rules might embrace, especially in case of affording aid to agriculturists, we are of opinion that an effective capital of 100,000*l.* at most would be sufficient for a commencement, and that from caution this might even at first be limited to 50,000*l.* or 60,000*l.*, making reserve for the extension or developement of business which ought to follow from the formation of such an establishment in a city and province so important as Brussa, and by its soil, products, and industry conjointly one of the most considerable in the Ottoman Empire.

(Here follow the signatures.*)

Certified as a correct translation and true list,

D. SANDISON,

Her Britannic Majesty's Consul, Brussa.

* The original is in my possession.— J. L. F.

Extract from Official Report to the Foreign Office, by Mr. Sandison, Her Britannic Majesty's Consul at Brussa, February 14th, 1857.

To give regularity and more extension to the trade of Brussa, the two desiderata are, further, a good road to the coast (at least by the completion of that in progress, which must lead to others connectively in the sequel), and the establishment of a branch bank.

Extract from Official Report to the Foreign Office, by Mr. Sandison, Her Britannic Majesty's Consul at Brussa, February 11th, 1861.

There is great need of monied capital in Brussa; the rate of interest is so enormous as to appear almost incredible, at the lowest it is 15 to 20 per cent. per annum, but many transactions, rather the majority, are on a scale ascending from 20 to 40, and even to 100 per cent. per annum for a limited term, whether on valuable pledges in hand, landed security, or whatever be the solidity and credit of the borrower. But a branch bank to be serviceable must adapt its operations to the nature of the country, without confining itself rigidly to discounts for a few months' term; and at little risk it would obtain rates of interest or discount not under 10 to 12 per cent., which all would be content to pay as suitable and just.

Specification and Value of the Importations and Exportations of the Province of Brussa during the year 1859 :—

IMPORTATIONS.

	Piastres.
Cotton manufactures	25,000,000
Woollen do.	8,000,000
Cotton twist	9,000,000
Iron, wrought and unwrought	8,500,000
Ironmongery	2,000,000
Arms	2,500,000
Glass-wares and window-glass	2,300,000
Sugar, coffee, &c.	3,500,000
Silk stuffs	1,500,000
Clothes (ready-made)	300,000
Drugs, medicines	800,000
Total	Piastres 63,400,000

EXPORTATIONS.

	Okes.	P.	Piastres.
Silk, raw	145,000 at	620	89,900,000
,, ,,	16,000 ,,	450	7,200,000
,, Cocoons	210,000 ,,	200	42,000,000
,, Silkworms' eggs	2,000 ,,	1200	2,400,000
,, (waste, &c.)			1,540,000
Wool	70,000 ,,	10	700,000
Cotton	10,000 ,,	15	150,000
Opium	4,000 ,,	300	1,200,000
Chromate of iron			5,000,000
Wines and spirits of wine			2,000,000
Hides			2,000,000
Salted olives			12,000,000
Sundries			4,500,000
Total			Piastres 170,590,000

CHAPTER XI.

TREBIZOND.

TREBIZOND (the ancient Trapezus) is the principal commercial port on the Black Sea, and, from its position, is the natural entrepôt of the trade of Armenia, north Persia, and Georgia with the west.

The following Table of the imports and exports from the year 1853 to the year 1859 inclusive will give an idea of the immense increase in the trade and commerce of Trebizond:*

Years.	Imports. Value in Pounds sterling.	Exports. Value in Pounds sterling.	Total.
1853	1,742,693	728,849	2,471,542
1854	2,023,073	289,173	2,312,246
1855	2,432,160	342,220	2,774,380
1856	2,816,304	No returns.	—
1857	3,293,422	1,483,334	4,776,756
1858	3,750,529	1,228,794	4,979,323
1859	3,255,762	955,741	4,211,503

It will be seen from the above that the imports and exports in 1858 were more than double the amount of those in 1853. This large increase is accounted for

---

* There are few spots on the earth richer in picturesque beauty, or abounding in more luxuriant vegetation, than the south-eastern shores of the inhospitable Euxine. The magnificent country that extends from the mouth of the Halys to the snowy range of Caucasus is formed of a singular union of rich plains, verdant hills, bold rocks, wooded mountains, primeval forests, and rapid streams. In this fertile and majestic region, Trebizond has been, now for more than six centuries, the noblest and the fairest city.—*Finlay's Empire of Trebizond.*

by the facilities which an extended steam communication has afforded. Within the last six years the French *Messageries Impériales* have run their boats regularly every week, bringing Trebizond in almost a direct communication with the Turkish provinces in Roumelia and Syria, with the Danube, Greece, Italy, and France, in all which places the produce of certain Russian provinces on the Caspian, as also of Persia, Georgia, Erzerum, and Trebizond, are largely consumed. In 1858 a Russian boat commenced running every fortnight between Odessa and ports on this coast, linking thereby the Crimea, Sea of Azof, Abassah, and Circassia, Daghistan, Tiflis, and the Russo-Georgian provinces of Guriel, Mingrelia, and Immeritia with Trebizond. Again, the establishment of a monthly English steamer between Liverpool and Trebizond connected the latter port, in a commercial point of view, with various towns of Turkey in Europe, and with Egypt; those vessels touching at Salonica and other places, upon the outward voyage, and, frequently, at Alexandria, on their return to England. Such an extensive communication necessarily facilitated trade, and, with time, there can be no doubt that a great number of new branches of commerce hitherto unknown will spring therefrom.

During the spring of last year commerce was very brisk in Persia, and gave much activity to the Trebizond market; the trade with Circassia and Georgia was also very lively, particularly during the first six months of the year. Circassia exported to Trebizond large quantities of grain, receiving in return manufactures, colonials, salt, and tobacco. The Russian stations on the same coast supplied several cargoes of boxwood, as also important quantities of bees'-wax, ox hides, skins, and wool; while Georgia provided silk, salt fish, and caviar, taking in return British cotton goods, colonials, tea, and beer, and French haberdashery, wines, spirits, and machinery. The various qualities of grain grown in Circassia and Georgia are inferior to those produced on the Danube and in Russia, and are therefore cheaper, and better suited to the wants of the lower classes.

The crop of nuts in the district was larger last year than has ever been remembered. Trebizond and Kierrasond together produced 220,000 to 250,000 cwt. Upwards of 10,000 cwt. were exported to Great Britain, and also large quantities to Russia, Constantinople, Smyrna, and Egypt. The present price is 30 to 40 per cent. lower than in 1857. Tobacco was likewise produced extensively, and its cultivation around Trebizond is daily increasing. Fruit was very abundant, upwards of 10,000 packages of apples and pears having been sent by the steamers to Constantinople.

The following Tables show the gross amount of British and foreign trade, at the port of Trebizond, during the year ending 31st December, 1858:—

IMPORTATIONS.

Nationality.	Number of Vessels.	Tonnage.	Number of Crews.	Value of Cargoes.
				£
Austrian	48	30,920	2,131	1,168,839
Turkish	89	27,030	2,470	1,040,703
French	51	15,740	1,785	681,080
British	19	8,798	448	514,492
Egyptian	14	5,242	482	201,412
Dutch	2	736	31	60,301
Greek	34	6,034	317	35,212
Russian	63	10,675	1,073	23,728
Prussian	1	555	13	21,390
Wallachia, Moldavia	3	340	38	3,372
Total	324	106,070	8,788	3,750,529

EXPORTATIONS.

Nationality.	Number of Vessels.	Tonnage.	Number of Crews.	Value of Cargoes.	Specie.
				£	£
Turkish	80	25,630	2,360	482,126	
Austrian	48	30,920	2,131	352,161	
French	50	15,380	1,750	268,271	
Egyptian	14	5,242	482	61,561	
Russian	63	10,675	1,073	46,039	
British	19	8,798	448	18,418	
Greek	34	6,034	317	5,018	
Dutch	2	736	31	200	
Prussian	1	555	13	..	
Wallachia, Moldavia	3	340	38	..	
Total	313	104,310	8,643	1,228,794	994,130

It may be remarked, from the foregoing returns, that the amount of the imports is double that of the exports. It were, therefore, well to observe that the province of Kurdistan receives a large portion of its supplies of European merchandise from Trebizond, by way of Erzerum, and makes returns for same in cattle, overland, to the Constantinople market. It is calculated that 400,000 sheep, 6,000 oxen, and 2,000 to 3,000 horses, are annually sent in this manner. Again, large remittances from Persia, as well as Turkey, are made in paper. Tiflis also offers much facility to Persia in its remittances to Europe, viâ Odessa; and finally, travellers carry large amounts of specie on their persons, to avoid paying a steam freight. If it were possible to make an approximate estimate of the above four items, and add the same to the amount of exports in merchandise and specie, the import and export trade would nearly balance.

The English steamers which plied between Liverpool and Trebizond in 1858 now terminate their voyages at Constantinople, and there has consequently been a considerable diminution in the number of British vessels entering the port. In 1859, there were only nine British ships against nineteen in 1858, and during the first six months of 1860 but one British vessel, a collier from Swansea, entered the port of Trebizond. The navigation for the half year ending 30th June, 1860, was as follows:—

Entered.

Nationality.	Number of Vessels.		Tonnage.
Austrian	{ Steamers .. 26 Sailing Vessels 4 }	30	21,047
Russian	{ Steamers .. 17 Sailing Vessels 8 }	25	17,274
Turkish	{ Steamers .. 20 Sailing Vessels 23 }	43	15,295
French	Steamers.	26	10,410
Greek	Sailing Vessels	8	2,372
Sardinian	,,	3	1,059
Tuscan	,,	2	522
British	,,	1	384
Mecklenburg	,,	1	231
		139	68,594

Cleared.

Nationality.	Number of Vessels.	Tonnage.
Austrian	30	21,047
Russian	25	17,274
Turkish	42	15,085
French	26	10,410
Greek	7	2,030
Sardinian	3	1,059
Tuscan	2	522
British	1	384
Mecklenburg	1	231
	137	68,042

The following Tables show the quantities and description of the various articles imported into and exported from Trebizond during the year 1858:—

IMPORTATIONS.

Arms	. .	522 cases
Anchors	. .	5 do.
Amber	. .	1 case
Aniseed	.	4 bags
Beer (in bottles)		510 casks
Bottles (empty)		50 crates
Books	. .	44 cases
Boards (deal)	.	2,746 do.
Boxwood	. .	730 tons
Barley	. .	9,006 quarters
Biscuits	. .	44 cases
Bricks (knife)	.	4 casks
Baggage	. .	176 packages
Blacking	. .	9 casks
Butter	. .	7 do.
Brooms	. .	1 bale
Baskets (empty)		1 do.
Coals	. .	6,198 tons
Coffee	. .	3,616 bags
Corn (Indian corn)		25,638 quarters
Cochineal	.	989 cases
Cotton twist	.	308 bales
Cordage	. .	494 do.
Carpeting	.	73 do.
Crockery and earthenware		467 casks
Cotton braiding		57 bales
Cotton (raw)	.	127 do.
Cloth, called "Abbah"		72 do.
Cloth	. .	208 do.
Clocks (wooden)		5 cases
Caviar	. .	152 casks
Canvas	. .	12,500 measures
Chickpeas	.	31 bags
Chains (for Marine use)		6
Candles (tallow)		90 cases
Candles (composite)		23 do.
Candles (wax)	.	3 do.
Caps (skull)	.	19 do.
Copper (sheet)	.	314 packages
Cheese	. .	15 do.
Clothing (old)	.	28 bales
Cutlery	. .	62 cases
Chalk	. .	5 casks
Cigars	. .	14 cases
Cirecloth	. .	3 bales
Chocolate and confectionery		7 packages
Carriages	. .	2
Drugs	. .	201 cases
Furniture	. .	249 packages
Flour	. .	1,123 bags
Fruit (dry)	.	292 casks
Furs and skins		123 bales
Fish (salt)	.	73 casks
Grates (iron)	.	2 cases
Glass ware	.	619 do.
Glass plates	.	267 do.
Gum (Benjamin)		8 do.
Galoches (Indian rubber)		3 do.
Hardware	.	1,596 packages
Haberdashery	.	357 do.
Hides (ox and cow)		2,040
Honey	. .	20 casks
Hemp	. .	21 bales
Hooks (fishing)		1 box
Horses	. .	7
Indigo	. .	151 cwts.
Iron chests and safes		13
Instruments (musical)		1 case
Iron bedsteads	.	4 packages
Iron	. .	4,265 bars
Iron (sheet)	.	74 bundles
Iron (rod)	.	385 do.
Ink	. .	1 box
Jewellery	.	6 cases
Jewellery (false)		1 case

THE RESOURCES OF TURKEY.

Khenna	. .	23 cases
Lemons	. .	235 do.
Logwood	. .	200 cwt.
Lentils	. .	9 bags
Linen stuffs	. .	55 bales
Leather	. .	12 packages
Liquors	. .	106 cases
Lead (white)	.	13 boxes
Lime (marble)	.	20 packages
Lead	. .	11 pigs
Locusts (car-rubs)		150 bags
Manufactures	.	74,953 trusses
Manufactures	.	1,133 bales
Marble flags (for furniture)		13 bales
Mirrors	. .	111 cases
Matches (lucifer)		372 do.
Manufactures (Asiatic)		296 packages
Madders	. .	64 bales
Medicines	. .	42 cases
Millet	. .	14 bags
Maccaroni and paste		67 cases
Mastic (gum)	.	4 casks
Nails	. .	514 kegs
Needles	. .	14 cases
Oats	. .	900 quarters
Oranges	. .	182 cases
Olives	. .	290 casks
Oil (olive)	.	756 do.
Oil (salad)	.	832 cases
Oil (fish)	. .	166 casks
Oil (linseed)	.	2 jars
Perfumery	. .	11 cases
Pipe bowls	.	29 do.
Plated ware	.	16 do.
Paper (common)		111 do.
Pickles	. .	70 do.
Paints	. .	194 packages
Porcelain	. .	77 cases
Pepper	. .	68 bags
Provisions	.	85 cases
Pearl barley	.	16 casks
Rice	. .	3,885 bags
Rum	. .	1,061 casks
Rochu (Arrak)		581 casks
Refined loaf sugar		4,646 hhds. 11,907 cases
Sugar (crushed)		346 barrels
Salt (Marine)	.	16,800 quarters
Soap	. .	2,784 packages
Stores (Military)		303 do.
Silks	. .	164 cases
Satins	. .	61 do.
Silk (raw)	.	322 bales
Steel	. .	725 cases
Spices	. .	74 do.
Stoves	. .	13 do.
Sacking	. .	54 packages
Spirits of wine	.	47 casks
Shot (lead)	.	22 do.
Salt (rock, or basket)		4 do.
Shoes	. .	1 package
Saltpetre	. .	2 do.
Sulphur	. .	2 do.
Sal-ammoniac	.	30 casks
Sailcloth (Cutnina)		2 packages
Stationery	.	5 cases
Saddlery	. .	4 do.
Sweetmeats	.	28 casks
Spelter	. .	40 slabs
Sundry merchandise (not detailed)		10,586 packages
Tallow	. .	182 casks
Timber, for house building		600 tons
Tea (chiefly black)		2,638 cwts.
Tin (in bars)	.	134 casks
Tobacco	. .	5,938 bales
Tin plates	.	40 cases
Trays	. .	4 do.
Toys	. .	3 do.
Trays (silver)	.	4
Tarpaulin	.	5 bales
Thread (cotton sewing)		4 cases
Tamarinde	.	1 case
Thread (gold)	.	3 packages
Tinder (Punk)	.	5 bales
Tomb stones	.	40

TREBIZOND. 123

Umbrellas (cotton)	} 3 cases	Wax	. .	142 packages
Velvets . .	15 do.	Wearing apparel	}	856 do.
Valonia . .	107 bags	Wines	. .	1,981 cases
Vinegar . .	92 casks	Watches .	.	13 packages
Vegetables (fresh & dried)	} 68 packages	Woollen tissues		99 bales
Varnish . .	6 casks	Wire (brass and iron)	}	12 packages
Vitriol . .	1 case	Wheat	. .	7,500 quarters
Wool . .	174 bales	Zinc .	. .	4 packages

EXPORTATIONS.

Apples & pears	6,300 packages	Horns (mixed) .		5 bales
Apricots (dry) .	202 do.	Horses . .		122
Almonds . .	52 bags	Hardware .		98 packages
Arms . .	17 packages	Iron . . .		13 tons
Beans . .	4,108 bags	Insect powder .		106 bags
Boxwood . .	904 tons	Henna . .		28 do.
Butter . .	266 packages	Leeches . .		496 cases
Berries (yellow)	208 bags	Linen (Rizeh)		184 bales
Baggage . .	123 packages	Lemon trees .		72
Books . .	22 cases	Lemons . .		67 cases
Beer (in bottles)	61 packages	Leather . .		26 packages
Bronze and brass work	} 4 do.	Liquors . .		7 do.
		Lackered work .		116 do.
Charcoal . .	282 bags	Meat, dried (Pasturmah)	}	1,854 do.
Copper utensils	41 packages			
Copper (in slabs)	3,900 cwt.	Meat, salted (Cavoonnah)	}	64 do.
Coals . .	94 tons			
Carpets and rugs	283 bales	Manufactures .		900 do.
Corn (Indian) .	1,850 quarters	Manufactures, Aleppo	}	5 do.
Coffee . .	144 bags			
Cochineal .	7 do.	Nuts . .		11,196 bags
Caviar . .	602 casks	Nets (fishing) .		378 packages
Dyes . .	427 packages	Olives . .		66 casks
Drugs . .	42 do.	Olive oil . .		35 do.
Earth (potters')	196 do.	Oakum . .		53 bales
Eggs . .	56 do.	Orpiment. .		92 packages
Furs . .	31 do.	Oranges . .		34 do.
Flour . .	11 do.	Packing materials	}	670 bales
Galls . .	1,207 bags			
Gums . .	184 do.	Pitch . .		72 barrels
Goldsmiths' sweepings	} 13 do.	Potatoes . .		1,532 bags
		Planks (deal) .		423
Glass plates .	19 packages	Paper . .		9 packages
Hides (ox and cow)	} 3,580 bales	Paints . .		18 do.
		Rum . .		1 package

Rice	15	packages
Raisins	15,978	do.
Rags	28	do.
Reeds, for writing	198	do.
Salt	11,000	bushels
Slippers	78	bales
Straw, for chair bottoms	42	tons
Skins (goat and sheep)	982	bales
Sundries (not detailed)	2,983	packages
Silk	5,992	bales
Safflower	706	do.
Silk (cocoons)	609	packages
Silkworm eggs	132	do.
Silk (refuse)	122	bales
Silks (tissues)	5	do.
Shawls	338	do.
Steel	22	packages
Soap	27	do.
Sulphur	2	packages
Sugar	674	do.
Tobacco (called Tumbeky)	15,068	do.
Tallow	522	do.
Tobacco (leaf)	6,196	do.
Tin (in bars)	9	do.
Thread	1,027	do.
Tea	566	cwt.
Tar	18	casks
Wax	782	do.
Wheat	566	do.
Wool (goat's tiftic)	185	packages
Wool	342	do.
Wool (camel's)	26	do.
Walnut wood	902	pieces
Walnuts	233	bags
Vegetables	94	packages
Vegetables (cabbages)	2,780	cwt.

Agricultural Products.—The following is an average estimate of the quantity of agricultural produce annually raised in the Pashalic of Trebizond:—

Articles.	Quantities.		Articles.	Quantities.	
Indian corn	520,000	bushels.	Rice	275,000	lbs.
Wheat	110,000	,,	Tobacco	15,500	cwts.
Barley	25,000	,,	Hemp	3000	,,
Oats	35,000	,,	Flax	1000	,,
Beans	80,000	cwts.	Olives	1300	,,
Nuts	160,000	,,	Olive oil	500	,,
Potatoes	10,000	,,			

Provisions are abundant. The present prices are—

	Per oke—2¾ lbs.	Piastres.		Per oke—2¾ lbs.	Piastres.
Bread, 1st quality		4	Butter		12
,, 2nd ,,		1½	Milk		2
Beef		2½	Rice		2¼
Mutton		3	Beans		1
Fish		3	Fowls, each		4
Vegetables		2	Olives, per oke, 2¾ lbs.		2¼
Cheese		5			

Forests.—The forests in the Pashalic of Trebizond

are very extensive. They abound with oak, beech, elm, chestnut, walnut, red and white pine, box, and maple. The oak is well adapted for ship-building, and the chestnut is much used in the construction of houses. All kinds of timber might be easily exported, if a conveyance existed, either by land or water, from the forests to the coast. Small wood only, such as is intended for fuel and dwellings, can be floated down the streams; while all boxwood for exportation is carried down by horses and mules.

Mines.—The silver mines of Goomooshhanah are eight in number, but only three of them are now open. They are worked on Government account, and yield annually 15 to 20 okes of silver, and 40,000 okes of lead. In the time of Sultan Mustapha III. these mines produced 600,000 okes of lead, and 6000 okes of silver per annum.

The copper mines of Helsah, near Goomooshhanah, produce at present only about sixty to one hundred thousand okes of ore, containing 70 to 80 per cent. of copper. The copper mines of Figaneh and Graoordagh have been closed for the last seventy-five years. The Esserley mines, near Triboly, which are farmed out to various individuals, yield, under very unskilful management, about 150,000 okes of copper, 27,000 okes of lead, and 30 okes of silver; but, although they are situated within eighteen miles of the coast, there is no road by which the ore can be conveyed for shipment.*

* It is obvious that the want of proper means of communication must

The iron mines, near Vono, are neglected. The alum pits of Karahissar, which formerly supplied all Turkey, are very nearly abandoned; while the coal, near Kierrasond, remains altogether untouched.

Fisheries.—There is only one fishery off the coast, that of the porpoise, which yields upwards of 250,000 okes of oil per annum. A portion of the oil is consumed for light by the lower classes, and the rest finds hence, wheat and other commodities, that might, under more favourable circumstances, be brought down to the ports, have now a mere local value. Instances are numerous where the people have been in a state of comparative famine in one section of the country, from scarcity of breadstuffs, whilst in others wheat, &c., might be purchased at nominal prices. To bring wheat down 36 and 150 miles, the average cost of transport may be computed at 4s. and 16s. sterling a quarter, whereas, over good roads, it might be reduced to 1s. and 4s. a quarter respectively; the difference being upwards of 13 and 112 per cent. on the farmer's gross receipts.

In dealing, however, with the means of transport and communication in foreign countries, a grave error has been almost invariably committed by the concessionaires, who, misled by splendid schemes, have induced the public to embark their money in enterprises which carry with them the seeds of their own failure. It is fatal to such undertakings to judge them by the standard of results in this and other equally advanced countries. The scale of such works is usually too far in advance of the state of developement of the country, and many an enterprise, which might have been profitable on a proper scale, has been ruined by the magnitude of the plans adopted. Already this has been found the case even in England, and it will be wise to apply the experience, which has cost so much, to obtain from it a compensating profit.

Well-constructed horse tramroads will, probably, be found, in practice, the most successful measure to introduce into Turkey for facilitating transport. A good system of such roads would permit of an immense increase of traffic, and would not require the costly skilled labour necessary in combination with the ordinary railway system. Such roads are already being introduced in many of the agricultural districts of France, and the small cost of their construction and maintenance is a strong argument in their favour. There can be no doubt that the adoption of some such scheme as I have here suggested must precede any great increase of Turkish trade, and, as the safety of investments depends upon the power of the debtor to pay, it is obvious that any means which can tend to augment that power must operate as an additional guarantee for the faithful observance of obligations.

a market at Constantinople. Fish for domestic use is abundant and excellent, particularly the turbot, skate, herring, mullet, smelts, and sprats. The two last are taken in such vast numbers, that after the natives have provided for their own wants and salted sufficient for the winter's consumption, a considerable quantity is turned into oil, or made use of as manure. It is not at all unusual to see a horse-load of sprats sold for four piastres.

Manufactures.—A considerable quantity of silk veils, linen and cotton shirting, woollen aprons, &c., are made by the lower classes. The beautiful linens, used in the harems of the rich, are manufactured at Rizeh, to the extent of from 50,000 to 75,000 pieces annually, and sold chiefly to Constantinople, Egypt, Baghdad, and Mosul. Twenty thousand to thirty thousand pieces of a common description are used in the local consumption of this and the neighbouring provinces. Rizeh also manufactures annually about 1,500 bales of linen thread, and 250 bales of fishing nets, which are principally exported to Constantinople. Trebizond is famous for its copper and brass utensils, as well as for its manufacture of slippers and saddlery. A coarse-grained gunpowder, suitable for blasting purposes, is also made at Trebizond, and various dyeing and printing establishments give employment to about 200 individuals.

CHAPTER XII.

SAMSOUN.

A GLANCE at the amounts of the imports and exports by British shipping at the port of Samsoun from 1853 to 1856 will give the best idea of the immense increase which has taken place in the trade within four years:—

Years.	No. of British Vessels.	Tonnage.	Imports. Value in Pounds sterling.	Exports. Value in Pounds sterling.
1853	26	14,105	30,100	45,378
1854	36	24,920	150,762	154,613
1855	96	69,081	157,194	356,972
1856	167	174,988	319,326	220,749

The total number of vessels of all nations which entered and cleared at the port of Samsoun in the year 1853 was 203: the value of their inward cargoes amounted to 329,007*l.* in merchandise, and 80,019*l.* in specie; the outward cargoes amounted to 235,529*l.* in merchandise, and 192,316*l.* in specie. In 1856 the total number of arrivals was 433: the value of their inward cargoes was 702,418*l.* in merchandise, and 99,951*l.* in specie; the value of their outward cargoes was, in merchandise, 581,917*l.*, and in specie, 44,999*l.*

The following is a general statement of the gross amount of merchandise and specie which passed through the port of Samsoun during the year 1860:—

IMPORTS.

In French, Austrian, Turkish, and Russian Steam
Vessels (156 Vessels) :—

Merchandise	£326,251	16	8
Specie	53,932	19	0
	£380,184	15	8
In 69 Sailing Vessels :—			
Merchandise	71,673	12	6
Total	£451,858	8	2

EXPORTS.

In Steam Vessels :—			
Merchandise	£320,485	18	8
Specie	124,840	4	2
	£445,326	2	10
In 69 Sailing Vessels :—			
Merchandise	64,856	5	0
Total	£510,182	7	10

More than three-quarters of the manufactures imported are British, the remaining quarter consisting of Swiss and French manufacture. The total number of packages of goods brought to Samsoun during the year 1857 by vessels belonging to the Austrian, French, and Turkish Steam Navigation Companies amounted to 34,523, and those exported to 53,072.

The accompanying detailed note of the different kinds of merchandise imported and exported by British vessels during the year 1856 will give a correct idea of the principal articles of commerce. Tobacco, one of the staple productions, has become an article of very great importance; 13,662 bales, equal to 2,049 tons weight, figure in the list of exports by English ships, and, as the value has risen nearly 300 per cent., its cultivation is now greatly attended to. The tobacco from Samsoun chiefly goes to Russia and Egypt. The production of silk cocoons is annually increasing in the neighbouring district of Amassia, and has lately attracted a good deal of attention from several French mercantile houses at Marseilles. The French *Messageries Impériales* Company has lately taken up the line of steam communication between Constantinople and Samsoun, in connection or continuation of their line of steamers between that capital and Marseilles. The communication is regular and weekly, as is also that of the Austrian Lloyd's Company; and, in consequence of the competition arising between the different steamers, merchandise is now brought to Samsoun for one-third of the freight which used to be paid for it a few years ago. The same may be said of the goods exported. If the construction of the railway which is now projected between Samsoun and Sivas take place, an impetus to trade, to an incalculable extent, will certainly be the result throughout this part of Asia Minor; and its effect will be of equally incalculable advantage to British industry in every way.

Return and Specification of the Imports and Exports at the Port of Samsoun, in British Vessels, during the year 1856.

IMPORTS.		EXPORTS.	
Names of Articles.	Value in Pounds sterling.	Names of Articles.	Value in Pounds sterling.
European manufactures	198,528	Tobacco	81,972
Coffee	7570	Native manufactures	17,759
Paper	1000	Pasturmah *	5720
Sugar	8270	Tchirish †	2232
Soap	612	Yellow berries	4389
Henna	1680	Copper	47,640
Hardware	2565	Leather	3598
Tin	925	Leeches	1000
Spirits	1835	Mahlep ‡	444
Nails	263	Skins	960
Fruit	748	Flour	1608
Skins	405	Silk	3520
Iron	25,827	Silk cocoons	4280
Horses 623		Hides	2725
Mules 1858	14,440	Carpets	3712
Buffaloes 100		Wheat	2311
Sundries	55,258	Barley meal	397
		Wax	540
		Butter	300
		Tallow	644
		Fruit and dried vegetables	2164
		Sheep 10,532 Bullocks 2520	11,566
		Sundries	21,268
Total	319,926		220,749

* "Pasturmah"—beef cut into long strips, pickled with garlic and spices, and dried in the sun.

† "Tchirish"—a paste used by shoemakers, made from a bulbous root.

‡ "Mahlep"—a small aromatic seed, used by bakers to sprinkle over bread.

CHAPTER XIII.

SALONICA.

SALONICA (*anc. Thessalonica*) is, next to Constantinople, the principal seat of commerce in European Turkey. The population amounts to 80,000, viz. :—

Mussulmans	30,000
Greeks	36,000
Jews	12,000
Franks	2,000
	80,000

The imports and exports have, of late years, considerably increased. In 1851, the value of the principal articles imported into Salonica by sea amounted to 433,919*l.*; in 1852, to 599,216*l.*; in 1853, to 571,555*l.*; and in 1854, to 754,074*l.* The exports by sea, which, in 1851, amounted in value only to 179,070*l.*, increased in 1852, to 489,648*l.*; in 1853, to 695,210*l.*; and in 1854, to 1,098,596*l.*

IMPORTS.

The demand for British cotton manufactures of all descriptions daily increases, and every year there is some new outlet of sufficient importance for the establishment of agencies in the interior by the importers at Salonica, hence the prospect of an increase of the import trade in proportion with the increasing value of the export trade. The Austrian and Saxon manufacturers have, however, again turned their attention to this part of Turkey, and are now sending large parcels of low cotton goods into the country. The principal imports are:—

FROM GREAT BRITAIN.	Manufactured cotton and woollen goods, tin, lead, iron, clocks, watches, jewellery, and colonials.
FROM GERMANY.	Woollen cloths, calicoes, muslins, glass-ware, porcelain, steel, copper.
FROM ITALY.	Woollen cloths, firearms, glass, silks, velvet, paper, red caps.
FROM HOLLAND.	Colonials and woollen cloths.
FROM RUSSIA.	Silk, velvet, gold thread, gold lace, furs.
FROM FRANCE.	Woollen cloths, caps, embroidery, coffee, sugar, indigo, cochineal, pepper, logwood, drugs, paper, lead and small shot.
FROM EGYPT.	Mokkha coffee, flax, linens, gum, incense, sal-ammoniac,* drugs, and henna-powder.†
FROM SMYRNA.	Soap, madder, and dry fruits.
FROM CANDIA.	Oils, soap, lemons and oranges.
FROM THE ISLANDS OF THE ARCHIPELAGO.	Fruits, wines, silks.
FROM CONSTANTINOPLE	Silk stuffs, gold and silver brocades, yellow moroccos, worked amber, valuable pipes, &c.

EXPORTS.

Cotton.—The cottons known under the name of the

---

* Sal-ammoniac is received in small loaves, both round and broad. Some writers have asserted that this salt proceeds from the urine of the camel, sublimated in African sand; this, however, is a popular error. The Egyptians burn camels' dung, mixed with straw infused in urine, and it is from the soot which proceeds from this that they draw, by sublimation, the sal-ammoniac. Sal-ammoniac is employed as a dissolvent by the Turkish tanners. It assists the sublimation of imperfect metals, heightens the colour of gold during fusion, and is used in making *aqua regia*. At the present time sal-ammoniac is manufactured in England from the impure ammoniacal liquors obtained as secondary products in the manufacture of coal-gas and animal charcoal.

† Henna is a shrub of the family of *Salicares*, whose leaves, when pulverized and wrought into a pulp with lemon juice, are made use of as a cosmetic.

cottons of Salonica are gathered in the district of Serès, a city of Macedonia, celebrated throughout European Turkey for the richness of its market, and situated fifteen leagues to the north-west of Salonica, in the midst of a vast plain, watered and fertilized by the river Strymon. The annual harvest of cotton in the valley of Serès was, fifty years ago, estimated at 70,000 bales; of which, 30,000 bales were exported to Germany, 12,000 to France, 4,000 to Trieste, 1,500 to Leghorn, and as many more exported to Genoa. Upon the whole, there were exported 50,000 bales. Of late years, however, the production of this staple has very much decreased.

Corn.—The total annual produce of corn in the districts of Salonica, Volo, and Orphano is estimated at eight hundred thousand imperial quarters, of which three hundred thousand are exported.

Wool.—There is no country of the globe more agreeably diversified than Macedonia; it is the compendium of every climate. Plants which grow between the tropics flourish in its plains, and those of the most northern countries become acclimatized on its mountains. The lands which do not allow of cultivation produce spontaneously thyme, creeping or wild thyme, sweet marjoram, and aromatic plants. Such a country as this, possessing excellent pastures, must be singularly well adapted for the support of cattle and sheep, of which there are numerous herds and flocks. It supports also, during six months of the year, all the flocks of the neighbouring regions, for the Albanian shepherds, driven from the mountains by the severity of winter, come to the mild climate of Macedonia in quest of more substantial and more plentiful pastures, and they there enjoy the privilege of going from place to place, over all the uncultivated lands.

The wools of Salonica are brought from Jénidgé, from Doiram, Strumzza, and from Serès, and are held in the greatest estimation in the Levant. The total exportation from those districts, as well as from the fine plains that surround Salonica, is estimated at 2,200,000 lbs.

Silk.—The district of Zagora, in Thessaly, produces the greater part of the raw silk exported from Salonica. The climate of that district is so mild, the air so pure, and the sky so bright, that the silk-worms spin in places open on every side.

Tobacco.—The cultivation of this plant occupies an eighth part of the ploughed lands, and supports a population of 20,000 families. The annual harvest or gathering of tobacco in Macedonia is estimated at one hundred thousand bales. European Turkey consumes forty thousand bales; Egypt, thirty thousand; Barbary, ten thousand; and Italy, twenty thousand. The other principal articles of export from Salonica are oil, wax, opium, yellow berries, gum, hides, hare-skins, leather, and carpets.

From Mr. Calvert, Her Britannic Majesty's Consul at Salonica, May 2nd, 1859.*

In reply to your letter of the 19th ult., I hasten to express to you my opinion that the formation of a Branch Bank at Salonica would be attended with very great advantage to the local trade, and I beg to assure you that several of the leading merchants with whom I have spoken on the subject are in favour of its establishment.

* Mr. Calvert is now Her Britannic Majesty's Consul at Monastir.

You have only to look at the map and see what a large radius inland the trade through Salonica, as the nearest seaport, must cover. From 2,000 to 3,000 horse and mule loads of merchandise are calculated to pass out of the gates of this town every week for the interior, and when trade is very active they have been known to exceed 5,000 loads. I calculate the imports and exports at a million and a half sterling, at least, annually. Every point, offering fewer facilities of access from the Adriatic or from the frontiers of Austria, is reached from Salonica for the introduction of British, French, and German goods; at Serès, only 18 hours inland on the road to Belgrade, the trade with Austria is exceedingly active at certain seasons. The trade in silk and silk cocoons is very important at Salonica. Several large fairs are held in this district every year.
. . . . . . There is here a horde of small money-dealers who play with the currency of the place. One advantage of a bank would be their suppression, and the better regulation of the currency and the exchanges. The English sovereign is now at 180 piastres; last year, at this date, it was at 168 piastres, and all the coins rise in proportion.

A vast amount of cash lies buried underground in the country for security, but producing no fruit, and I imagine that, so soon as the operations of a bank give sufficient confidence, much of this money will come to light again, in order to be deposited in it.

Report by Mr. Richard Wilkinson, jun., Her Britannic Majesty's Consul, on the Inducements for forming a Branch Bank at Salonica.

The subjoined approximate returns of the trade at the port of Salonica for the year 1860 will at once show the magnitude and importance of its commerce, and the vast field open to banking operations.

It must, however, be observed, with reference to the subjoined returns, that the year 1860 has been, as regards the quantity and value of the exports, far below the average of former years, owing to the partial failure of the grain crops. Tobacco, Indian corn, wheat, barley, silk, and cotton, constitute the staple products of Macedonia and Thessaly. Sesame, oats, rye, rice, and wine are also raised, but scarcely in sufficient quantities to meet the requirements of local consumption. A good deal of olive oil, to the amount of upwards of 2,000 tons, is on an average exported annually from the port of Volo, in Thessaly.

The usual rates of interest here are the same as in most other parts of Turkey, 12 per cent. being the lowest figure charged.

The want of monied capital, combined with the complete absence of good roads, and the abuses exercised under the tithe system, are evils which obstruct the developement of agriculture in this country, and fetter whatsoever there is of energy in its inhabitants. The soil is everywhere of great fertility. Capital, good roads, and a fair assessment of the taxes, are only required to increase tenfold the present productions, by bringing under cultivation immense tracts of fertile lands, which are now let run to waste.

There are, properly speaking, no real banking establishments here. A few native saraffs occasionally discount bills and promissory notes, usually charging interest at the rate of 12 per cent. per annum on first-class paper.

Considering the scarcity of money and the high interest it commands — and, above all, the natural propensity of the inhabitants, the Christians particularly, to engage in commercial pursuits whenever they can command some capital, however small the amount, to enable them to do so—I think a capital of from 100,000*l.* to 150,000*l.* could be easily and beneficially employed here in banking operations, which could, of course, be increased with the increasing prosperity of the country, which the facilities afforded by a bank for obtaining loans at a reasonable interest would be sure to develope the more, as there is every reason to believe that the Turkish Government will soon take measures to alter the present mode of levying the taxes, and abolish altogether the system now in vigour of farming them to the highest bidder. And as orders have already been given for making roads, the moment is certainly most propitious for the establishment of a branch bank in Salonica.

Imports by Sea in 1860.

British goods . . . . . Value	£350,000
Foreign . . . . . . „	150,000
Total . . .	£500,000

Exports by Sea in 1860.

Tobacco	£5,000
Cotton	1,000
Silk	50,000
Indian corn	30,000
Wheat	100,000
Barley	30,000
Other produce	80,000
Total . . .	£296,000

Tobacco and cotton, which constitute two of the most important articles of export from Macedonia, figure for a small amount only in the above returns, Cavalla and Orfano being the principal outlets for those products.

RICHARD WILKINSON, jun., Consul.

Salonica, February 25, 1861.

CHAPTER XIV.

VOLO.

The district of Volo contains a population of about 75,000 souls, who reside chiefly in the twenty-four villages of Mount Pelion. Some of these villages might be ranked as towns, as well from their extent and the style of the buildings as from the number of inhabitants, which, in some cases, reaches 6,000. In all of them considerable industrial activity prevails, and wealth to a large amount is often amassed, although it is more frequently hoarded than put into circulation.

There remain about 1,000 Mussulmans in the district, but, small as is this number, it is continually diminishing, for, as the Turks are habitually averse to industrial pursuits, they are, one after another, obliged to mortgage whatever property they possess; and as the general rate of interest is 20 per cent. they soon become deeply involved, bankruptcy follows, and then they migrate to any place where their co-religionists are to be found in large numbers. The vacant space is at once occupied by the Greeks, who are remarkable for their industry and intelligence.

The surface of Mount Pelion, nearly to the summit, consists of a light soil, fit for pasture and tillage, but agriculture has not yet received any benefits from modern science. Nevertheless, considerable quantities of grain are produced, together with potatoes, and most of the vegetables used in England. Fruits of excellent quality grow in abundance, and light wines are made in large quantities. The summit of Pelion is thickly wooded with beech and oak; the chestnut abounds on the eastern side, but the great staples are the mulberry and olive. The latter clothes the eastern and southern slopes of the mountains for miles together, and receives additions every year. Cotton is grown in small quantities, but the quality is indifferent, as the farmers do not seem disposed to give it increased attention. The soil and climate, however, are well suited for it, as also for nearly all European grains, fruits, and vegetables.

It is now well known that Mount Pelion contains vast mines of argentiferous lead, as also of copper, iron, manganese, and arsenic. Much has been done to explore this wealth, and it is to be hoped that the skill and capital (upwards of 50,000*l*.) already expended will be followed out to advantageous results. The fisheries of the Gulf form another source of local wealth. Sponges of the best quality are annually taken to the value of 2,000*l*., and fish might be caught in great quantities.

Volo, being the only port of Thessaly, is the commercial entrepôt of the whole province, and, as a safe roadstead and a capacious harbour, it has not a superior in Europe. The subjoined figures show its principal imports and exports, but the capabilities of the province are not to be judged of by its present returns, for there is not upon the earth a country of greater and more varied resources:—

Imports at Volo in the year 1858.

Names of Articles.	Where From.	Quantity.	At. £ s.	Value. £
Salt	Sicily	20,000 tons.	1 8	28,000
Soap	Candia	70 ,,	28 0	1,960
Sundries				100,000
		Total		£129,960

Exports at Volo in the year 1858.

Names of Articles.	Where To.	Quantity.	At. £ s.	Value. £
Wheat	England, France, and Trieste	185,000 qrs.	0 17	157,250
Barley		100,000 ,,	0 10	50,000
Sesame	Trieste	18,000 ,,	1 8	25,200
Silk cocoons	France	145 tons.	450 0	65,250
Olive oil	Constantinople, Smyrna, Salonica	1,785 ,,	—	56,580
Tobacco	Do. & Alexandria	1,230 ,,	46 0	56,580
Wool	France and Trieste	490 ,,	37 0	18,130
Sundries				50,000
		Total		£478,990

CHAPTER XV.

MONASTIR.

THE foreign trade of Monastir, and its two dependent Sandjaks of Ochrida and Castoria, is, to a certain extent, carried on through the port of Durazzo, in Middle Albania, but its principal channel is Salonica, situated in Macedonia.

The total value of foreign commodities imported during the year 1856 was estimated at 813,000$l.$, viz. :—

From Great Britain	£422,000
„ Austria	340,000
„ Holland	35,000
„ France	16,000
Total	£813,000

The imports from Great Britain consist of :—

Cotton Manufactures: Prints, Longcloths, Shirtings, Cambrics, Shawls, Handkerchiefs, and Cotton Twist	£305,000
Colonial Produce and Dyes	100,000
Tin, Ironware, Nails, Shot, &c.	15,000
Earthenware and Glass	2,500
Total	£422,500

The imports from Austria consisted chiefly of woollen

cloths, demi-cottons, furs, silk-stuffs, and Nuremburg wares; those from France, of silk manufactures, and from Holland, of colonial produce.

The amount of exports during the year 1856 has been computed at 220,000*l*. They consisted almost entirely of grain, and exhibit a great falling off from the exportation of the previous year, which was reported to have exceeded half a million sterling in value. Such fluctuations, however, in the amount of exports are inevitable, and must continue as long as the means of communication between the outports and the interior remain so defective.*

Although the export of grain has very much declined, other but less considerable branches of trade have improved. The trade in furs, which is the staple of some of the chief towns of the province, viz., Monastir, Ochrida, and Castoria, displayed, during the year 1858, unusual activity. Monastir also supplies not only Roumelia, but other provinces of European Turkey, with articles of clothing ready made, both embroidered and plain; the former, since the introduction of European fashions among the official and wealthier classes, are much less in vogue than they used to be, but the demand for plain clothing has increased. The quantity of wool produced for exportation is, as well as can be ascertained, more abundant now than in former years; the shepherds, some of whom carry on their operations on a large scale, descend every year with their flocks,

* In 1859, the Turkish Government granted 700,000 piastres for the construction of a road from Monastir to Salonica; but this sum was never expended upon the road, as the Governor of the province found other and more agreeable means of spending it. In the present state of the road, one horse can carry two-hundredweight in four days from Monastir to Salonica, but upon a well-made road he could in the same time convey with a cart at least eighteen-hundredweight.

from the mountains of Roumelia, into the plain of Salonica, and, after wintering there, and disposing of their wool, return to their families with the proceeds, so that the profits of the trade contribute to the resources of Monastir. To these may be added the gains of certain seats of local industry; for instance, of Kuprili, Veles, and Perlippe: the tanners of the first, and the braziers of the latter town, are much esteemed, and find customers for their wares all over European Turkey. Besides these, there is in the mountainous districts of Roumelia an itinerant and migratory class of artizans (*courbetchis*), composed chiefly of masons, builders, joiners, bakers, &c., who carry on their trades in every part of the Ottoman Empire, and, after a certain number of years, return to their homes with the fruits of their industry. On a moderate computation, it is supposed their number must amount to 25,000, and their average savings to 15*l*. a year, which will give 375,000*l*. This sum being subsequently consumed at home, or converted into capital, may be justly considered as augmenting the ways and means of their native province.

The sales effected in the year 1858, of the produce and manufactures of Roumelia, in other provincial markets and at Constantinople, consisting of olive oil, tobacco, butter, tallow, wool, woollen stockings, coarse cloth (*abbas*), and ready-made and embroidered wearing apparel, amounted to about 260,000*l*. This, as well as can be ascertained, was balanced by purchased commodities, the growth and manufacture of other parts of Turkey; such as Brussa-silk, silk cord, gold and silver cord, as also carpets, shawls, furs, arms, iron, rice, fruit, jewellery, amber, and soap.

The following is a statement of all the vessels that arrived at and sailed from the port of Durazzo during the six months from the 26th of May to the 25th of November 1858:—

Nationality.	Entered.		Cleared.	
	Vessels.	Tons.	Vessels.	Tons.
Turkish	213	8,227	210	8,113
Ionian	114	2,148	115	2,206
Austrian	98	4,771	99	4,810
Steamers	55	10,481	55	10,481
Neapolitan	30	1,432	30	1,432
Greek	11	692	10	483
Papal States	8	538	9	564
French	1	101	1	101
Total	530	28,390	529	28,190

The principal articles of export in 1859 were grain and skins; most of the other productions having been used for home consumption, or sold in the neighbouring provinces of Ochrida and Uscup, as well as in central and northern Albania.

The following is an approximate estimate of the exports *viâ* Salonica and Belgrade:—

VIA SALONICA.

	£	£
Wheat, 98,840 imp. qrs., average price 21s.	103,782	
Silk cocoons	2,500	
		106,282

VIA BELGRADE.

Manufactured sheep-skins, average price per skin 1s. 5d.	3,670	
Manufactured sakhtians, or goats'-skins, at 3s. per skin	15,380	
Lambs'-skins (raw material), at 10d. per skin	5,380	
Goats'-skins (raw material), at 2s. per skin	5,500	
Sheep-skins (raw material), at 1s. 1d. per skin	4,400	34,330

Carried forward £140,612

MONASTIR.

Brought forward	£140,612
Hare-skins, at 5d. per skin	£4,500
Wool (unwashed), per oke of 2¾ lbs., 1s. 5d.	3,000
Woollen socks, at 6d. per pair	1,000
	8,500
Total	£149,112

Besides the above, there is also a large transit trade in olive oil, produced in the district of Ochrida, which is conveyed through Monastir to Servia and Wallachia.

The imports in 1859 were as follow :—

VIA SALONICA.

	£	£
Coffee, from 1s. 6d. to 1s. 10d. the oke of 2¾ lbs.	42,000	
Sugar, from 1s. 2d. to 1s. 4d. the oke	84,000	
Rum, from 1s. to 1s. 4d. the oke	23,000	
Rice, from 6d. the oke	3,000	
Soap, from 11d. the oke	10,000	
Iron rods, from 4d. to 5d. the oke		
Iron nails, from 8d. to 10d. the oke		
Sheet iron, from 5d. to 9d. the oke	76,000	
Lead, from 6d. to 7d. the oke		
Tin, in boxes, 1l. 3s. to 1l. 6s.		
Cotton goods (all British manufacture):		
Water twist, Nos. 4 to 14, 12s. per bundle of 10 lbs.		
Ditto, Nos. 16 to 24, 14s. ditto		
Ditto, Nos. 26 to 32, 17s. 1d. ditto		
Ditto, Nos. 38 to 42, 1l. 1s. 5d. ditto		
Ditto, Nos. 48 to 52, 1l. 4s. 2d. ditto		
Printed calicoes, 7s. 10d. to 11s. per piece of 28 yards		
Ditto, 12s. 2d. to 1l. 3s. per piece of 36 yds.		
Madapolams, 11s. to 18s. 7d., pieces of 40 yards	298,000	
Shirtings, Nos. 1, 2, 3, 4, 5, 11s. to 18s. 7d. pieces of 40 yards		
White tangibs, 4s. to 6s., pieces of 20 yards		
Blue cloths, 6s. to 11s., pieces of 28 yards		
Coloured shirtings, 12s. to 15s. per piece of 40 yards		
Pocket handkerchiefs, coloured, 2s. to 5s. per dozen		
	Carried forward	£536,000

	Brought forward	£536,000
Indigo, 10s. to 1l. the oke	£6,000	
Cochineal, 1l. 3s. to 1l. 10s. the oke	2,000	
Copper-plates, at 4s. the oke	8,000	
Silks	7,500	
		23,500
VIÂ BELGRADE.		
Glass	8,000	
Gold embroidery	4,000	
Cloth	50,000	
Fezes	22,000	
Demi-cottons	28,000	
Pocket handkerchiefs	4,000	
Sheep, at 8s. per head	8,000	
Oxen, at 4l. per head	40,000	
Horses, at 6l. per head	24,000	
		188,000
Total		£747,500

Extract from Official Report to the Foreign Office by Mr. Longworth, Her Britannic Majesty's Consul at Monastir.

The amount of disposable capital at Monastir has been considerably augmented of late years; as a proof of which we have only to refer to the rate of interest, which, with fair security, is as low as 12 per cent.; while in other parts of European Turkey, where capital is wanting, it rises to 20, 30, 40, and even to 60 per cent. per annum.

This comparative low rate of interest at Monastir indicates a certain accumulation of capital, and this, it might naturally be supposed, would lead to its employment, to some extent at least, in works of public utility; for it has been seen elsewhere that there is a period in accumulation, when capital overflows the narrow limits of individual enterprise, and when banks and joint-stock companies are called into existence as the only efficient machinery by which undertakings on a large and collective scale can be accomplished.

Railroads, to which the attention of European capitalists has been chiefly directed, offer by no means the only profitable mode of investment; more secure and more advantageous employment of capital must occur, in many shapes, to those acquainted with the country. Among others may be specified the cultivation of silk and of cotton, the adaptation of the abundant water-power everywhere available to industrial processes; to saw-mills, for instance, and the spinning of woollen yarn. To these may be added mining operations, and the draining of marshy grounds; and, above all, as immediately conducive to the extension of the export trade, the improvement of inland navigation, and the means of land transport. The substitution of carriage by carts and waggons, instead of the primitive conveyance of pack-horses and camels (which naturally involves the construction of roads and bridges), presents, I believe, if prudently prosecuted, one of the safest forms of speculation in which capital could be here embarked. Far from interfering with the formation of railroads, it is evident these improvements would greatly facilitate, and indeed, in the natural course of things, ought to precede it.

For the accomplishment of these objects, the capital and industry of the country itself are, I repeat, wholly inadequate. Branch banks, connected with a directing establishment at Constantinople, and founded on foreign capital and enterprise, would, I am persuaded, afford the only practical medium.

The capital, skill, and industry of Western Europe, in connection with branch banks, would undoubtedly accelerate the developement of the same elements of progress in Turkey, and a great advantage likely to result from their establishment would be the gradual diffusion of that confidence which is essential to undertakings of any magnitude, and without which trade and agriculture must remain but imperfectly developed.

CHAPTER XVI.

BOSNIA.

Bosnia is rich in pasture grounds, which are particularly adapted for rearing cattle. The vast forests of oak in the north are likewise admirably calculated for fattening swine, whilst some parts of the province, owing to the coolness of the climate, and the quality of the vegetation, are not less favourable for the rearing of sheep, and for the production of a superior quality of wool, much esteemed in the markets of Europe. Thus it is that cattle and sheep form a considerable portion of the wealth of the inhabitants, and likewise a vast proportion of the trade that is carried on with their neighbours. The northern districts of Zvornik, Bania-luka, and Bihka produce oxen, swine, and horses; the southern districts of Yeni-Bazar, Hersek, and Serajevo produce sheep. Seinitza, Novi-Bazar, Priepoli, and Novi-Varosh produce the best quality of wool, while Serajevo, Tashlija, and Koprez come next. Tanneries have, for a considerable time, existed in the country, and leather is not an unimportant article of its commerce.

Of the vegetable productions, plums, of which large quantities are consumed in Bosnia, are the most important. A great deal of spirit is distilled from them, and considerable quantities are exported. Grain comes next in importance, and yields a great profit, 800 per cent. being the average return to the cultivator. The climate is too cold for the culture of the olive-tree or the cotton-plant, but mulberry-trees thrive, and the silk-worm might be introduced into the country with every prospect of success. Tar is produced, as well as resin, from the fir and pine trees, and timber of every description abounds.

Of the mineral riches of the country, the iron mines are the only ones at present worked to any extent by the natives.

The following are the positions of the principal mines in Bosnia :—

Gold and Silver.—The mountains round Bosnia-Seraï contain gold and silver; and in a forest near Travnik, the excavations of the celebrated gold mine of Ilatnizza (literally signifying gold in the Bosnian tongue) are still visible. There are silver mines near Preberniza on the Drina, Kruppa on the Unna, and Kamengrad, within a short distance of the Verbas.

Iron.—The iron of Bosnia is of excellent quality, resembling the best variety of Swedish. Some mines are worked in the vicinity of Bosnia-Seraï by gipsies, who have a number of smithies, in which horse-shoes, nails, locks, iron-plates, and other wares are manufactured. There are also iron mines at Vakup, Kamengrad, Kreshovo, Ossoji, Babgaravan, Foinitza, Bussovatz, Varesh, Slari, Maidan, and Borrovitzo.

Lead.— Olovo, Kladem, Shedni, Kreshovo, and Zvornik.

Copper.—The copper ore is very rich, yielding on an average 35 per cent. of pure copper, but that amount could be still further increased if the appliances of European science were introduced, as fully 8 per cent. of metal remains in the refuse of the furnace. There are mines at Kreshovo and Foinitza.

Mercury.—Kreshovo, Inact.

Zinc.—Zinc is found in considerable quantities in the basin of mines surrounding the town of Kreshovo, 25 miles north-west of Serajevo.

Arsenic.—Kreshovo, Ivitza, &c. It is abundant throughout the province in the form of orpiment and realgar: the ore is very fine, and would, no doubt, prove exceedingly remunerative.

There are also two mines of cinnabar in Bosnia, both of which have been worked for some time past, but, owing to a fault in the vein, the works have been discontinued, as the technical knowledge of the miners is not sufficient to enable them to recover the trace of the ore. There are also fine quarries of freestone and mill-stones, alabaster, and marble. Rock-salt is found in large quantities near the town of Jusla, and mineral and hot springs abound throughout the province. Coal is also plentiful.

The superficial area of Bosnia (including Herzegovina) is 2,300 square miles, and the population, about 1,150,000, is thus divided:—

	Christians.	Mussulmans.	Total.
Sandjak of Serajevo	42,823	58,964	101,787
Teavnik	103,026	54,912	157,938
Banialuka	127,833	35,764	163,597
Bihutah	103,165	76,023	179,188
Svoinik	127,950	110,865	238,815
Novi-Bazar	46,225	49,350	95,575
Herzegovina	120,000	80,000	200,000
Jews	...	...	3,100
Gipsies	...	...	10,000
	671,022	465,878	1,150,000

Very few articles of British manufactures are consumed in Bosnia; not that the native trader is ignorant of their superior quality, but because his means do not permit him to enter into the trade. The native merchants are obliged to receive from their consignors at Trieste whatever the latter choose to send, which is usually the cheapest and most worthless of Austrian manufactures, and as the trader, in the absence of branch banks or such institutions, is unable to give his foreign correspondent any tangible security, he is obliged to pay heavy interest for these investments, and the eventual purchaser suffers accordingly.

Cotton cloth forms a principal article of import, and seems to be, in most cases, of British manufacture, but the price it bears is nearly one-half as much again as in England. Cotton twist is purchased by the peasantry, who find it cheaper to weave their own cloth than pay the high prices demanded for foreign manufactures. Fine woollen fabrics of French or German manufactures are worn by the Mussulman portion of the inhabitants, who do not condescend to wear the coarse cloth of the country. Green and scarlet are the colours most in request.

Of the colonial produce consumed in the country, coffee comes from Marseilles, through Trieste, and is probably the production of the French colonies; the sugar is of Belgian manufacture; and the rice is imported from Egypt. The rum imported is made from beet-root in the neighbourhood of Trieste. The iron wire and sheet iron are said to be of British manufacture, as likewise the tin-plates imported.

The articles of importation and exportation that constitute the principal trade of Bosnia and the Herzegovina may be classed under these two heads in the following manner:—

Importations.		Exportations.	
Names of Articles.	Value in Pounds sterling.	Names of Articles.	Value in Pounds sterling.
Manufactures of Mixed cotton & wool	45,000	Oxen, 75,000 head	450,000
Chintz	30,000	Cows, 25,000 ,,	87,500
Longcloth	18,700	Pigs, 80,000 ,,	104,000
Twist	20,000	Sheep, 15,000 ,,	7,125
Red caps	2,000	Horses, 1,000 ,,	4,500
Gold lace	2,500	Plums	60,000
Furs	1,500	Leather	10,000
Watches	4,000	Wool	3,000
Paper	1,200	Sheep-skins	3,000
Cloth	8,000	Wheat	8,620
Sugar	18,700	Indian corn	865
Coffee	15,800	Wax	1,800
Rice	5,400	Iron	12,000
Salt	8,600	Sundries	20,000
Raki	21,500		
Sundries	50,000		
Total	252,900	Total	772,410

CHAPTER XVII.

RHODES.

THE trade of Rhodes has increased considerably during the last eight or ten years. In 1851, the importations amounted to 39,561*l*., and the exportations to 15,477*l*.; whereas in 1858 the value of the former was 113,599*l*., and of the latter, 102,958*l*. Formerly, a merchant found it difficult to dispose of a hundred sacks of coffee in a year, whereas the quantity sold by him now in Rhodes amounts, on an average, to a thousand sacks per annum. This same ratio of increase is particularly applicable to British manufactures, which have replaced those of Switzerland and Germany throughout the entire Ottoman Archipelago. This increase in the consumption of British manufactures is not caused, however by the wants of the scanty population of Rhodes, but by the wants of the inhabitants of the surrounding islands, and especially by those of the people on the neighbouring coast of Asia Minor, from Boudroum to Adalia inclusive. From the coast of Anatolia, British manufactures are carried into the interior, where they are beginning to be extensively used; and it is the opinion of many intelligent merchants at Rhodes, that if one of our English commercial houses had depôts in that island of Manchester and Birmingham goods, enormous profits would be speedily realised, as Asia Minor imports annually British manufactures to the amount of several millions of piastres. A great drawback, however, to the extension of our trade exists from there being no direct steam communication between Great Britain and Rhodes. At present, all British goods reach the islands of the Ottoman Archipelago by indirect routes. They are first landed at Syra, Smyrna, Constantinople, Beyrout, or Alexandria, and afterwards re-shipped for their respective places of destination, thus making them liable to heavy charges; for example, the freight and expenses on British goods from Smyrna to Rhodes cost about as much as from Liverpool to Smyrna. There can be no doubt that if the English Company, which has a line of steamers between Liverpool and the coast of Syria, would cause their vessels to touch at Crete, Rhodes, and Cyprus, great profits would be obtained by them. The deviation from the course would be but slight, and the exportation from Great Britain of our cotton manufactures, ships' gear of all kinds, especially anchors and chain cables, metals, hardware, and crockery, would furnish the said vessels with valuable freights, while the return cargo by them of silks, fine sponges in cases, yellow wax, madder roots, valonia in sacks, dried fruits, and wheat, could not fail to be equally advantageous.

The following Tables will show the total amount of the trade of Rhodes for the five years ending 31st December 1858, and the respective countries with which it has been carried on:—

IMPORTATIONS.

Where From.	1854.	1855.	1856.	1857.	1858.
	£	£	£	£	£
Turkey	152,045	139,804	103,564	102,824	89,558
France	13,983	14,194	15,581	9,556	8,658
Great Britain	4,420	10,900	2,800	7,707	7,900
Greece	5,080	5,057	5,521	4,635	1,034
Egypt	6,837	7,313	3,931	3,368	3,858
Austria	5,180	4,436	3,936	1,684	884
Sardinia	—	—	—	—	1,667
Total	187,545	181,704	135,334	129,773	113,559

EXPORTATIONS.

Where To.	1854.	1855.	1856.	1857.	1858.
	£	£	£	£	£
Turkey	56,300	60,834	54,932	13,542	19,092
France	23,440	24,900	26,247	32,697	34,000
Great Britain	6,950	450	..	38,462	25,000
Austria	14,143	11,600	6,581	6,769	22,083
Egypt	6,110	10,000	3,735	3,372	1,950
Greece	980	1,100	1,197	854	..
Sardinia	2,000	—	2,949	—	833
Total	109,923	108,884	95,641	95,696	102,958

The following Table shows the value of the various articles imported into and exported from Rhodes during the year 1856 :—

IMPORTATIONS.		EXPORTATIONS.	
Names of Articles.	Value in Pds. sterling.	Names of Articles.	Value in Pds. sterling.
Coffee	11,410	Sponges, fine	34,872
Sugar	4,009	„ common	25,385
Pepper	1,068	„ coarse	4,487
Drugs and medicines	4,273	Honey	2,051
Cotton twist	12,393	Wax	6,094
„ manufactures	4,274	Wheat	2,991
„ printed calicoes	6,154	Onions	3,504
Cloths	2,564	Wine	4,915
Woollen manufactures	3,205	Sundries	11,342
Grey goods	6,923		
Silk, various kinds	2,222		
Sail cloth	1,538		
Coals	6,800		
Tin	5,128		
Cattle	2,137		
Wheat	9,829		
Rice	2,479		
Timber	4,274		
Leather	2,709		
Sundries	41,945		
Total	135,334	Total	95,641

IMPORTATIONS.

Colonials.—The importation of colonials was valued at about 12,000*l.* in 1858; whereas, in 1848, their value only amounted to 4,000*l.*

Manufactures.—The articles most in request have been, and still are, printed calicoes, madapolams, grey goods, and woollen stuffs. The value of these goods imported in 1858 amounted to 40,000*l.*; in 1848, to 20,000*l.* If our manufactures were brought direct from Great Britain to Rhodes, instead of by way of Smyrna, as at present, from which last place the merchants are obliged to purchase them, enormous expenses would be saved; the inhabitants of all the islands, as well as Anatolia, would then obtain our goods much cheaper, and, as a natural consequence, the importation thereof would be considerably extended.

EXPORTATIONS.

Sponge Fishery.—Sponges form the principal article of exportation; within the last few years the number of boats employed in this fishery has increased one-third, while the number of men has nearly doubled, as is shown by the subjoined return:—

Average Number of Boats and Men employed by each Island in the Sponge Fishery.

Islands.	In 1854.		In 1858.	
	Number of Boats.	Number of Men.	Number of Boats.	Number of Men.
Calymnos	120	840	254	2000
Symi	120	840	190	1450
Halki	60	420	65	480
Castel Rosso	40	280	40	300
Leros	30	210	30	210
Stampalia	10	70	12	90
Telos	—	—	7	56
Cassos	—	—	2	14
Total	380	2660	600	4600

The sponges are of three different qualities, namely—fine, common, and coarse. In the fine sponges there is but one in ten of the first, or superior quality; the rest are of a second, or inferior fine quality. In the common sponges there is but one in four of a first quality, the rest are of a second common quality. In the coarse, one-half are of first quality, and the other half of a second coarse quality. Thus it will be seen that the fine, common, and coarse kinds of sponges may be divided into two qualities each.

The following is the value, in round numbers, of the sponges sold during the five years ending 31st December 1858:—

Years.	Amounts Sold.			Total.
	Fine.	Common.	Coarse.	
	£	£	£	£
1854	30,000	20,000	4000	54,000
1855	33,000	22,000	5000	60,000
1856	35,000	25,500	4500	65,000
1857	51,000	25,000	5000	81,000
1858	35,000	50,000	5000	90,000

Of the sponges purchased in these islands, about two-thirds of the fine, one-quarter of the common, and one-quarter of the coarse (all of the first qualities) are sent to London; half of the best common quality to France (none of the other qualities are exported to that country); one-eighth of the common, and many of the coarse (all second quality) to Trieste. The refuse of the fine, common, and coarse sponges are sent to Constantinople. Lately, a few good fine sponges have been sent to the United States of America.

The following Table shows the total amount of

shipping, with the value of the imports and exports, at Rhodes, Mitylene, Scio, and Cyprus, during the year 1859:—

	Number of Vessels.	Tonnage.	Value of Imports.	Value of Exports.
Rhodes . .	2687	166,967	137,780	97,476
Mitylene . .	1401	231,728	319,800	292,700
Scio . . .	1959	131,520	143,383	163,361
Cyprus . . .	678	63,817	103,380	107,550
	6725	594,032	704,343	661,087

From Mr. Campbell, Her Britannic Majesty's Consul at Rhodes.

Money here is scarce, and high interest is paid for it to the native merchants. The sponge fishers, particularly, who require large pecuniary advances to enable them to carry on their sponge-fishing operations, always borrow money at the rate of 3 to 4 per cent. per month —36 to 48 per cent. per annum.

CHAPTER XVIII.

MITYLENE.

The island of Mitylene, the ancient Lesbos, is situated in the Ægean sea, opposite to Asia Minor, and lies between the Gulf of Adramyti on the north, and that of Smyrna on the south. It is supposed to number 80,000 inhabitants, and contains mines producing iron, coal, emery, and antimony, as well as forests of considerable extent, one of which, that of Tchiamlik, is nearly seven leagues in circumference, and is, in one part, within one-and-a-half leagues from the sea. Unfortunately, however, its fine natural harbours are filled up with rubbish, and, in the whole island, there is not one road fit for a carriage.

The city of Mitylene, in which the Governor, the Greek Archbishop, and the Vice-Consuls of the various European powers reside, is built on a peninsula, at the extreme point of which stands a fort dating back to the time of the Genoese occupation. It possesses two harbours — one on the north, which is very nearly choked up, and one on the south, which is now only accessible to vessels of 100 tons. The population of the city and suburbs amounts to 10,000 souls :—

Mussulmans		2,000
Christians—Greek Church	7,000	8,000
Armenians, Catholics, &c.	1,000	
		10,000

IMPORTS.

The imports consist chiefly of wheat, barley, maize, Levant tobacco, sugar, coffee, Russian butter, soda, rum, lead, French leather, English and Russian iron, cotton and woollen manufactures from England and Germany, arms, furniture, &c. The value of cereals imported from 1854 to 1858 was:—

Year.	£	s.	d.
1854	150,660	0	0
1855	114,400	0	0
1856	129,366	0	0
1857	201,295	8	0
1858	180,436	12	0

EXPORTS.

The exportations consist of olive-oil, soap, silk, silk cocoons, valonia, skins, wool, figs, fresh fruit, lambs, brandy, cheese, &c. The oil is exported to Turkey, France, England, and Austria; the valonia to Trieste; the cocoons to France, and the other articles to various ports in the Levant. The value of the annual exports is as follows:—

Year.	£
1854	98,453
1855	33,632
1856	112,476
1857	114,309
1858	143,233

In 1859, the total imports and exports were:—

Number of Vessels.	Tonnage.	Value of Imports.	Value of Exports.
1,401	231,728	£319,800	£292,700

The prices of provisions were doubled by the Crimean war, and have not since then undergone any sensible variation. They are at present:—

			s.	d.
Bread, per oke of 2¾ lbs.			0	4
Beef	,,	,,	0	8
Kid	,,	,,	0	6
Lamb	,,	,,	1	0
Fish	,,	,,	0	10
Kidney potatoes	,,		0	2
Onions	,,	,,	0	2
Dried vegetables	,,		0	4
Fresh	,,	,,	0	2
Wine	,,	,,	0	8
Oil	,,	,,	1	0
Butter	,,	,,	3	0
Milk	,,	,,	0	6
A fowl	,,	,,	1	8
A turkey	,,	,,	5	0

The Christians of Mitylene rank very high in the Levant for their skill in masonry, rough joinery, rough casting and painting. There are about 4,000 employed in these trades, half of whom emigrate every year, in search of employment, to Smyrna and Constantinople. The wages have considerably risen since 1854, viz. :—

	In 1854.		In 1860.	
	s.	d.	s.	d.
Ship-caulker, per day	3	0	5	0
Carpenter ,,	3	0	4	2
Painter ,,	2	4	4	0
Mason ,,	1	10	3	0
Reaper ,,	1	6	2	4
Labourer ,,	1	4	2	0
Hodman ,,	0	10	1	6
Female Olive-gatherer	0	5	0	8

CHAPTER XIX.

SCIO.

THE island of Scio possesses an area of 340 square miles, and is divided naturally into two districts: the highlands, comprehending the villages situated in the north and west, and the lowlands, containing those of the centre and south. The number of these villages is sixty-six, of which thirty-six are in different parts of the north, inhabited by a population of 17,000 souls; nine, including the city, lie in the centre, with a population of about 20,000 souls; and twenty-one in the south, with 23,000 inhabitants. The total population of the island before the revolutions of 1821 and 1827 amounted to more than 120,000 souls; but in the year 1830, the number was scarcely 20,000. As the births, however, are in excess of the deaths, in consequence of the healthiness of the climate, the population has sensibly increased, and the number is now estimated at 60,000, viz:—

Mussulmans	1,800
Greeks	57,400
Roman Catholics (descendants of the ancient Genoese)	400
Jews	200
Negroes	200
Total	60,000

The inhabitants of Scio are laborious, intelligent, economical, honest, and enterprising, and devote themselves chiefly to the three following branches of industry: agriculture, commerce, and navigation. They are remarkable for ability, activity, and a determination to overcome every difficulty, and possess, in the highest degree, a natural predilection for commerce, and turn to some account whatever produces money. In confirmation of this, it may be stated that the largest proportion of the commercial establishments in Turkey are owned by natives of Scio, and that the richest Greek merchants in Europe have nearly all come originally from that island. The two distinctive traits in the character of the natives of Scio are, great honesty and great economy. The latter, indeed, sometimes verges on parsimony, for the richest native of Scio will often deny himself important necessaries to save expense, and will not ordinarily enjoy his easy circumstances, but continue to toil on for the purpose of amassing money. A case of burglary, murder, or assassination is hardly ever known in the island. The Turks are not very fanatical; they take but little interest in commerce, living generally on the revenues of their land, and are on very good terms with the Christians.

PRODUCE.

The chief products are: mastic, oranges, lemons, almonds, silk, cereals, beans, lentils, grey peas, oil, wine, cotton, leather, brandy, confections, which are the commodities exported; and grapes, caroubs, walnuts, figs, apricots, prunes, pistachios, peaches, &c., which are consumed at home.

Mastic.—All the twenty-one villages of the south produce this gum. Before the cold of 1850, they produced from 45,000 to 50,000 okes; but, in consequence of many of the trees having been killed by the frost, the amount collected was much reduced. Since then, however, the quantity has greatly increased, and in 1858 as much as 20,000 okes were collected. Mastic, one of the chief resources of the island, is a kind of gum which oozes from the trunk of a tree of the same name, but it can only be cultivated in the southern part of the island. All endeavours to propagate this tree, whether in other parts of the island or in other countries, have totally failed. The tree which produces mastic rarely exceeds eight feet in height; its leaves are evergreen, and resemble those of the turpentine-tree. To extract the mastic, incisions are made on the main trunk, and from them the gum issues.

Lemons and Oranges.—The cold of the same year, 1850, injured also the orange and lemon trees, the value of the produce of which had hitherto been as high as from 6,000,000 to 7,000,000 piastres. The old stocks have, however, since put out new shoots, and the quantity of oranges and lemons increases every year. Their present value is about 2,000,000 piastres, and it is hoped that the former prosperity will be soon attained.

Almonds.—The quantity of almonds varies much; sometimes it is as great as 400,000 okes, and sometimes as low as 40,000 or 50,000 okes only. They are esteemed some of the best in Turkey. These great variations in the quantity of almonds are owing to the unseasonable warmth occasionally experienced in the early spring, which brings the blossoms too forward, and then the high winds in the beginning of summer cause them to fall, and there remains thus but little to gather.

Silk.—The cocoon harvest is estimated at about from 15,000 to 16,000 okes annually, from which, formerly, the silk was taken on the island; but now the cocoons are usually bought by French merchants, who have the silk spun either at Smyrna or in France.

Wheat and Barley.—Scio does not produce more than 75,000 to 80,000 kilos of wheat, which only supply the home demand for three months. During the remaining nine months, the island is dependent on corn brought by Scian vessels from the Danube, Roumelia, Karamania, and Egypt. These vessels carry corn also to the neighbouring coasts of Tchesme, Alazata, &c., which are without cereals. Barley is very little cultivated or imported, and animals are fed generally with hay and beans.

Pulse.—The average crop of beans is from 16,000 to 18,000 kilos; that of lentils from 1,500 to 2,000 kilos, and that of grey beans from 4,000 to 5,000 kilos. These vegetables are of excellent quality, and are mostly exported to Constantinople.

Oil.—The supply of oil ranges from 25,000 to 30,000 okes, which were formerly consumed in the island, but its excellence having in time been discovered at Constantinople, the largest portion is now exported there, and Mitylene and Candia send what is wanted by the island.

Wine.—The wine of Scio, once highly esteemed, has lost much of its former reputation. Before the disease of the grapes, about eight years ago, the crop amounted to from 200,000 to 250,000 okes; it has since much diminished, and it is now necessary to import for home consumption.

Cotton.—From 600 to 800 kintals of cotton are annually produced. This cotton is used in the local manufacture of the cloth employed for the sails of ships. The British Vice-Consul made a free distribution, some time ago, of American cotton seed, which has succeeded well, and will contribute to increase the cultivation of this plant.

Madder.—This has only been cultivated since 1853. It has been exported to England, and its success has induced many landholders to plant it; in a few years, it is expected that this root will become one of the chief branches of commerce in the island.

Leather.—In Scio there are several tanneries, which are supplied with skins from Egypt and Buenos Ayres. When tanned, the skins are exported to the islands of the Ottoman Archipelago. These tanneries promise well, and business has already been transacted with Anatolia, Syria, and even Dalmatia.

Brandy.—The brandy is considered the best in Turkey, chiefly on account of the mastic put with it, which gives it a peculiar flavour. It is sent to Constantinople to the value of nearly 1,000,000 piastres.

Confectionery.—Scio is renowned for its confections and preserves. Many people carry on trade in this branch with the capital and the principal cities of the Ottoman Empire.

Grapes.—Many merchants buy the grapes of Tchesme for export to France, Hamburgh, England, and Trieste. The island produces but few grapes.

COMMERCE.

The commerce consists not only in the exportation of the chief products of the island, such as mastic, lemons, oranges, almonds, brandy, leather, vegetables, &c., and the importation of the articles which the island does not afford, such as wheat, oil, &c., together with colonial produce, manufactured goods, hardware, &c., &c., but likewise in external mercantile enterprises.

The latter are conducted through the medium of native ships, maintained by the merchants of Scio, which enter foreign ports for the purpose of speculating, and load cargoes on their own account. The products of which the island is in want are procured chiefly from Turkey; wheat, however, which is required as well for the neighbouring coasts and islands as for Scio itself, and the imports of which amount to about 300,000 kilos, comes from the Danube, Roumelia, Karamania, and Egypt. Oil is brought from Candia and Mitylene; wine from Cyprus; the larger portion of manufactured goods and hardwares from Smyrna, Constantinople, and England; chains, iron, anchors, and rigging are imported from Europe; sugar, coffee, &c., exclusively from France. All these articles come to Scio in native vessels. Schooners and other vessels used in the coasting trade are generally employed in the voyages to Anatolia, whence they convey wheat for the use of Scio and the other islands. These vessels make a twofold use of their journey, by carrying at the same time such products from Scio as may be in demand, and very often taking over European goods, such as manufactures, hardware, and earthenware, &c., which they have purchased at Scio itself. The greater part of the imports from the European markets is also conveyed by native vessels, which likewise bring cereals from Russia and the Danube to Marseilles, Trieste, Leghorn, and England.

The total capital employed in the import and export trade, and in the construction of ships, &c., exceeds annually 60,000,000 piastres. In addition, the capital sunk in shipping belonging to the island, including the expenses of their equipment, exceeds 40,000,000 piastres;

thus making a total of more than 100,000,000 piastres. There are at Scio two insurance companies, held in shares by merchants of the island, which insure native vessels only. The annual amount insured in these companies is calculated at about 50,000,000 piastres. Failures are uncommon, but if one occurs, it is submitted to a severe examination; and, if the merchant is found guilty of fraud, he is condemned to prison for a longer or shorter period, according to the offence.

The following Table will convey some idea of the value of the various commodities imported and exported during the year 1858:—

IMPORTS.

Names of Articles.	Weights and Measures.	Quantity.	Value.
			£
Wheat	quarters	28,280	54,359
Barley	,,	3,150	2,872
Manufactured goods	bales	435	15,697
Coffee, sugar	chests	3,193	15,966
Drugs	,,	324	3,769
English iron, chains	cwts.	5,040	3,948
Timber	,,	..	3,846
Rigging	,,	..	5,385
Pewter and copper	pounds	16,875	649
Hardware	cases	215	2,743
Paper	bales	157	1,555
Cotton yarn	,,	74	2,376
Raw hides	pounds	235,000	6,632
Pottery, glass	cases	401	2,436
Salt fish	hogsheads	1,780	2,692
Butter, cheese, &c.	pounds	287,500	7,650
Spirits of wine	..	..	6,648
Sundries	..	..	7,600
Tobacco and salt	..	..	4,872
Total	..	..	151,695

EXPORTS.

Names of Articles.	Weights and Measures.	Quantity.	Value.
			£
Wheat	quarters	6,870	14,102
Mastic	pounds	43,750	22,325
Silk cocoons	,,	43,750	11,992
Grapes	cwts.	11,715	10,521
Almonds	pounds	100,000	17,735
Brandy	..	..	11,282
Confectionery	cases	750	4,100
,,	pounds	46,250	21,598
Oranges and Lemons	packages	11,500	12,778
Madder	cwts.	1,760	3,700
Shrubs	number	2,500	684
Sundries	..	..	7,692
Sail cloth	pieces	2,000	1,368
Vegetables	..	..	4,102
Oil	pounds	100,000	2,051
Totals	..	..	146,030

NAVY.

The island of Scio possesses about 120 ships, of from 150 to 200 tons, with crews of 15 or 16 persons; 140 schooners, of from 30 to 100 tons, with crews of 7 or 9 persons; and 160 to 170 small sailing boats, employed in the coasting trade between the islands and the neighbouring coast of Anatolia. All these vessels belong to merchants or captains of Scio, and it is calculated that the capital sunk in them, including the salaries of the captains, amounts to a sum of 40,000,000 piastres. Native ships not uncommonly make the voyage of the Black Sea and the Mediterranean, and within the last few years they have even undertaken the voyage to England. The Scian ships are preferred generally to all other Greek vessels, on account of the integrity and naval skill of their captains. It is seldom at Scio that a vessel belongs to a single owner; almost all are the property of joint owners, among whom is the captain, and the largest merchants have an interest in several ships. Both captains and sailors are natives of Scio, and come principally from the village of Vrondado, which is situated about two miles from the city, and has about 6,000 inhabitants, who are mostly seafaring. The shipping of the island increases every year.

The following Table shows the amount of shipping, together with the value of imports and exports, during the six years from 1854 to 1859 inclusive:—

Years.	Number of Vessels.	Tonnage.	Value of Imports.	Value of Exports.
			£	£
1854	1,056	69,579	135,540	104,425
1855	864	79,320	141,250	104,030
1856	891	119,906	191,900	170,070
1857	842	120,262	156,655	142,470
1858	890	122,420	151,695	146,030
1859	1,959	131,520	143,383	163,361

CHAPTER XX.

CYPRUS.

The island of Cyprus is separated from the coast of Karamania by a channel of about twenty-five leagues in width. Its area approximates to 1,000 square leagues, which may be subdivided in the following manner:—
One-fifth, having a mountainous character, is adapted chiefly for the growth of timber; but, nevertheless, a portion could be turned to account for the culture of the vine. This mountainous district of the island offers immense resources; the forests of Thrados alone, which lie in this section, if properly managed, would produce annually a considerable number of pine-trees. Oaks are also seen in thousands on the declivities of this mountain district, which extends, for five leagues, close to the sea. Two-fifths of the island are occupied by hills, on which grow chiefly olives, mulberries, vines, and fruit-trees of all sorts. The remaining two-fifths are composed of magnificent plains and extensive open country, which, though wanting in rivers and streams, are still very productive in cereals; in fact, the eastern portion of the island, where is situated the ancient port of Famagosta, has always been the granary of the island.

Soil.—The soil of Cyprus, which is of very great fertility, and which formerly supplied the wants of a population exceeding a million and a half, still responds too kindly to the natural indolence and want of skill of its present inhabitants, of whom hardly one-fourth are devoted to agriculture.

Agriculture.—Labourers use a kind of plough, a rude and miserable implement, without wheels, drawn by two oxen, and driven by one man; like the earliest plough, it penetrates the soil scarcely more than two inches. It is used in the tillage of the plains, and the cultivation of the vineyards and vegetable gardens. The husbandmen wait generally till the autumnal rains have softened the soil, and then, after ploughing up twice, they sow the seed, and merely level the earth with a common plank. Any young man, though far from able-bodied, can drive one of these ploughs, sow, and, with the aid of the women, reap and store the produce. The few districts in the island which have the advantage of running water are chiefly devoted to the culture of cotton, barley, and wheat; sesame and vegetables are but little cultivated. The water is, at stated times, distributed over the different meadows, but, as these are not well levelled, the earth is unequally moistened—and often, indeed, the water soaks away without rendering any service.

Products.—The island produces cereals in abundance, wool, cotton, madder, silk, flax, sesame, tobacco, colocynth, oil, wine, figs, currants, oranges, honey, pitch, skins, yellow, red, and green umber, butter, and cheese. The products, which have been more abundant in later than in preceding years, will continue to increase in proportion with the importance acquired by the agricultural population of the island; for immense tracts of waste land exist, which might be cultivated successfully for every purpose. The cultivation particularly of the vine and mulberry would be followed by satisfactory results. The silkworm at Cyprus furnishes two harvests in one year: the first generation produces the cocoon in the early part of April, lays eggs, revives, and in thus reviving spins a second cocoon about the end of May. This has often been confirmed by experiments. The silk harvest at Cyprus will always be in proportion to the number of hands engaged in that branch of industry; mulberry-trees flourish, and the silkworm-sheds may be erected in the open air.

Mineral Products.— The mineral products of the island have hitherto been unexplored; it is, however, certain that many mines would be discovered of sulphur, coal, copper, iron, and perhaps also of gold and silver. Tradition and romance speak much of treasures concealed in the Isle of Cyprus. As far as is known, no one ever yet explored the island who was cognizant of these matters. In the neighbourhood of Cape Blanc, sulphur may be seen on the surface of the soil, and the entire character of the island promises most satisfactory results to those who would develop its mineral productions.

Salt-pits, &c.—Cyprus possesses two rich natural salt-pits, one of which is situated half a league from Larnica, and the other a third of a league from Limassol. There are also coloured earths, trees, and roots, adapted for dyeing; pot-herbs grow wild in the fields and prairies, while on the hills exist rich pasturages, which would feed numerous flocks.

Manufactures.—At Cyprus the arts and trades remain stationary; machinery and all other contrivances for simplifying work and saving hand labour are quite unknown. At Nicosia, at Larnica, at Killani, and some other places, silk tissues for the consumption of the island are prepared, which are good and solid, but of coarse execution. Woollen bags and slippers are also made, especially the red and yellow ones used by the Turks. Besides these there are manufactured—lace, stuffs, and other articles; but the production is hardly adequate to the demand, and there is, consequently, a large field for speculation in manufactures, metals, different tools, &c.

Ports.—Larnica, the residence of all the European Consuls, is the chief seaport of the island, and carries on a considerable commerce. War steamers and sailing vessels coming to Cyprus usually cast anchor in the roadstead, which is formed by the two capes of Pilla and of Kitti, and affords a tolerable anchorage. Through Larnica pass all the manufactured goods imported, as well as almost all the cereals, and a considerable part of the wines, caroubs, and silks exported from the island. The population amounts to 15,000, of whom a third are Turks.

Limassol is the chief port for the wine and bean trades, and has acquired considerable importance within the last few years on account of the demand for wines and spirits. It would be difficult to calculate the possible produce of Cyprus, after some years of active and scientific cultivation, if the island contained a million of agriculturists, for the entire place is one unworked mine of enormous wealth. The hills alone which surround Limassol might produce annually, to an almost unlimited extent, the currants so highly prized in Europe; and, although there is not a single vine in a circuit of more than four leagues from the town, Limassol nevertheless sends out a million barrels of wine as the produce of the mountains of the province, of which hardly one-tenth is cultivated. The olive and caroub trees grow together on the chain of mountains encircling Limassol, without any cultivation being bestowed on them, while the hills are covered in some places with the oaks planted in the time of the Venetians. Limassol contains between 5,000 and 6,000 inhabitants, of whom one-third are Turks.

Famagosta, so famous under the Venetians, possesses an excellent spacious port, which, however, is now so choked up with mud, that it can only hold about a dozen small craft. It is well sheltered from all winds, and, if deepened, which could be done at a small expense, would contain hundreds of large ships.

Commerce. — The export of the products of the island, such as cotton, silk, madder, wool, lamb-skins, wheat, barley, new commanderie wine, caroubs, linseed, colocynth, sesame, and currants, is for France, England, Trieste, Malta, the Ionian Islands, Leghorn, Genoa, and Venice; the other products are exported to Alexandria, Constantinople, Smyrna, Syria, and the islands of the Archipelago. To France is sent all the silk, and a large portion of the cotton, madder, wool, sesame, and flax-seed. To England, cereals and madders. To Trieste and Venice, commanderie wine, cottons, madders, beans, flax-seed, colocynth, lamb-skins, sesame, and currants. To the Ionian Islands are exported cereals and beans. To Leghorn, commanderie wine, wool, cotton, madder, and cereals. To Constantinople, Alexandria, Smyrna, Syria, Karamania, and the Isles of the Archipelago, common wines, brandy, spirits of wine, beans, cereals, pitch, tar, cheese, onions, and vinegar. The present prices of products sold free on board, including every expense, are as follow:—

Cotton	per oke of 2¾ lbs.	7½	piastres
Madder	,, ,,	6	,,
Wool	,, ,,	6	,,
Silk	,, ,,	250	,,
Flax seed	,, ,,	2¼	,,
Sesame	,, ,,	3	,,
Colocynth	,, ,,	10	,,
Currants	,, ,,	2½	,,
Commanderie wine	,, ,,	3	,,
Common wine	,, ,,	2	,,
Brandy	,, ,,	6	,,
Spirits of wine	,, ,,	34	,,
Vinegar	,, ,,	1	,,
Beans, per kintal		40	,,
Wheat, per kilo		30	,,
Barley ,,		15	,,

The imports are limited to the mere necessaries of local consumption. Formerly, Cyprus furnished to the neighbouring coasts of Syria and Karamania the articles which she now imports. These are sugars, coffee, leather, cotton yarn, copper boilers and saucepans, iron, steel, paper, glass, small shot, fowling-pieces, woollen cloths, silks, rice, soap, candles, vitriol, alum, logwood, sal-ammoniac, codfish, sardines, eels, indigo, boards, &c. All cotton goods and indigo come from England by Beyrout. France furnishes colonial produce, leather, woollen cloth, small shot, silk stuffs, gums, and codfish. Trieste contributes glass, steel, iron, nails, wrought copper, paper, wax candles, boards, and sardines. Rice comes from Egypt; soap and eels from Syria.

The following approximate Table will give some idea of the general navigation, and the imports and exports of the single port of Larnica, during the five years ending 31st December, 1858:—

Year.	Number of Vessels.	Tonnage.	Crews.	Value of Imports.	Value of Exports.
				£	£
1854	320	47,643	4,451	87,750	179,690
1855	385	59,629	5,478	60,125	136,060
1856	563	64,347	7,358	60,890	140,300
1857	799	66,892	7,015	61,910	131,070
1858	715	76,993	7,415	57,939	131,110

Population.—In the time of the Venetians, the population of Cyprus was 1,000,000. In 1840, the entire population of the island was only 100,000; it is now, however, calculated at 180,000, distributed amongst 605 towns or villages, of which 118 are exclusively inhabited by Turks, 248 by Christians, and 239 by a mixed population. The number of Turkish families is 7,299, and of Christian families 19,215, making a total of 26,514 families.

Condition of the Inhabitants.—Those inactive masses who live from hand to mouth are not to be found in Cyprus; all who wish for employment can obtain it. The want of hands is so much felt, that anyone having a distaste for the calling of fisherman or boatman can find employment at once, as cooper, porter, wine-gauger, broker for foreign captains, &c. There is probably no country where living is so easy as at Cyprus; even the beggars, who are generally blind, maimed, or worn out by age, and have mostly a small house of their own, are able to live quietly at home, without begging more than one or two days in the week. The country enjoys perfect tranquillity; thefts are very rare, and robberies are unknown. Many years have passed since an assassination occurred in the island; and altogether Cyprus enjoys the reputation of being the most peaceable island in the world. Its present state is that of a country which once was celebrated, rich, and populous; which now is but the shadow of its former days; but for which a better destiny may be reserved.

Extract from Official Report to the Foreign Office, by Mr. Campbell, Her Britannic Majesty's Consul at Cyprus.

There is not a single bank in all the island; and, as capitalists are rare in Cyprus, the want of an establishment of the kind is sensibly felt, especially within the last few years, in which commerce, both in imports and exports, has been so much developed. At present, merchants find themselves compelled to negotiate at Beyrout their drafts on Europe, which causes them delay, expense, and risk, while it fetters the course of their transactions.

CHAPTER XXI.

COS.

THE island of Cos is twenty-three miles in length, and five miles in width, and contains a population of about 8,000 souls, of which two-thirds are Greeks, and the remainder Turks and Jews.

This island is remarkably fertile, and well cultivated, considering its scanty population. In 1850, the frost destroyed or seriously damaged, as in many other islands of the Archipelago, the greater part of the lemon, orange, and other fruit trees. Previous to that year, the exportation of lemons was from 25 to 30 millions; of oranges, 4 millions; of raisins, of five different sorts, from 20,000 to 23,000 kintals; of fresh grapes and other fruits, from 90,000 to 100,000 okes; of red and white wine, from 90,000 to 100,000 okes; of spirits, only a small quantity; of almonds, from 1,300 to 1,500 kilos; and of white Indian corn, from 20,000 to 30,000 kilos.

Everything is, however, gradually improving, and the principal articles now annually exported are:—7,000 cantars of raisins, sold at 140 to 150 piastres the cantar; 6,000,000 lemons; 150 cantars of wool; 2,000 cantars of onions; 4,000 kilos of sesame seed; 1,000 kilos of almonds; 30,000 to 40,000 kilos of salt; some figs, melons, and water melons, and a small quantity of olives. Cotton, hemp, and silk are also exported, but not in any great quantities; 40,000 kilos of wheat, and 90,000 to 100,000 kilos of barley.

The principal articles imported are:— Oil, butter, rice, soap, oxen; manufactures from England and France: coffee, sugar, iron, cotton twist, cloths, and printed calicoes.

The following is a general return, showing the amount of the populations of all the islands under the jurisdiction of the Governor-General at Rhodes:—

Islands.	Population.
Rhodes	30,000
Cyprus	180,000
Scio	60,000
Mitylene	80,000
Cos	8,000
Lemnos	24,000
Tenedos	4,500
Samothraki	2,500
Imbros	8,000
Mosco Nissi	6,000
Castel Rosso	4,000
Cassos	5,000
Scarpantos	7,000
Halki	2,000
Symi	8,000
Telos	2,000
Nissiros	2,500
Stampalia	1,500
Calymnos	9,500
Leros	5,000
Patmos	3,500
Nicaria	7,000
Psarà	2,000
Total	460,000

Shipbuilding is carried on to a considerable extent in the above islands, particularly in the islands of Cassos, Castel Rosso, Halki, and Symi. The greater part of the vessels built in the two former islands, which, on an average, amount to about sixty a year, are sold at Constantinople, Trieste, Marseilles, Greece, &c.; so that shipbuilding is becoming in these two islands an important branch of commerce. The total number of vessels built in all the islands of the Ottoman Archipelago amounts annually, on an average, to about one hundred and fifty, of from 100 to 500 tons each, besides numerous smaller craft.

At present, the trade throughout the Archipelago is carried on in these vessels, which, when the weather is at all rough, often take a fortnight to beat up a distance of eighty or ninety miles against the strong northeasterly winds that prevail during nine months of the year. If steam-vessels, however, say from 200 to 300 tons, were to ply among these islands, there can be no doubt that, in a few years, an immense increase of trade would be the consequence.

CHAPTER XXII.

CRETE.

CRETE is well known to be one of the largest islands in the Mediterranean Sea. Homer describes it as an extensive island in the midst of the stormy main, the soil being rich and fertile; containing an immense number of inhabitants, and adorned with a hundred cities.

At present, the island produces corn, wine, oil, opium, liquorice, flax, cotton, silk, caroubs, oranges, lemons, dates, &c., and, besides the common domestic animals, game, wild sheep, chamois goats, bees, and fish are very abundant.

In 1832 the population was estimated at 153,000, but by the year 1851 it had increased to 221,265, divided as follows:—

Greek rural population	143,050
,, city ,,	7,181
	150,231
Mohammedan rural population	39,784
,, city ,,	28,216
	68,000
Armenians	100
Jews	284
Foreigners	2,650
Total	221,265

The population has since gone on increasing (in the year 1855, the Greek births at Canea were exactly double the deaths), and is now considered to be about 260,000 souls. As a natural consequence, the agricultural produce has also considerably increased. In the year 1837, the value of the tithe on agricultural produce was estimated to be 5,675,000 piastres, exchange at 100 piastres per pound, say 56,750*l.*; whilst, for the two years, 1856-1857, commencing on 1-13 March, it was farmed out to several individuals for 22,499,170 piastres, making, at the exchange of 115, 195,645*l.* for two years, or 97,822*l.* 10*s.* for one year, being an increase of 41,072*l.* If to this sum of 97,822*l.* 10*s.* we add 10 per cent. as the probable expense of collection and profit to the farmer of the tithes, we have 1,076,040*l.* as the actual value of the agricultural produce of Crete for one year, exclusive of the value of animals.

At a rough calculation, this amount may be divided as follows:—

Olive oil	£342,410
Barley	186,000
Wheat	127,075
Oats	71,800
Beans	20,955
Wine	124,404
Silk	47,499
Raisins	32,044
Cheese	31,936
Caroubs	22,484
Wool	15,176
Oranges and lemons	14,770
Almonds	11,130
Chestnuts	10,000
Honey	6,462
Cotton	5,545
Valonia	4,330
Wax	3,395
Brandy	758

The following is a comparison of the imports and exports for the years 1836, 1837, 1856, and 1857:—

	1836.	1837.	1856.	1857.
	£	£	£	£
Imports	151,654	127,804	406,832	435,628
Exports	161,703	64,440	433,240	402,556

The following Table shows that a considerable increase has taken place in the number of vessels entering the ports of Canea and Candia:—

Nationality of Vessels.	1838.		1855.		1856.	
	Number.	Tonnage.	Number.	Tonnage.	Number.	Tonnage.
Turkish	133	6,172	443	22,166	495	25,877
Greek	389	14,235	138	4,822	203	8,897
Ionian	63	1,507	167	4,605	152	4,270
French	5	630	23	3,022	18	2,484
Sardinian	7	543	18	3,001	16	1,979
British	4	419	13	2,226	11	1,884
Neapolitan	—	—	10	508	19	1,370
Austrian	32	4,856	1	100	5	753
American	—	—	—	—	1	288
Tuscan	4	167	1	75	2	194
Samiote	—	—	1	30	4	192
Roman	—	—	—	—	1	32
Norwegian	—	—	3	325	—	—
Russian	7	993	—	—	—	—
Syrian	1	130	—	—	—	—
Total	645	29,652	818	40,880	927	48,220

Of the manufactures, the chief is that of soap, which is highly esteemed all through the Levant. Any person can hire a soap manufactory for one single operation—that is, to make seven to eight tons of soap; so that to become a manufacturer of this article does not require any considerable capital. At Canea, about eight tons of soap are produced per week from one boiler; but at Candia, ten to eleven tons are made at one time. In the year 1837 there were only twenty-three soap manufactories; there are now fifty-one.

At Canea and Candia, manufactories for reeling silk in the Italian manner have been established; and improved machinery for expressing oil from the refuse of the oil mills has been introduced, with considerable profit.

Some researches into the mineral resources of the island have also been lately made, and the result is, that iron and lignite are said to be abundant. Manganese, nickel, and sulphur have likewise been discovered.

The following is a list of the number of houses, shops, and soap manufactories in the three cities of Crete:—

Cities.	Houses.	Shops.	Soap Manufactories.
Canea	2,117	825	23
Candia	3,620	1,314	20
Retimo	935	403	8
Total	6,672	2,542	51

WALLACHIA AND MOLDAVIA.

CHAPTER XXIII.

IBRAÏLA.

IBRAÏLA, situated on the left bank of the Danube, and fifteen miles south from Galatz, is the chief shipping port of Wallachia, whence the corn and other products of that principality are exported. The town has of late years risen rapidly in extent and importance, and its population, which in 1838 amounted only to 6,000, is now estimated at 20,000.

The trade of Ibraïla has considerably increased, for whereas in 1847, a year of extraordinary exportation, in consequence of the famine in Ireland, there were exported from Ibraïla and Galatz 1,836,647 imperial quarters of corn (wheat, maize, rye, and barley), in 1852, a year of ordinary consumption, 1,769,799 imperial quarters were exported. In the latter year, the value of the total exports from Ibraïla amounted to 916,933*l.*; but in 1855, they increased to 1,696,929*l.*

The following Table shows the quantities and value of the different articles exported from Ibraïla during the year 1852:—

Names of Articles.	Quantities.	Value in Pounds sterling.
Grain, Wheat	343,584 quarters	343,584
Barley	80,278 ,,	40,139
Rye	1,296 ,,	778
Maize	725,259 ,,	489,550
Millet	5,180 ,,	3,108
Linseed	849 ,,	1,358
Rapeseed	2,554 ,,	3,320
Wool	254,667 lbs.	8,489
Tallow	12,084 cwts.	18,126
Butter	274 ,,.	544
Cheese	912 ,,	593
Staves	334,020 pieces.	5,567
Bones, calcined	282 tons.	917
Sundries		860
Total		916,933

The imports into Ibraïla during the year 1852 were—British manufactured goods, 261,140*l*.; Turkish manufactures, 1,260*l*.; cotton yarn, 10,215*l*.; sugar, refined and crushed, 65,800*l*.; tea, 500*l*.; coffee, 5,852*l*.; rum, 2,828*l*.; tin plates, 5,368*l*.; iron, in bars, rods, and sheets, 12,600*l*.; nails, 5,660*l*.; coals (645 tons), 645*l*.; oil, 20,666*l*.; olives, 1,567*l*.; wine, 800*l*.; champagne and other wines, 2,220*l*.; spirits, 814*l*.; raisins, 5,398*l*.; figs, 1,505*l*.; lemons and oranges, 2,343*l*.; rice, 1,133*l*.; tobacco, 16,355*l*.; salt fish, 3,960*l*.; aniseed, 1,110*l*.; window glass, 4,500*l*.; dressed leather, 3,000*l*.; sundries, 10,667*l*.; total, 447,906*l*.

CHAPTER XXIV.

GALATZ.

GALATZ, on the left bank of the Danube, is the chief seat of commerce in Moldavia. Its trade, like that of all the other ports in the Ottoman Empire, has been of late years considerably augmented. In the year 1848, the importations into Galatz amounted to 319,405l.; and in 1855, to 624,880l. The value of the exportations in 1848 was only 333,271l.; whereas, in 1855, the amount had increased to 1,271,209l.

The following Table will show the steady increase that has taken place in the imports and exports since the year 1848 :—

Years.	Imports.	Exports.
	£	£
1848	319,405	333,271
1849	410,644	528,342
1850	435,090	367,700
1851	500,803	496,368
1852	441,759	567,110
1853	559,440	542,080
1854	121,440	148,280
1855	624,880	1,271,209

It will be seen from the above that the imports in 1855 almost doubled those in 1848, while the exports during the former year were nearly four times as much as the exports during the latter year.

The quantities and value of the exports in the year 1852 were as follow:—

Names of Articles.	Quantities.	Value in Pounds sterling.
Grain, Wheat	187,555 quarters	206,310
Barley	468 "	211
Rye	96,900 "	62,985
Maize	329,279 "	271,655
Linseed	1,351 "	1,824
Wool	229,120 lbs.	9,547
Tallow	866 cwts.	1,472
Preserved beef	170,280 lbs.	2,128
Bones, calcined	197 tons.	634
Wine	30,200 gallons.	1,007
Planks and deals	193,000 pieces.	3,217
Masts and spars	8 rafts	5,600
Sundries		520
Total		567,110

The importations into the port of Galatz during the year 1852 were:—British manufactured goods, 211,695*l.*; manufactures not British, 6,150*l.*; cotton yarn, 990*l.*; sugar, refined and crushed, 55,602*l.*; tea, 2,160*l.*; coffee, 6,264*l.*; rum, 3,780*l.*; tin plates, 11,427*l.*; iron (rods, bars, &c.), 13,050*l.*; nails, 1,056*l.*; coals, 13,690*l.*; sal-ammoniac, 1,500*l.*; cotton wool, 1,055*l.*; soap, 4,098*l.*; oil, 18,869*l.*; olives, 1,959*l.*; wine in barrels, 765*l.*; champagne and other wines in cases, 2,060*l.*; raisins and figs, 20,985*l.*; lemons and oranges, 7,586*l.*; almonds, 810*l.*; rice, 8,526*l.*; tobacco, 8,950*l.*; cigars, 3,094*l.*; caviar, 8,775*l.*; fish, salted, 5,523*l.*; earthenware, 1,570*l.*; leather (dressed), 4,780*l.*; skins, 1,870*l.*; sundries, 13,120*l.*; total, 441,759*l.*

GENERAL REVIEW OF THE TRADE OF IBRAÏLA AND GALATZ.

The following Table shows the great increase which has taken place in the exports of grain since the year 1837:—

Years.	From Ibraïla.	From Galatz.	Total.
	Imp. Quarters.	Imp. Quarters.	Imp. Quarters.
1837	128,247	185,344	313,591
1840	281,227	419,605	700,832
1843	612,321	251,887	864,208
1846	668,014	523,635	1,191,649
1849	523,178	493,918	1,017,096
1852	1,155,597	614,202	1,769,799
1855	1,172,009	890,630	2,062,637
1858	1,278,982	347,531	1,626,513

Table of estimated Value of all Articles exported from Ibraïla and Galatz.

Years.	From Ibraïla.	From Galatz.	Total.
	£	£	£
1838	148,238	172,168	230,406
1841	225,610	189,036	414,646
1844	551,044	303,885	854,929
1848	611,958	333,271	945,229
1852	916,933	567,110	1,484,043
1855	1,696,929	1,271,209	2,968,138
1856	1,294,181	792,258	2,086,439
1857	891,572	595,386	1,486,958

Total Number of Vessels Loaded at Ibraïla and Galatz in the years 1838, 1848, and 1858.

Years.	At Ibraïla.	At Galatz.	Total.
1838	451	517	968
1848	726	397	1123
1858	1291	490	1781

Number of Vessels Loaded at Ibraïla and Galatz direct for the United Kingdom in the years 1843, 1845, 1848, and 1858.

Years.	At Ibraïla.	At Galatz.	Total.
1843	3	4	7
1845	35	9	44
1848	115	115	230
1858	443	162	605

Number of Vessels, under different Flags, which Loaded at Ibraïla and Galatz during the years 1838, 1848, and 1858.

Nationality of Vessels.	Years.		
	1838	1848	1858
Greek	259	432	667
British	6	132	219
Turkish	358	247	211
Sardinian	120	66	124
Austrian	90	99	115
French	8	8	75
Dutch	1	—	61
Wallachian	12	24	55
Ionian	40	28	55
Norwegian	—	—	34
Hanoverian	—	—	28
Danish	—	1	20
Oldenberg	—	—	18
Swedish	—	—	15
Moldavian	—	17	14
Samian	8	5	13
Tuscan	—	1	12
Prussian	—	—	12
Neapolitan	2	1	9
Russian	61	56	8
Servian	—	—	5
Mecklenburg	—	—	2
Hamburg	—	—	2
Bremen	—	1	2
Jerusalem	—	1	2
Roman	1	2	2
Belgian	2	2	1
Total	968	1123	1781

In 1860, the value of all articles exported from Ibraïla and Galatz to Great Britain alone amounted to 2,252,246*l*., viz.:—

Principal and Other Articles.	Quantities.			Value in Pounds Sterling.		
	1856	1858	1860	1856	1858	1860
				£	£	£
Corn : Wheat . qrs.	124,671	133,556	97,400	333,494	262,807	260,979
„ Barley . „	11,135	203,324	539,826	15,589	223,314	769,951
„ Maize . „	196,706	431,597	656,054	314,730	633,800	1,123,333
„ Other kinds „	——	14,799	22,590	——	18,903	31,922
Seed : Linseed and Flaxseed . . „	1,844	1,059	——	5,025	2,770	——
„ Millet . . cwts.	14,631	5,818	47,793	9,510	1,745	10,305
„ Rape . . qrs.	——	21,540	15,976	——	64,800	47,444
Tallow . . . cwts.	2,045	——	1,104	4,857	——	3,058
All other Articles value	——	——	——	1,577	5,177	5,254
Total . .	——	——	——	684,782	1,213,316	2,252,246

CHAPTER XXV.

ISMAIL AND RENI.

THE territory recently annexed to Moldavia, and known as New or Bessarabian Moldavia, differs in no respect from that of the province to which it now belongs. The land is equally fertile, and capable of producing a very large amount of grain, and other articles of commerce.

The chief towns in the interior are Bolgrad, Cahul, and Leova; and on the banks of the Danube, Ismaïl, Reni, Kilia, and Vilcof. The two principal ports from whence shipments are made by sea-going vessels are Ismaïl and Reni; the grain produced in the neighbourhood of Kilia and Vilcof being almost entirely sent in small river craft to Ismaïl, which is well adapted for all purposes of shipping, having a long extent of open natural quay, with deep water, where upwards of 100 vessels can commodiously load at one time.

The chief articles of export are grain and oleaginous seeds, wool, tallow, hides, cheese, butter, oxen, and sheep.

The quantity of grain and seed exported from Ismaïl and Reni during the year 1857 was as follows:—

Grain						
Wheat	.	.	.	.	38,845	Kisloz.
Indian corn	.	.	.	.	47,636	do.
Rye	.	.	.	.	1,859	do.
Barley	.	.	.	.	37,685	do.
Oats	.	.	.	.	1,178	do.
Millet	.	.	.	.	4,545	do.
Linseed	.	.	.	.	1,470	do.
				Total .	133,218	Kisloz,*
			equal to	199,827	Imperial Quarters.	

In 1858 the exports of grain from Ismaïl and Reni were:—

Grain.	From Ismail.	From Reni.	Total.
	Imp. Qrs.	Imp. Qrs.	Imp. Qrs.
Wheat	73,337	18,337	91,674
Indian corn . . .	24,843	34,423	59,266
Barley	75,192	28,476	103,668
Rye	14,066	4,073	18,139
Oats	5,847	2,309	8,156
Total . . .	193,285	87,618	280,903

* 1 kisloz equal to 1½ imperial quarters.

SYRIA.

CHAPTER XXVI.

SYRIA.

WHEN Greece was in her infancy, and long before Rome had even been founded, the coast of Syria was covered with magnificent and wealthy cities. On the north stood Aradus (the Modern Rouad); eighteen miles to the south, Tripolis; at a similar distance Byblos (Djebail), with the temple of Adonis; again, farther south, Berytus (Beyrout); at a like distance Sidon; and, finally, about fifteen miles farther, stood the "Queen of the Waters," the stately Tyre. From the latter city arose commerce, civilization, the arts and sciences, and, above all, that great instrument of social progress, the gift of letters. To its inhabitants, the Phœnicians, we are indebted for the knowledge of astronomy and arithmetic, as well as for the discovery of weights and measures, of money, of the art of keeping accounts or book-keeping; for the invention, or at least for the improvement, of ship-building and navigation, and likewise for the discovery of glass. They were also famous for the manufacture of fine linen and tapestry; for the art of working in metals and ivory; for their skill in architecture, and especially for the manufacture of that rare and costly article of luxury, the Tyrian purple.*

A new and formidable rival, however — Alexandria

* See Heeren on the "Manufactures of the Phœnicians."

—at length competed with Tyre, and the trade of the latter became, to a considerable extent, transferred to that great city founded by the Macedonian conqueror. Nevertheless, when subsequently reduced to a Roman province (B.C. 65), Syria lost nothing of her material prosperity; for the commerce which created her wealth, far from decreasing, received an unexpected impulse, and found a new source of profit in the luxurious habits of her masters. Another and a more remunerative market was immediately opened, as the conquerors, having once tasted the delights of Asia, soon felt wants unknown to their frugal forefathers, and eagerly demanded her perfumes, her silks, and her precious stones, which they paid for with the spoils of the world. The ports of Syria continued to send forth ships filled with rich and costly merchandise; with gold, silver, tin, and other metals; with vessels of brass, slaves, mules, sheep, and goats; pearls, precious stones, and coral; wheat, balm, honey, oil, spices, gums, woven silk, and wine. Berytus (Beyrout) was famous for her immense exportation of corn, oil, and the choicest wines. The cedars of Lebanon furnished the Romans with wood for the manufacture of magnificent ornaments, as well as for the domestic architecture of the rich, and the adornment of the temples of their gods. The dates of Syria were well known; for Galen, in one of his treatises, mentions their properties, and compares them with those of Egypt. The plums and other fruits of Damascus appeared, among various exotic luxuries, upon the tables of the epicures; and Virgil tells us of a delicious species of pear, the cultivation of which had been, in his time, introduced from that country into Italy.

Since the fall of the Roman ascendency, however

(A.D. 638), this wondrous and classic land has been the scene of many contests, and the battle-field on which the destinies of many kings have been decided. But the details of these contests are foreign to the purpose of this work. Notwithstanding, however, all the vicissitudes through which the country has passed, and the oppression under which the people have groaned, the Syria of to-day is as rich and fertile as the Syria of twelve hundred years ago. Upon her fruitful soil, wheat, barley, maize, rice, cotton, spring up with the same luxuriant abundance. The sugar-cane and tobacco, those two modern sources of wealth, abound; and the white mulberry trees afford food for myriads of silkworms, which supply the manufactories of Lyons with their precious products. Limestone, sandstone, basalt, slate, coal, iron, and copper are plentiful in the mountain districts; timber of every description may be had for the felling; while sycamores of enormous size spread their branches wide enough to cover a whole caravan with their grateful shade. Here are valleys where everything useful or beautiful in the vegetable kingdom is produced, by the most superficial cultivation, in rich and prodigal abundance. Here are gardens where the rose, the orange-flower, the jasmine, mingle their perfumes into one delicious odour, almost too powerful for the senses. Avenues of fig-trees shade the roads; growths of oleander follow the course of the rivers; red-flowered grass blends its hues with a thousand gay flowers that enamel the meadows; above is the beautifully blue vault of heaven, and between stretches the clear ocean of pure, pellucid atmosphere. In the poetry of the Turks, this favoured region has been called "the odour of Paradise;" in that of the Hebrews, "a garden planted by God for the first man;" and in that of the Arabs it is described as a country "where the mountains bear winter on their heads, spring upon their shoulders, autumn around their bosoms, while summer is ever sleeping at their feet."

For some years past, a very extraordinary improvement in the commercial prosperity of Syria has been everywhere apparent, despite the disadvantages arising from a want of that internal communication which is so necessary to the extension of trade. For example, in the year 1851 the imports at Aleppo amounted to only 486,060*l*., whereas in 1855 they increased to 1,414,059*l*. In 1854 the exports were 993,630*l*., but in 1855 they amounted to 1,254,130*l*. At Beyrout, the imports in 1841 were only 66,748*l*.; in the year 1848 they had increased to 546,266*l*.; in the year 1853 they amounted to 722,864*l*.; in 1856, to 1,162,676*l*.; in 1857, to 1,324,550*l*.; while during the year 1859 they still further increased to 1,448,860*l*. The exports in 1841 amounted only to 25,128*l*.; in 1848 they were 253,648*l*.; in the year 1853 they increased to 624,544*l*.; in 1856, to 795,657*l*.; in 1857, to 983,398*l*., and in the year 1859, to 1,698,456*l*.* At Alexandretta, Latakia, Tripoli, Sidon, Kaïffa, and Jaffa, signs of an increasing commerce have been also evident, and there can be little doubt that, now the Lebanon has been pacified, the country will soon resume its former activity, trade will revive, and plenty will again spread happiness over the land. The traffic between India and Europe, so long carried on through the Atlantic

* The value of our exports to Syria (the produce and manufactures of Great Britain, exclusive of foreign and colonial produce), in the year 1848, was 258,186*l*.; in 1853 this amount increased to 306,580*l*.; in 1854, to 366,993*l*.; in 1857, to 703,375*l*.; and in 1858, to 760,497*l*.

and Indian Oceans, is gradually returning to its more direct and natural course; and it is by no means improbable that the route by the Mediterranean and the Persian Gulf will shortly prove to be the best and cheapsest, a it is decidedly the shortest. The royal cities of Nineveh and Babylon are, it is true, no more, and the mean towns of Mosul and Hillah alone mark the places where they stood; but the great rivers, the Tigris and the Euphrates, which contributed to their grandeur, are still capable of being made important arteries of commerce.* The Jordan, although only sixty

* On the Tigris and Euphrates, the same means of communication that prevailed centuries ago are still in use, without the slightest attempt at improvement. Rafts made of skins form the only means of transport, and these even are only available for descending the stream. A raft is composed of 110 inflated sheep-skins, which cost each about one shilling and twopence. They are fastened together by poplar poles, of which also a rough flooring is made. Each raft is navigated by two men, whose wages, from Diarbekhr to Mosul, are about thirteen shillings. The ordinary hire of a raft is between five pounds to six pounds, and each carries about fifty-four cwt. of merchandise. From Diarbekhr to Mosul, and thence to Baghdad, merchandise and produce are usually conveyed by these rafts, but from Baghdad and Mosul to Diarbekhr all goods are conveyed by pack animals — camels, horses, mules, and asses. The latter, in fact, form the only means of conveyance between Diarbekhr and the Black Sea, or between Baghdad, Diarbekhr, Aleppo, and the Mediterranean. These animals are capable of carrying as follows: —

Camel	5 cwt.
Mule	$3\frac{3}{4}$,,
Horse	$3\frac{1}{4}$,,
Ox	$2\frac{1}{4}$,,
Ass	$1\frac{1}{2}$,,

Some few years ago it was estimated that Baghdad sent annually, even as far as Erzerum, two thousand mule-loads of pearls, silk, cotton, stuffs, shawls, coffee, gall-nuts, indigo, &c.; still more to Mosul, Diarbekhr, and Orfa, and five thousand to Aleppo. The making of good roads, and the substitution of carriage waggons for these primitive and expensive methods of conveyance, would form one of the safest modes of speculation in which capital could be embarked in Turkey.

feet wide, is in some places twenty feet deep, and might easily be rendered navigable; while the Orontes rushes through the plain with a velocity and a headlong impetus that have induced the Arabs to call it El-'Asy, or The Rebel. The maritime cities of Syria are despoiled and neglected. Tyre, whose "merchants were princes, and her traffickers the honourable of the earth," has become "a place for the spreading of nets in the midst of the sea;" but the old Berytus still remains, bereft, to a great extent, of her artificial splendour, yet possessing those natural beauties which time cannot destroy, and reviving, by her increasing trade, the memory of the vast commerce which she once enjoyed, and that greatness to which, from the advantages of her position, she is now again so likely to attain. The eyes of Europe are, once more, eagerly turned towards this land for whose deliverance the proud chivalry of Christendom once shed its blood and won its victories in vain. This land, endeared by so many hallowed recollections, made famous by the superhuman prowess of a Richard Cœur-de-Lion and a Salah-ed-Dîn; this land, teeming with untold wealth, and whose soil bursts spontaneously with productiveness, is now being quietly and gradually occupied by the descendants of those who, nearly eight hundred years ago, fought and fell upon its plains; and civilization, which here had its birth, but which fled in terror before rude and ignorant barbarians, finding a refuge in the West, is now coming back again upon the wings of Peace, seeking for its ancient but still remembered home.

CHAPTER XXVII.

BEYROUT.

BEYROUT is the port of Damascus, and the entrepôt for the commerce of the Druses and Maronites of Mount Lebanon, who are the most industrious and intelligent of all the native populations of Syria: hence its thriving condition, and the steady augmentation of its trade and affluence. Within the last few years, a new town seems to have sprung up from the ruins of the old. The means and appliances of European civilization have been introduced; streets have been paved, and spacious warehouses erected.* No longer than fifteen years ago, there was scarcely any steam communication between Beyrout and Europe. Now, the mails leave London for Syria every Friday, *viâ* Marseilles, and every Monday, *viâ* Trieste; while English steamers run regularly between Beyrout and Liverpool. In the year 1853, only thirty-nine British vessels entered the port of Beyrout, tonnage 8,546; while in 1855 there were 113, tonnage 39,132. The line of steamers belonging to the "*Messageries Impériales*" and "Austrian Lloyd's Company" has also been increasing: thus, ninety-two of the former, tonnage 21,049, entered Beyrout in 1855; while in 1856

---

* Here, in Beyrout, turn which way you will, houses are being erected on every vacant space, and land for building purposes has risen in value more than a hundred per cent. during the last eighteen months. The greatest improvements, however, are the roads, which, having been begun in one long trunk road by the Damascus Road Company, are now being carried on in various directions by the government. Anyone who left Beyrout, even so late as a year ago, would hardly know where he was, if put down now in many of the suburbs of the town.—*Beyrout Correspondent of the Levant Herald, April 2, 1862.*

there were 106, tonnage 41,354. Of the "Austrian Lloyd's," fifty-eight steamers, tonnage 22,812, entered in 1855; and sixty-six, tonnage 28,278, in the year 1856.

The following Tables show the trade with foreign countries during the years 1853, 1856, and 1857:—

Return of Imports at the Port of Beyrout in the years 1853, 1856, and 1857.

Where from.	1853. Value of cargoes in Pounds sterling.	1856. Value of cargoes in Pounds sterling.	1857. Value of cargoes in Pounds sterling.
Great Britain	225,875	434,166	276,472
Austria	268,569	268,081	353,005
France	109,020	260,788	453,580
Turkey	89,205	184,820	230,635
Jerusalem flag	3,540	—	—
Neapolitan and Roman	8,899	—	—
Sardinia	4,420	7,354	3,355
Tuscany	6,821	4,156	3,065
Greece	3,200	1,342	2,878
Russia	1,300	—	—
Norway	1,015	—	—
Holland	1,000	1,969	1,560
Total	722,864	1,162,676	1,324,550

Return of Exports at the Port of Beyrout in the years 1853, 1856, and 1857.

Where to.	1853. Value of cargoes in Pounds sterling.	1856. Value of cargoes in Pounds sterling.	1857. Value of cargoes in Pounds sterling.
Great Britain	41,995	45,330	66,912
Austria	333,878	267,062	341,390
France	161,016	247,244	286,787
Turkey	67,820	202,239	254,934
Jerusalem flag	1,470	—	—
Sardinia	1,145	17,632	5,050
Tuscany	1,000	12,115	8,208
Greece	5,400	3,779	2,517
Russia	1,050	—	—
U. S. of America	9,000	256	16,000
Holland	770	—	1,600
Total	624,544	795,657	983,398

Return and Specification of Imports at the Port of Beyrout in the year 1857.

Names of Articles.	From France and under French flag.	From Austria and under Austrian flag.	From Great Britain.	From Turkey.	From Sardinia.	From Tuscany.	From Greece.	From U.S. of America.	From Holland.	Total.
	£	£	£	£	£	£	£	£	£	£
Coals	—	4,181	14,200	—	—	—	—	—	—	18,381
Corn, rice, wine, &c.	764	5,548	360	123,025	230	310	1,960	—	—	132,197
Colonials—viz., coffee, sugar, indigo, &c.	25,207	3,120	6,940	24,804	110	206	—	—	1,560	61,947
Copper and lead	38,240	27,832	966	7,386	—	—	—	—	—	72,424
Drugs and medicine	1,973	3,440	—	440	94	44	—	—	—	5,991
Earthenware	319	3,160	620	985	360	250	—	—	—	5,694
Fezes or caps	15,025	11,880	—	1,550	602	540	—	—	—	29,597
Glassware	432	3,240	—	1,080	210	320	—	—	—	5,232
Hardware and toys	84,022	18,220	830	2,160	310	—	—	—	—	105,542
Iron & steel, wrought and otherwise	14,452	14,970	1,562	1,395	—	—	—	—	—	32,379
Manufactures, cotton	168,932	117,960	240,974	48,460	850	640	110	—	—	577,926
,, silk	8,496	37,010	60	13,500	—	—	—	—	—	59,066
,, woollens	79,905	69,900	—	450	—	—	—	—	—	150,255
Paper and registers	3,425	840	300	120	180	215	—	—	—	5,080
Various articles not included under the above heads	14,388	31,704	9,860	5,280	409	540	808	—	—	62,789
TOTAL	453,580	353,005	276,472	230,635	3,355	3,065	2,878	—	1,560	1,324,550

Return and Specification of Exports at the Port of Beyrout in the year 1857.

Names of Articles.	For Austria.	For France.	For Turkey.	For Great Britain.	For Sardinia.	For Tuscany.	For Greece.	For U. S. of America.	For Holland.	Total.
	£	£	£	£	£	£	£	£	£	£
Corn and eatables	3,738	—	842	—	—	2,800	1,212	—	1,800	10,192
Colonials—viz., coffee, &c.	6,120	—	2,034	2,000	—	—	—	—	—	10,154
Drugs	448	—	682	—	—	—	—	—	—	1,130
Fruits, dry	5,915	320	3,025	160	—	—	240	—	—	10,260
Gums, galls, &c.	540	1,754	510	—	—	350	—	—	—	8,154
Hides, hair, &c.	2,460	—	1,410	—	—	—	—	—	—	8,870
Hardware	7,268	850	600	—	—	—	615	—	—	8,828
Manufactures, cotton	124,000	31,500	43,170	—	—	—	—	—	—	199,345
" silk	126,304	4,320	55,770	—	—	—	—	—	—	186,464
Maulders	130	9,000	1,470	10,320	1,150	1,042	—	—	—	30,680
Oil and soap	12,060	—	4,040	—	—	—	—	—	—	18,932
Silk and cocoons	34,945	217,830	28,440	27,500	—	—	—	—	—	308,715
Tobacco and tumbac	4,905	180	107,245	112	—	—	—	—	—	112,442
Wool	2,700	11,083	—	13,330	3,900	4,010	—	16,000	—	51,029
Various articles not included under the above head	9,777	9,230	4,300	4,480	—	—	450	—	—	28,313
TOTAL	341,390	286,787	254,034	66,012	5,050	8,208	2,517	16,000	1,800	983,398

Description of Cotton Manufactures Imported into Beyrout during the year 1857.

- Grey T cloths.
- Madapollams.
- Water twist.
- Handkerchiefs.
- Lapetz, English manufacture.
- Lapetz, imitation of Syrian manufacture.
- Veils for the face, called yasmi.
- Levantines.
- Calico shirting and sheeting.
- Zebra shawls.
- Coton satiné.
- Curtains.
- Cambrics.
- Cotton velvet.
- Coloured yarn.
- Chintz.
- Printed calicoes.
- Shirts.
- Muslins.

Comparative Statement of the Number of British Vessels that Entered the Port of Beyrout during the years 1855 to 1859 inclusive.

Years.	Number of Vessels.	Tonnage.
1855	113	39,132
1856	92	35,003
1857	66	26,381
1858	73	30,837
1859	63*	25,661

The foregoing statistics of the importations into Beyrout are well deserving the serious consideration of English merchants, for they disclose a state of things by no means flattering to our pride as a commercial nation. The growth and extension of our external trade is, no doubt, highly gratifying, and evidences the intensity and universality of our business enterprise.

* Consisting of twenty-eight colliers, seven sailing vessels in ballast, three ditto with general cargoes, and twenty-five screw-steamers.

Not only are we keen competitors with other nations in almost every mart where the standard of civilization has been planted, but an incessant war is waged between our merchant princes, as the representatives of social advancement, on the one hand, and uncivilised tribes, who strenuously resist the encroachments of modern ideas, on the other. To open new markets for the produce of our looms and furnaces, is a distinct profession in the world of commerce — a profession which is followed with such earnestness and devotion as, in the absence of other evidence, to induce the belief that our trade with old countries has been pushed to its utmost development consistent with commercial safety. Such, however, is unfortunately not the case. Our shipowners complain, yet the carrying trade of the Levant is passing from our hands into those of the Greeks and kindred races; and our merchants bewail the quietness of markets and paucity of orders, whilst our neighbours in Europe are, in many places, monopolising the trade and pocketing the profits which by right ought to be ours.

Syria is one of those countries where British commerce has not attained the developement of which it is susceptible. For example, the imports at Beyrout, which in the year 1853 were only 722,864*l.*, rose in the year 1856 to 1,162,676*l.*, and in the year 1857 to 1,324,550*l.*, or nearly double in the short space of four years. The exports also steadily increased from 624,544*l.* in the year 1853, to 795,657*l.* in the year 1856, and to 983,398*l.* in 1857. The imports from France, in the year 1853, were 109,020*l.*; and this amount increased in 1856 to 260,788*l.*, and in 1857 to 453,580*l.* The imports from Austria, which in the year 1853 were 268,569*l.*, did not much vary during 1856; but in the following year they increased to

353,005*l.* The imports from Great Britain in 1853 were 225,875*l.*, which increased in 1856 to 434,166*l.*; but were only 276,472*l.* during the year 1857. So that, with an increasing demand for the products of Western Europe, we find the French and Austrian trade steadily and rapidly increasing, whilst the value of the imports from this country diminished in the course of a single year to the serious extent of nearly one-half. The number of British ships which entered the port of Beyrout during the year 1855 amounted to 113; whereas, in 1859, there were only sixty-three, of which twenty-eight were colliers. In fact, with the single exception of the article of coal, we would seem to have resigned the trade of Beyrout into the hands of Austria and France. For example: in the year 1857, whilst the value of the copper and lead imported at Beyrout under the Austrian flag was, in round numbers, 28,000*l.*, and under the French flag 36,000*l.*, the total declared value from this country was under 1,000*l.*; in the articles of iron and steel, we only exported to the extent of one-eighteenth of the united French and Austrian value, which two countries divide with us the articles of cotton manufacture; and in woollen goods, while the value of the French exports amounted to 80,000*l.*, and the Austrian to 70,000*l.*, the exports from Great Britain were *nil.**

It cannot be supposed, for one moment, that the countries I have named can compete with us, in an open market, in the articles of metals, and cotton and woollen goods. These are our specialties; and it is

---

* It is also worthy of remark that, whilst the total trade between Turkey and Great Britain increased from 7,000,398*l.* in 1851, to 10,963,329*l.* in 1860, that between Turkey and France increased, during the same period, from 2,899,254*l.* to 8,385,156*l.*

just possible that our merchants may neglect the Syrian trade until they find themselves practically excluded from all profitable participation in its benefits. It is idle to seek an excuse for this state of things in the geographical position of Austria and France. We possess means of production and of transport far more considerable than these two countries; yet we permit ourselves to be outstripped by them in the Syrian markets. One cause, however, which may have contributed, in some measure, to this undesirable result, is the want of sufficient banking facilities between Great Britain and Syria; and the following resolutions, unanimously adopted by the leading merchants of Beyrout, relative to the establishment of a branch bank in that city, testify how much such accommodation is required by the mercantile community: —

"1. That the importance of the affairs and the progressive developement of the commerce of Syria, render daily more apparent the necessity of a new bank at Beyrout.

"2. That an establishment of this nature, under the supervision of a local committee of management, would secure beforehand the sympathies of the whole mercantile community, and would unite the elements of undoubted success.

"3. That it is, therefore, of the highest moment for the mercantile community of Beyrout that the projected bank should be forthwith carried out."

(Signed)

(Here follow the signatures.) *

"I hereby certify and attest that the signatures attached to the foot of the original declaration, exhibited at this Con-

* The original is in my possession.—J. L. F.

sular-office, and whereof the foregoing is a faithful and correct translation, are known to me to be those of the subscribing firms respectively, that the said firms are of standing and respectability, and that the native houses subscribing are the leading Arab firms of Beyrout.

"NOEL TEMPLE MOORE,
"Her Britannic Majesty's Vice-Consul, Beyrout."

The usual rate of discount in Beyrout for first-class paper, with two or three indorsements, and not having more than ninety days to run, is about sixteen per cent. per annum; but in the bazaars the native saraffs, or bankers, charge as much as from twenty-four to thirty-six per cent. per annum on advances for two or three months, the security required being either lands, houses, goods, or gold ornaments.

To a person unacquainted with the country, this rate of interest may perhaps appear excessive, particularly when he considers that there is a large amount of wealth accumulated in the towns; but it must be borne in mind that wealth is not necessarily capital; and that although we may be, like Midas, surrounded with gold, yet, if that gold be unproductive, it is commercially valueless. 'The essence of wealth consists in the capacity of supplying the wants and ministering to the desires of men, and not in the capacity of being accumulated;'* and it is, therefore, only when wealth is made use of for the purpose of reproduction that it becomes really useful, and takes the name of capital. In Syria, there is a great deal of wealth, but very little capital.

* M'Culloch's "Principles of Political Economy."

The insecurity of property, which existed for so many years under the Ottoman rule, and the total absence of any establishments in which money could be safely deposited, compelled the Syrians to invest their gains in the most valuable and, at the same time, the most portable articles. In consequence of this, a considerable proportion of the wealth of the place consists in jewels; and it is startling, when visiting at the private houses of the native population, to see the quantity of diamonds and other precious stones worn by the females of the family. The head-dress is generally one mass of brilliants; and the long hair, braided with silk, hangs over the shoulders loaded with gold ornaments and coins.

The harem has always afforded a place of security; it is the sanctuary of the wife, and has ever been held sacred and inviolable; there is no instance of a pasha, or officer of any description, forcing his way into its hallowed precincts. No matter what political change may affect the husband, the property of the wife is always secure; under all circumstances, it remains her own; nor is it in any way liable for her husband's debts, any more than the trust-property of a married woman in England secured under settlement. And this applies to all her property whatever—not only that which she possessed before marriage, but, if her husband subsequently purchase lands or houses in her name, they belong to her absolutely, and no claim of any kind against the husband will reach them. The natives have largely availed themselves of this mode of investment for their savings, and thus, instead of being made use of in the ordinary way for the purposes of trade, the accumulated wealth of centuries has been uselessly hoarded, and diverted from its proper function of reproduction.

The following letters, received from an English merchant, for many years established at Beyrout, give some interesting particulars relative to the extensive field existing in Syria for the investment of capital:—

'The resolutions which have already been forwarded to you, signed by the leading merchants of Beyrout, are, I should think, conclusive proof of the unanimous feeling prevailing here upon the subject of establishing a new bank; and I scarcely imagine that I can throw any further light upon a matter with which, from practical experience, you are yourself so well acquainted, and, consequently, so well able to elucidate. Nevertheless, as you appear to think that my opinion may be of some importance, I can have no hesitation in stating that there is plenty of room, not only for one but for two or three banks in this city, and that, so far from injuring, they would respectively aid and create business for each other. In this opinion every mercantile man in Beyrout coincides. As regards the probability of success which such an establishment as a branch bank would have in Beyrout, I feel assured that, inasmuch as the whole mercantile community anxiously desire its formation, and as it would be cordially and well supported by every respectable house in the place, you would safely divide a net profit of 12 per cent.; and if the paid-up capital of the bank permitted your making advances out of the town, where the rates of interest are much higher, you might with safety expect a net profit of 15 to 18 per cent. I am now speaking alone of Beyrout, and I leave altogether out of the question the profits to be derived from the operations of the bank at Aleppo and Damascus, where at present no banking facilities exist, and where, consequently, the rates of interest are even higher than they are here.

THE TRADE OF BEYROUT.

As all banking must depend more or less upon the commercial movements of the place for which the bank is intended, I have taken some pains to compile the following Tables of the imports and exports at Beyrout upon an average struck from the last five years, and taken from official papers of the different consulates, as well as of the custom-house, duly compared one with another:—

Importations and Exportations at Beyrout, taking an average of the last Five Years.

IMPORTS.

	Value in Francs.
Flour, corn, &c.	1,357,172
Tarbooshes (red caps)	347,400
Coffee and colonials	1,058,450
Cotton yarn, water twist, &c.	2,287,953
Other Manchester goods	10,477,704
Coal	585,750
Wines	94,227
Hardware	638,422
Cloth	1,282,000
Drugs	596,964
Copper, lead, &c.	75,470
Specie	7,597,903
Paper	311,113
Silk goods	2,306,812
Sugar (refined)	842,220
Iron and steel	546,580
Glassware	339,325
Sundries	1,357,172
Total	Fr. 34,241,214

EXPORTS.

	Value in Francs.
Raw silk and cocoons	10,131,825
Corn	4,076,360
Madder roots	160,175
Wool	344,150
Wax, gum, &c.	129,255
Oil	1,496,322
Camel skins	35,500
Soda	24,700
Specie	7,425,440
Tobacco	2,617,175
Fruits	415,500
Manufactured goods	7,181,977
Silk tissues	4,722,000
Old copper	4,145
Sundries	1,235,722
Total	Fr. 40,190,246

The foregoing Tables do not include the imports and exports on the coast, at Jaffa, Kaiffa, St. Jean d'Acre, Tyre, Sidon, Tripoli, and Latakia, the counting-house and banking business for which is transacted in Beyrout.

THE DIFFERENT KINDS OF BUSINESS WHICH A BANK MIGHT DO IN BEYROUT.

1. Discounting the bills given to importers by the native merchants against purchased Manchester, Swiss, or French goods. These bills are chiefly at 60 and 90 days for fine goods, and at 30 days for the more ordinary kinds of cloths. They are almost always paid punctually; but, in the event of non-payment or delay, can be enforced quite as well as in England. The discount in ordinary times ranges from 12 to 16 per cent. per annum, and this even by selecting only the very best paper.

2. Granting cash credits, on the Scotch system, to

the merchants of the place, upon undoubted security, charging interest at the same rate as that for discounting bills, with the addition of a stipulated commission.

3. Receiving money on deposit, at rates of interest varying according to the time for which such money was deposited. This would, after some time, be a source of considerable profit to the bank, as the security afforded by such an establishment would create a confidence in the minds of the native population which would result in their preferring to deposit their savings in the bank, at a stipulated rate of interest, instead of, as at present, making unremunerative purchases of diamonds, &c., or, as is often the case, hiding it under ground.

4. Making advances on produce. For these advances, which are perfectly safe, and are paid at the season of the proprietors' harvest, interest at the rate of 24 per cent. is freely given, and I have frequently known 30 per cent. paid. Take one article of produce alone, viz., oil. I know a firm here that has often turned 50 per cent. in the course of the year by lending money to the proprietors of olive gardens, and this, too, on first-rate collateral security. The same may be said with regard to another most important article of produce, viz., silk.

5. A great deal of business might be done in making advances upon goods in store in Beyrout, but for which at the moment there is no market. The small importers often sell these at a considerable loss, in order to remit to cover their European correspondents; whereas, if the bank would advance two-thirds of their invoice value, the importers would be able to redeem them when the market got higher, and would

gladly pay 1½ to 2 per cent. per month (18 to 24 per cent. per annum) for the advance.

From a consideration of the above, I do not think I have overstated the profits of a bank doing a purely local and legitimate banking business in Beyrout; on the contrary, I feel confident, and so do all the merchants with whom I have spoken on the subject, that a net profit of at least 15 per cent. should be realised, and that only doing a perfectly safe business.'

'Yours of the 2nd inst. reached me on the 15th, and, according to the best of my abilities, I hasten to answer the questions therein contained.

1.—The gross yearly agricultural produce of the Pashalic of Acre (of which Beyrout is the chief town) amounts in sterling money to 4,200,000*l.*

2.—This could be extended (and the same remark applies to Syria generally) to almost any amount by the introduction of capital, and wherever capital has been invested in the drainage of land, &c., the return has been little short of 50 per cent. per annum net profit. I am personally acquainted with many individuals who have in four or five years made large sums of money (I might, indeed, say large fortunes) by renting villages and using capital in planting mulberry trees, draining, sinking wells, and so forth, and I am certain that in many parts of the Acre Pashalic any one with a capital of 2,000*l.*, setting to work the right way, would make at least an income of 1,000*l.* per annum.

3.—The gross yearly produce of cocoons in Beyrout and the neighbouring parts of Lebanon, together with the reeled silk made in the same district, represents in English money between three and four millions.

4.—This amount is capable of being considerably extended, were a bank or discount company established which would make advances, on good security, to cultivators and reelers in Lebanon. The security given would be the title-deeds of their land and filatures,* together with the bond of wealthy men in Beyrout. Fifteen per cent. would be freely given. The advances would have to be made in May or June, and would all be repaid by the end of September without the slightest risk. This is a business which the large Marseilles agency houses find exceedingly profitable. The silk is sold in the Lyons market for the account and risk of those who have borrowed the money.

5.—In Beyrout and the neighbourhood there are about 1,700 native reels, 12 large filatures containing 1,000 reels, and 40 small filatures containing 500 reels.

6.—The investment of capital in filatures is highly profitable, and is calculated, one year with another, at not less than 25 per cent. per annum net.

7.—The land in the neighbourhood of Beyrout, and all over the country, is freehold.

8.—The population of Beyrout, and that portion of Lebanon depending upon Beyrout, is as follows:—

Beyrout	50,000
Lebanon, namely, the Kesrawân (region of the Maronites), and country of the Druses	200,000
To which may be added as the population of Sidon, Tyre, Tripoli, Latakia, &c., for all of which Beyrout is *de facto* the counting-house	100,000
Total	350,000

* Filature—Silk-reeling manufactory.

Of these 350,000, there are 250,000 Christians, &c., and 100,000 Mohammedans. The population of Beyrout is divided into the following sects:—

Mohammedans	20,000
Orthodox Greeks	15,000
Greek Catholics	5,000
Roman Catholics	1,000
Maronites	7,000
Armenians	500
Jews	1,000
Different Sects	500
Total	50,000

From the "LEVANT HERALD."

'Mr. Lewis Farley, in his work on Syria (*Two Years in Syria*), supplies a mass of statistical and other data in support of his appeal to capitalists which certainly demonstrates, as far as figures and statements of notorious accuracy can do so, the want of banking accommodation in Beyrout, and, consequently, the certainty of a profitable return to shareholders. "The usual rate of discount (says Mr. Farley) on the Beyrout market for first-class paper, with two or three indorsements, and not having more than ninety days to run, is from 12 to 16 per cent." And again—"The Syrians have great faith in everything English; this confidence opens a wide field for commercial enterprise, and no undertaking would be more successful at the present moment than a well-conducted and properly-managed bank. The security thus afforded would cause much of the hoarded wealth to find its way into the bank in the shape of deposits." That all this is in strict accordance with fact and probability will be at once admitted by those of our readers who know the country and are aware of the *prestige* which, like the scent from a broken vase, still hangs around the British name from Aintab to Hebron. Without going deep into the figures before us, we observe that the imports into Beyrout alone were, in the years

| 1853 | 1856 | 1857 |
| £722,864. | £1,162,676. | £1,324,550; |

whilst the exports were

| 1853 | 1856 | 1857 |
| £624,244. | £795,657. | £983,398. |

During 1858, the effects of the crisis were still too severely felt to permit of any great increase in commercial enterprise, but we understand that, whilst during 1859 the imports at Beyrout have increased to 1,448,860*l.*, the exports in the same period have more than doubled what they were in 1853, forming a total of 1,698,456*l.*; thus for the first time exceeding the imports by upwards of 200,000*l.* This augmentation of exports is chiefly owing to the greatly increased, and still increasing, cultivation of the olive and mulberry, and the consequent production of oil and silk, all over the Lebanon, vast tracts being every year redeemed from waste and planted with those trees. Surely, in such a country, a good return can be had for almost any amount of capital which an English bank may bring into it ?'

CHAPTER XXVIII.

JERUSALEM.

From Mr. James Finn, Her Britannic Majesty's Consul at Jerusalem.

IT is with much pleasure that I learn from you the probable establishment of a bank in Constantinople, and I most anxiously wish to see a branch of the same in Jerusalem.

Jerusalem is not an emporium of commercial trade, but it is a place into which money is being continually poured from without. The great religious establishments, as Convents, Patriarchates, Episcopates, not to mention the six Consulates, all have money dealings, and would be benefited by a banking institution, with good capital and character.

At the Russian buildings now in progress, and which will continue four years more, they were lately paying for mere cutting of stone 500*l.* weekly. Those works began with a capital in hand of above a million sterling. The Greek convents also are spending considerable sums in agricultural works about us.

But almost all the money affairs here are in the hands of a few petty firms, who transact their business at enormous interest, and money, when obtained on loan, often costs at the usurious rates of 50 or 60 per cent. per annum: 24 per cent. per annum is considered very moderate.

A bank here would prove a great blessing, and under its operation I should expect to see credit generally revived, trade enlarged, even in lines not yet tried: coins of foreign currency (as they mostly are) less fluctuating in value and more uniform between one town and another in Palestine, with less possibility of Pashas playing tricks with the currency.

Any bank that would lend money at moderate rates upon security of jewellery or lands, might have a large business here.

(Signed)   JAMES FINN.

Jerusalem, January 15th, 1861.

Extract from Official Report to the Foreign Office, by Mr. Finn, Her Britannic Majesty's Consul at Jerusalem.

Of late years, an export trade of grain from this country to Europe has been opened up, from which the peasantry, notwithstanding the losses sustained by extortion of their own Sheikhs and of the tax-farmers, have accumulated an unprecedented degree of wealth; but in some cases they bury the coin in holes, and in others they make use of it in decorating the women.

We see the rapid change in the latter of these respects. The peasant women of Bethlehem and Bait Tala wear gold instead of silver coins on their heads, and the style of dress in which they formerly indulged only on wedding occasions is now adopted upon the road in walking from one town to another.

Money in coin is accumulating like heaps of manure over the country, but is employed in no wholesome direction.

CHAPTER XXIX.

DAMASCUS.

DAMASCUS, the capital of Syria, is situate in a fertile plain at the east base of the Anti-Lebanon, about 180 miles from Aleppo, and 60 miles from Beyrout. It is one of the most ancient cities in the world, and has been from the earliest times remarkable alike for the unrivalled beauty of its situation, the superiority of its manufactures, and the magnitude of its trade.

Standing on the high road between the Mediterranean and the Persian Gulf, it became, in the flourishing days of Phœnician commerce, an emporium for the trade between Europe and India; and, although subsequently overshadowed by the magnificence and grandeur of Palmyra, it rose to great wealth and power. In the time of Solomon, it was the capital of an independent kingdom, which afterwards, under the name of the Kingdom of Syria, was engaged in wars with the Jews. Subsequently Damascus was annexed to the empire of Assyria, as well as to that of Persia; it then fell into the hands of the Macedonians, the Romans, the Arabs, and lastly of the Ottoman Turks, when in A.D. 1517 it was taken by Sultan Selim I. Still, though so often taken and devastated, it has always risen again, and while the wonderful ruins of Baalbec and Palmyra mournfully attest the greatness of their former splendour, Damascus has remained the most opulent city in Syria. The population of Damascus amounts to 180,000, viz.:

Mussulmans	130,000
Christians	30,000
Jews	20,000

The city contains 60 places of worship, 31 khans, and large entrepôts for merchandise, besides the great Bazaar destined to receive the caravans, and capable of containing from 1,200 to 1,500 camels; 150 coffee-houses, some of which are considered the finest in the East; 750 dealers in damask stuffs, 185 dyers, 70 printers on stuffs, 200 dealers in handkerchiefs and fancy articles, 98 fringe makers, 72 saddlers'-shops, 78 tobacco manufacturers, and 48 pipe makers.

The Pashalic of Damascus extends, north to south, from Hamah on the Orontes down to the deserts of Arabia Petræa south-east of the Dead Sea, a length of about four degrees of latitude. It comprehends the country of Haurân and the other districts on the east side of the Jordan, the Lake of Tiberias and the Dead Sea, besides the greater part of Judæa west of the Jordan, including Jerusalem and Nablous. Corn, hemp, flax, madder, tobacco, cotton, silk, and cochineal are the chief products. The surface, except in the west, is level; and the land, susceptible of cultivation, is extremely fertile, capable of supporting a population of six millions of souls. The population at present, exclusive of the Bedawîn, is not more than 500,000.

From its favourable position, Damascus is the seat of an extensive trade. The productions of India, consisting chiefly of spices, pepper, cinnamon, nutmegs, Java and other sugars; musk, cardamoms, aloes, camphor;

cotton manufactures, coarse and fine muslins, gold stuffs; porcelain, indigo, &c., are in great demand and bring high prices. They are brought from India by the Persian Gulf, Bussora and Baghdad. The manufactures of Great Britain are much sought after and held in very high esteem, particularly grey T cloths, printed cottons and chintzes, grey calicoes, long-cloths, calico shirting and sheeting, jaconets, cotton handkerchiefs and silk and cotton shawls of gay colours, made in imitation of those of Cashmere. About 150,000 pieces of plain calicoes are annually used for local consumption; also 20,000 pieces of various kinds of printed calicoes, about 5,000 dozens cotton handkerchiefs, and 500,000 lbs. of cotton yarn used in mixing with silk in the manufactures of the place. Besides these, there are imported a considerable quantity of sheet copper, sheet and bar iron, tin in bars and plates, some refined sugar, West India coffee and spices.

The manufacture of sabre-blades, for which Damascus was formerly so celebrated, has long since declined; but the manufactures of silk stuffs, embroidered with gold, as well as of plain cotton, and cotton and silk mixed, are carried on to a considerable extent; while in the bazaars are to be seen the manufactures of almost every country in the world. Superb caparisons for horses from European Turkey; rich bridles, martingales and silver-embossed breastpieces from Persia; richly ornamented fire-arms from France and Germany; silk from India and China; furs from Russia, Georgia, Circassia and Armenia; velvets from Italy, and cottons from Great Britain, as well as various other articles of an inferior kind from England, Germany, and France.

The great Hadji caravan, consisting of from 50,000 to 60,000 pilgrims, goes every year from Damascus to

Mecca, and on its departure and arrival occasions considerable activity to trade. On its passage southward, it gives origin to a retail trade in English cotton manufactures, small articles of Persian manufacture, and, sometimes, jewellery. On its return, the Hadjis bring back Indian and Arabian produce, coffee, spices, aloe-wood, and various articles of Indian manufacture.

CHAPTER XXX.

ALEPPO.

THE Consular district of Aleppo comprises the Pashaliks of Aleppo, Adana, and Tripoli, and embraces within its jurisdiction the Vice-Consulates of Mersina, Alexandretta, Suedia, Latakia, Tripoli, all being on the seaboard of the Mediterranean, and Antioch, Aintab, Marash, and Orfa, in the interior. Of these, Alexandretta, Suedia, Antioch, and Aintab are included in the Pashalik of Aleppo; Latakia and Tripoli, in that of Saida, as it is now called; Mersina, in the Pashalik of Adana; while Marash and Orfa are themselves the seats of independent pashaliks.

The above districts, lying between 37° 40′ and 35° of N. latitude, and 35° and 39° of E. longitude, comprise an extent of territory of 22,250 square miles, divided in the following proportions:—

Pashalik of Aleppo, exclusive of the three Kaimakamliks following		2,450
Kaimakamlik of Aintab		2,800
do.	Antioch	1,500
do.	Alexandretta	500
do.	Latakia	2,800
do.	Tripoli	1,800
do.	Mersina	1,300
Pashalik of Marash		3,800
do.	Orfa	5,300
	Total	22,250

The town of Aleppo is built at the eastern extremity of a range of rocky hills, which terminate in the great plain extending to the Euphrates, and is watered by a river which runs from the neighbourhood of Aintab, 60 miles to the north. Its early history is involved in much obscurity. There is a tradition that an inscription in Hebrew on a stone tablet was found some fifty years ago, to the effect that Joab took possession of the castle in the name of King David, and a copy of this inscription is preserved in a Jewish family of the town. Some assert that it is the ancient Berœa, others Hierapolis, and others again Chalybon; but by whatever name it was known, it seems to have been indebted for its commercial importance as the entrepôt for Eastern trade to the fall of Palmyra and Baalbec, the traffic engrossed by which cities sought a new channel farther north through Aleppo, or Haleb, the name by which it has been known from the beginning of the Christian era to the present time. At that early period it became a frequent subject of quarrel between the Greek emperors and the kings of Persia, till in the year 637 it fell before the conquering sword of the Arabs in the reign of the Greek Emperor Heraclius, and was selected as a place of residence by the Hamdanian sultans. In the year 998 it submitted to the yoke of the Seljoukian sultans, and passed successively into the power of the Attabeks, the Fattimites, the Ayoubites, and the Tartars, who in 1260 took it by assault. The Mamelukes became its next oppressors; they were succeeded by the fierce Tamerlane in 1400, and it was finally incorporated in the Turkish Empire in 1517, under the reign of Sultan Selim I. Its prosperity, notwithstanding so many vicissitudes, continued unabated till the commencement of the eighteenth century, when it was supposed to contain 300,000 inhabitants, but the natural effects of misgovernment, and the increasing commerce by the Cape of Good Hope, checked its growth. It reached, perhaps, its lowest point twelve years ago, when a reaction took place, and a growing commercial activity has since then been observable. The houses are substantially built of cut stone, one or two storeys high, and are provided with a court, where a fountain of water may generally be seen playing. The town is clean for the East, and altogether wears an appearance of solidity which gives it an historical character; a castle of considerable strength, in the Saracenic style, and lofty walls, attesting its military importance.

The population amounts to 100,000, and is divided as follows :—

Mussulmans	66,500
Greeks	19,000
Maronites	5,000
Armenians	3,000
Syrian Catholics	2,000
Jews	4,500
	100,000

There are at present, in Aleppo, 5,644 shops, viz. :— 22 woollen-drapers' shops, 250 linen-drapers, 70 goldsmiths and jewellers, 220 dealers in hardware and glass, 170 druggists, 200 dyers, 300 cobblers, 250 butchers, 500 shops for the sale of butter and oil, 150 flour-dealers, 50 pastry-cooks, 100 cook-shops, 300 green-grocers, 170 barbers, 70 carpenters, 50 stone-cutters, 120 pewterers, 150 tailors, 50 shops for the sale of leather bottles and buckets, 50 gunsmiths, 60 dealers in powder and shot, 15 workers in tin, 50 upholsterers, 100 dealers in cotton, 400 spinners employing 6,000 workmen, 40 sellers of planks and beams, 30 turners, 40 pipe-sellers, 50 boot-makers, 60 pipe bowl-makers, 240 sellers of tobacco, 50 sellers of snuff, 40 sellers of coffee, 30 sellers of fine paper, 30 farriers, 25 saddlers, 37 baths, 80 coffee-shops, 25 sellers of sherbet, 100 bakeries, 60 horse mills, 40 water mills, 250 dealers in firewood, 15 furriers, 35 braziers, 15 house painters, 150 soap dealers, 250 sellers of ready-made clothes, 30 perfumers, and 40 dealers in earthenware. The number of workmen employed in these shops amount to 18,685.

Aleppo has ever been celebrated for its manufactures, which are sent to all parts of the East, on account of their strength and durability. In 1856, there were 5,560 looms at work, and last year no less than 10,000 were in full operation, consuming upwards of 40,000 cwt. of cotton twist, chiefly imported from Great Britain.

The following Table will show the number of looms, and the quantity of goods manufactured in 1856 :—

Articles.	Style and Texture.	No. of Looms.	No. of pieces.	Value in Piastres per piece.	Total value in Piastres.
Chitara	Cotton and silk stuffs	2500	1,200,000	25	30,000,000
Gazlich	Cotton-stuffs throughout	1000	600,000	11	6,600,000
Cottonee	Cotton and silk satinet	500	120,000	75	9,000,000
Alagai	Silk and little cotton	400	134,400	60	8,064,000
Sawà-ee	Silk and gold thread	100	9,600	200	1,920,000
Agabanee	Cotton embroidered with silk	50	12,000	50	600,000
Chekmak	Silk and gold thread with cotton	50	7,200	100	720,000
Atlass	Silk satins	15	3,600	70	252,000
Fontah	Cotton and silk aprons	50	48,000	10	480,000
Boshch	Silk handkerchiefs	25	24,000	20	480,000
Girdles	Cotton and silk coloured	20	4,800	20	96,000
Girdles	Cotton coloured	50	24,000	8	192,000
Kham	Cotton cloth, not dyed	200	134,400	20	2,688,000
Abee	Woven wool and cotton	100	28,800	25	520,000
Mandeel	Black cotton handkerchiefs	300	192,000	30	5,760,000
Mandeel	Coloured cotton do.	300	96,000	20	1,920,000
	Total	5560	2,638,800	Pias.	69,292,000

The growth of cotton, which is just now occupying the attention of manufacturers in England, is confined to two places in the Pashalik, namely, Idlib and Killis. Twenty years ago, three times as much cotton was grown, chiefly for local consumption; but the importation of English twist discouraged its cultivation, as the native manufacturer finds that he can weave more cheaply with the wrought material imported. If capital, however, were introduced and encouragement given to the cultivation of cotton, the natives would find it more to their advantage to supply us with the raw material and take our manufactures in exchange.

The following list of the caravans arriving at Aleppo, with the principal objects brought by each, will show that fine cottons form a large portion of the internal commerce.

1. From Bussora and Baghdad.—Pearls, cottons, shawls, Indian drugs, perfumes, porcelain.

2. From Mossul and Merdin.—Cotton yarn and cotton stuffs, galls.

3. From Diarbekhr.—Cotton and cotton stuffs, red cotton, thread, Morocco leather, goats' hair, galls.

4. From Marash.—Timber, furs, goats' hair.

5. From Orfa.—White cotton and cotton stuffs, Morocco leather, goats' hair.

6. From Aintab.—White cotton stuffs, wrought Morocco leather.

7. From Killis.—Cotton stuffs and cotton yarn, silks, galls, oil.

8. From Idlib and Kiha.—5,000 quintals of soap, oil.

9. From Van, Tiflis, and Kars.—Chiefly furs.

10. From Erz-rum and Sivas.—Furs, goats' hair, wax.

11. From Guzun.—Linens.

12. From Tokat.—Silk, furs, copper.

13. From Trebizond.—Cotton stuffs and lint.
14. From Malatic.—Cotton stuffs, dried fruits.
15. From Latakia.—Silk, coffee, rice, tobacco, and Egyptian produce.
16. From Constantinople.—Cotton and woollen stuffs of Germany, printed muslins, wrought amber and furs.
17. From Brussa.—Silk, satin, velvet sofa covers.
18. From Smyrna.—European cotton and woollen stuffs, hardware, horlogerie, &c.
19. From Tripoli of Syria.—Silk.
20. From Damascus.—Mokkah coffee, soap, silk, produce of Damascus looms, cotton yarn of India, dried fruit.
21. From Mecca.—Coffee, scented wood, pearls, ambergris, drugs of Arabia and India.

The imports and exports have been increasing considerably at Aleppo, viz. :—

Imports.			Exports.		
1851	.	£486,060	1854	.	£993,630
1855	.	1,414,059	1855	.	1,254,130

The imports from Great Britain consist chiefly of manufactured cotton goods. They amounted in 1851 to only 146,405*l.* ; while in 1855 they increased, as per the annexed Table, to 444,689*l.*

Imports from Great Britain to Aleppo in the year 1855.

Articles.	Quantities.	Price.	Total value in Pounds sterling.
Manufactures, cotton twist, calicoes, &c.	20,480 bales	£ 20 s. 0 per bale	409,600
Sugar	878 barrels	5 0 ,, brl.	4,390
Coffee	534 bags	4 10 ,, bag	2,403
Pepper and pimento	325 ,,	3 10 ,, ,,	1,137
Cochineal	97 cases	30 0 ,, case	2, 10
Indigo	48 ,,	100 0 ,, ,,	4,800
Drysalteries	1,231 barrels	3 0 ,, brl.	3,693
Sundries	5,252 packages	3 0 per pge.	15,756
Total			444,689

The exports in 1855, which amounted to 1,254,130*l*., were as follow:—

Articles.	Quantities.	Price.	Total value in Pounds sterling.
Wheat	120,000 quarters	£ 2 s. 0 per quarter	240,000
Barley	50,000 ,,	1 5 ,,	62,500
Millet	24,000 ,,	1 5 ,,	31,250
Sesame	5,000 tons	12 0 per ton	60,000
Galls	750 ,,	70 0 ,,	52,500
Cotton	500 ,,	40 0 ,,	20,000
Wool	1,500 ,,	72 0 ,,	108,000
Flour	—	—	150,000
Madder root, scammony, yellow berries, gums, &c.	—	—	100,000
			824,250
		Coasting trade	429,880
		Total	1,254,130

The following resolutions have been adopted by the leading merchants at Aleppo, on the expediency of establishing a branch bank in that city:—

"1. That the monetary state of the trade of Aleppo calls for the aid of a regular system of banking.

"2. That the establishment of a branch bank at Aleppo would be received as a boon by the mercantile community, and would be a profitable investment of capital.

"3. That it is therefore desirable that some such measure should be adopted with as little delay as possible." (Signed)
(Here follow the signatures.)*

"I hereby certify and attest that the above signatures are known to me to be those of the subscribing firms respectively, and that those firms are the leading commercial firms at Aleppo.

"J. H. SKENE,
"Her Britannic Majesty's Consul, Aleppo."

In reference to the above, Mr. Skene writes as follows:—

"It is needless to observe that in every country where a regular systematic banking establishment has been founded for the first time the development of trade has been an immediate consequence, and this fact borne in mind will, of course, render calculations based on existing commerce underrated, and an allowance for it should therefore be made. Such as it is, the trade of Aleppo can well support a bank. Money is scarce. Loans are next to ruinous, interest ranging from 3 to 6 per cent. per month (36 to 72 per cent. per annum). The exchange is variable to a degree which impedes remittances, and, above all, the practice of native saraffs or

* The original is in my possession.—J. L. F.

money-changers oppresses legitimate commerce. The transmission of bullion is often dangerous too. Credit is uncertain, and the best houses are accustomed to see their bills looked at with suspicion. Thus the opening for a bank cannot but be favourable.

The actual state of the market is deplorable. Every merchant is obliged to send money out of the country, the amount of importation being much greater than that of exportation. Cash has come to such an agio that the merchant's gains are greatly diminished, and his transactions necessarily decrease. Uncertainty, moreover, deprives him of courage to undertake many operations, when he fears not to be able to replace the money employed at the same or a profitable rate of exchange. When the importation from England rose last year to 346,000*l.*, money disappeared; in 1847, the best year of exportation, bills were abundant, and there was a consequent increase of 60 per cent. in the quantity of merchandise imported, yet no difficulty of remitting ensued. Now that difficulty is felt in every considerable counting-house of Aleppo. A bank would remove it, increase business, and not only enrich itself by existing trade, but also on the extension of it produced by the facility of remitting, besides all the concomitant advantages which are self-evident. The total amount of the imports and exports here is upwards of 2,500,000*l.* per annum. This is a wide field for one establishment, and I feel assured that a bank is a felicitous idea, and whoever turns this way with that view must make a fortune with common prudence.

I have mentioned the saraff system. It is the most absurd thing in the world. About ten or twelve saraffs, mostly without capital of their own, hold all the cash of the merchants, and issue cheques, nominally payable at sight, but rarely paid at all, except by an exchanging of cheques with other saraffs, and when paid in cash, or even at 15 or 20 days after sight, a discount of at least 2 per cent. is charged. These people thus rule the trade of Aleppo by an unsound system of credit, a currency unrepresented by security, while they carry on all sorts of illicit traffic, usury, &c., for their own advantage, with the money belonging to the merchants, to whom they pay no interest and offer no guarantee. I do not mean to say anything against a system of bank cheques, which is excellent; but let it be a solid system, such as a regular bank would establish to its own great advantage and that of trade, acting and re-acting on each other."

CHAPTER XXXI.

AINTAB.

The town of Aintab is situated sixty miles to the north of Aleppo, of which Pashalik it forms a part, and is governed by a Kaimakam, also dependent on the Governor of Aleppo. Its ancient name was Antioch ad Taurum, but all traces of its antiquity have disappeared, and nothing is left to remind the modern traveller of the existence of the ancient town. It is celebrated in Northern Syria for the salubrity of its climate, a character which it owes doubtless to its elevation, the consequent dryness of the air, and the abundance of the springs, which gush from the hills on which it is built, and run through the streets in every direction. The town covers three little hills and their intervening valleys, and is commanded by a castle which crowns the summit of an artificial elevation, exactly resembling that of Aleppo, though not on so large a scale. The houses are small but well built, being constructed of the loose boulder stones which strew the high lands for miles around, and in respect to cleanliness, it contrasts favourably with any other Turkish town.

The population amounts to about 27,000 souls; of whom 18,000 are Turks, 8,500 Armenians, and 500 Jews. Turkish is the language universally used; the

Armenians having completely forgotten their mother tongue, though in the books which they make use of they employ the Armenian characters, from their superior simplicity to the Arabic. The inhabitants of the country are chiefly Turks, who claim their property in the land as far back as the time of the old Seljoukian dynasty. They inhabit 320 villages, the population of which does not probably exceed 70,000, of whom about 10,000 are Christians. These villages are scattered over an extent of country, measuring 50 miles from north to south, by 30 from east to west. Of this extensive district, not more than two-thirds have been brought under tillage; and even of this cultivated portion, only one-half comes under the plough every year, owing to the defective system of agriculture, which allows the land that has produced a crop one year to lie fallow the next. This ignorance of the method of the rotation of crops, which has doubled the productive power of the soil wherever it has been introduced, tends naturally to keep down the population, and to check commercial activity, by diminishing the amount of agricultural produce which would otherwise be available for exportation.

The government derives an annual revenue of 930,000 piastres from the land tax, amounting to 10 per cent. of the net produce; which is farmed out to Turks residing at Aintab, who form the wealthy portion of its Mussulman population. The tax on houses and other immovable property amounts to 650,000 piastres; that on weights and measures, to 250,000 piastres; stamps, and other miscellaneous duties, bring in another 250,000; thus raising the revenues of the Kaimakamlik to about 2,000,000 piastres per annum.

The land produces wheat, barley, Indian corn,

millet, rice, lentils, sesame, olives, fruit of various kinds, castor oil seed, yellow berries for dyeing, gall nuts, scammony, tobacco, and wax. Of these there is a regular exportation of the six latter articles; and when prices in the European corn markets are sufficiently high to admit of a profit, wheat is added to the above exportations. The following Table will show more clearly the amounts annually exported from the province through its port Alexandretta, the prices and quantities quoted being taken to represent the annual average, since they vary considerably, according to the demand in Europe.

Articles.	Quantities Exported.		Prices free on board.	
	Shumbuls.*	Cantars.*	Piastres.	
			Per shumbul.	Per cantar.
Wheat	20,000	—	70	—
Castor oil seed	200	—	—	—
Yellow berries	—	30	—	1,000
Gall nuts	—	60	— from	1,500 to 2,300
Scammony	—	3	—	3,500
Tobacco	—	200	—	1,450
Wax	—	30	—	5,000

English imported goods have a limited sale, and are confined almost entirely to cotton and calico stuffs. From the circumstance of there being no British or other merchant corresponding direct with England, the cost prices are extremely high. Upon a rough estimate, there is an annual importation of English manufactured goods of 2,500 bales, of which 400 or 500 consist of cotton twist, selling at the rate of 2,600 piastres the bale, which, allowing a higher price for calicoes, would make

* Note.—3¼ shumbuls = 1 quarter; a cantar = 5 cwt.

a total of 7,000,000 piastres, or 54,000*l*. This internal commerce is quite of recent origin, the trade of former times having been confined to the transport, for the European markets, of the more costly productions of India, which were exchanged for manufactured goods intended for Aleppo, Baghdad, and the East. This inland trade has been thus instrumental in introducing our manufactures to the towns and villages of the interior, so that now even the wandering Arab delights to deck himself out in the gay coloured clothing woven in the looms of Manchester and Leeds.

The great bar to carrying on an active commerce consists in the absence of carriage roads, which obliges all goods to be transported on the backs of mules and camels, entailing an enormous expense on their original cost; and, as the distance between Aintab and Alexandretta is about 100 miles, which, at a camel's pace, cannot be traversed under five days in summer, and eight, ten, or even fifteen, in winter, only a few of the most valuable products of the country can bear such ruinous transport charges. Wheat, for example, which can be purchased at Aintab at 35 piastres a shumbul, by the time it reaches the sea, has incurred expenses which have raised its price to upwards of 60 piastres, consequently it is only exported when a scarcity in Europe calls for a supply. At the present moment, however, a company is in course of formation at Aleppo, for constructing a carriage road between that town and Alexandretta; and, an example once given, we may hope that the benefits derived from the undertaking will encourage native enterprise to make a network of roads, connecting the different towns of Syria.

The population of Aintab is almost exclusively trading and manufacturing, the operations of weaving, tanning of leather, and dyeing employing a great number of hands. There are also three soap manufactories, producing annually 9,000 cwt. of soap, two-thirds of which are sold in the neighbouring towns and district. The native hand-looms supply the middle and lower classes of the population with the striped woollen garments universally worn in the East; whilst the richer inhabitants have contracted a taste for the finer textures of Europe. A considerable part of the population is occupied in the cultivation of the extensive orchards and vineyards surrounding the town, the fruit of which is much esteemed for its flavour, and is sent to great distances, while the grapes produce excellent wine. The country people are quiet and orderly, and, as the tent of the Bedawy or Turkoman is never seen in the district, the pursuits of agriculture can be followed, and the harvests gathered in with perfect security.

CHAPTER XXXII.

MARASH.

THE town of Marash is situated at the junction of the Taurus with the Ghiaour Dagh, or Mount Amanus, in 37° 30′ N. latitude, and 37° E. longitude. It is the seat of a Pashalik of the second rank, and the territory comprised within its jurisdiction contains 18,000 square miles. The general character of the country is mountainous, as it extends over a considerable part of the Taurus; but it contains many large and fertile plains capable, if cultivated, of supporting a population of several millions.

The population of the town of Marash is 25,000, about 10,000 of whom are Armenians, and the rest Mussulmans. The local manufactories are engaged almost exclusively in the fabrication of a coarse striped cloth of cotton or wool, which is in general use in the country, and its durability and cheapness have obtained for Marash a provincial celebrity. The looms are, of course, worked by the hand, some 300 being in operation, giving employment to upwards of 1,000 workmen, principally Mussulmans. A few years since, the cotton twist used in the fabrication of these goods was all made in the district, from the raw material, then much cultivated; but it has been found that Manchester cotton twist is both cheaper and superior in every way to the native, which has consequently been entirely superseded. The manufacture of iron and saddlery are also pursuits employing many hands, while a considerable part of the poorer population is engaged in agriculture; rice, wheat, and barley being grown in the plain at the foot of the town, while the vine and various fruit trees flourish upon the higher lands on the mountain sides. The only necessaries of life, however, which may be considered cheap in this place are rice and wood. Of the former 1,500 quarters are annually produced, and sold at from 2*l.* 10*s.* to 2*l.* 15*s.* the quarter. Wood is largely felled in the mountains, and conveyed to great distances for fuel and building purposes, the whole of Northern Syria being supplied from the Marash forests.

The Christians of Marash are divided into three communities — Armenians, Armenian Catholics, and Protestants: the first numbering about 6,820; the Catholics, 2,560; and the Protestants rather above 1,000. They are the most industrious portion of the inhabitants of Marash, a large proportion being engaged in carrying on a commerce with Aleppo and Aintab; each merchant keeps his own shop, where he sells his merchandise, either wholesale or retail, but five or six only aspire to the title of wholesale merchants. The trade with Great Britain is carried on through the Aleppo houses, as there is no one engaged in direct trade with Europe.

The closest approximation that can be made as to the amount of British goods annually imported into Marash is as follows:—

Articles.	Quantities.	Value.	Total value.
		£ s. d.	£
Cotton twist	300 bales	19 0 0 per bale	5,700
Calico	400 ,,	22 5 0 ,,	8,900
Prints	70 ,,	44 0 0 ,,	3,080
Muslins	50 ,,	26 10 0 ,,	1,325
Linen kerchiefs	20 cases	45 0 0 per case	900
Miscellaneous linen, woollen, and cotton goods	30 bales	30 0 0 per bale	900
Copper	6 tons	188 0 0 per ton	1,128
Total			21,933

CHAPTER XXXIII.

ORFA.

ORFA (the ancient *Edessa*) is a large, well-built town, surrounded by high and strong walls, 7 miles in circuit, and contains between 40,000 and 50,000 inhabitants.

The district of Orfa produces the following articles in the quantities, and sold at the prices, set forth in the following Table:—

Annual Produce.	Annual Export.	Market Prices.
Wool, 1,500 cantars	1,000 cantars	500 to 1,000 piastres
Sesame, 5,000 ,,	4,000 ,,	250 piastres per cantar
Wheat, 2½ millions of Aleppo shumbuls	Mostly bought at Aleppo	35 to 50 ,, per shumbul
Barley, 1¼ millions of Aleppo shumbuls	—	13 piastres ,,
Lentils, 1,300 of Aleppo shumbuls	—	30 piastres ,,
Raisins, 1,000 cantars	500 cantars	300 ,, per cantar
Silk, 4 ,,	worked in Aleppo	2,100 ,, per rottolo
Cotton, 15,000 ,,	not exported	200 ,, per cantar
Wax, 53 ,,	50 cantars	20 to 22 ,, per oke
Sulphur . . .	150 ,,	uncertain
Butter, 2,000 cantars	1,000 ,,	36 ,, per rottolo

Two soap factories have lately been established at Orfa: within a few months they have produced 800 cantars of soap, which is sold in the town and surrounding villages at 1,200 piastres per cantar.

European manufactured goods (purchased at Aleppo) are sold annually to the amount of 15,000,000 piastres; and articles of consumption, such as sugar, pepper, coffee, cinnamon, and spices, to the amount of 5,000,000 piastres.

In 1857, about 7,000 camels, laden with manufactured goods, passed through Orfa, *en route* for Northern Syria, Asia Minor, and Baghdad; and about the same number *en route* for Alexandretta, laden with Persian silk, wool, and jumbar.*

The revenue of the district of Orfa amounts to 2,500,000 piastres, and the expenses to 2,000,000; leaving a net surplus of 500,000 piastres.

* Each camel carries one cantar, or five cwt.

CHAPTER XXXIV.

ALEXANDRETTA.

ALEXANDRETTA, or Iskenderoon, was founded by Alexander the Great, and called Alexandria ad Issum. It is the most important port on the coast of Syria, being situated on a bay of considerable extent (24 miles broad), capable of containing any amount of shipping, which can ride upon its waters in perfect safety during any season of the year; the anchorage is good, and it is well sheltered from all the prevailing winds by ranges of high mountains, some of them 4,000 feet above the level of the sea. Nevertheless, and although it is the port where all goods are discharged and shipped for and from the entire districts of Northern Syria, Mesapotamia, and Kurdistan, there is not a more neglected harbour in the Turkish dominions. There are but two miserable jetties in the place, and the lighters employed in conveying goods from the ships to the shore, and *vice versâ*, are of the most wretched description.

The climate of Alexandretta, in consequence of the marshes which surround the town, is most unhealthy, more particularly during the months of June, July, August, and September, at which season the few respectable inhabitants who reside there leave for the villages in the mountains, about two hours' distance, where they remain until the commencement of October. In the year 1832, an attempt was made by Ibrahim Pasha to drain these marshes, but it was left unfinished, and nothing has since been done in the matter. The sum required to complet ethe work is only 2,000*l.*, by the outlay of which about 1,500 acres of prime land would be brought into cultivation, and become the property of the person or company making the advance. The plain around Alexandretta is of the most fertile description, and well suited for the production of cotton, wheat, maize, barley, sesame, indigo, rice, &c.; in fact, for any produce which the East is capable of yielding. It could be irrigated to any extent, as there are several mountain streams running through it; notwithstanding which, and the advantages that are held out by the situation of the port for exportation, the cultivation of the soil is confined to the bare wants of the native population; thus a plain capable of supplying many of the largest cities of the United Kingdom with corn, does not at present produce sufficient to feed 2,000 people.

Another project, which would aid very much in the improvement of Alexandretta, is a carriage-road between that town and Aleppo; could this most desirable work be carried out, the entire of Northern Syria would be much benefited, and the trade with Europe be at least doubled before the end of two years after the completion of the road. The heavy carriage paid for goods between Alexandretta and Aleppo, a distance of 70 miles, is over 3*l.* per ton on the average throughout the year, being nearly as much as the freight of same to England: this, of course, prevents many parties embarking in the export trade with Europe, and thus causes large plains of fertile country to remain uncultivated for want of an outlet for the produce; but, even putting this part of the question aside, the large traffic which even at present passes between this port and Aleppo would in itself pay the shareholders of a company a handsome dividend on the capital required. Such an undertaking, while realizing large profits, would, at the same time, be of vast importance to the mercantile interests of both countries, and open a field for the immigration of small capitalists from England to cultivate the plains now lying waste and unproductive.

The imports and exports at the port of Alexandretta for the half-year ending June 30, 1858, were as follows:

Imports. — 6,866 bales manufactured cotton goods, 92 bales silk, 29 bales cloth, 1,215 casks sugar, 722 casks copper, 66 casks alum, 72 casks copperas, 24 casks saltpetre, 20 casks turmeric, 68 casks rice, 27 casks sal-ammoniac, 1,156 bags coffee, 53 bags pepper and pimento, 65 bags indigo, 24 bags cochineal, 498 boxes tin, 272 boxes oranges, 8,052 bars iron, 130 bars steel, 475 tons coals, $15\frac{1}{2}$ tons dye-woods, 300 crates glass, 500 chairs, and 3,276 packages sundries.

Exports. — 10,147 shumbuls wheat, 357 shumbuls maize, 12,211 shumbuls sesame, 69 sacks lentils, 167 sacks linseed, 2,347 sacks galls, 327 sacks peas, 106 sacks flour, 1,225 sacks raisins, 59 sacks pistachios, 30 sacks yellow berries, 1,379 bales manufactured goods, 4,181 bales wool, 385 bales cotton, 170 bales silk, 66 bales cocoons, 833 bales tobacco, 395 bales saffron, 80 cases soap, 88 cases gum, 69 cases wax, 9 cases scammony, 125 barrels eels, and 1,636 packages sundries. Valonia does not figure amongst the exports, but large quantities grow on the mountains around Alexandretta, and, if prepared and shipped with due care, would prove a valuable export to Great Britain.

CHAPTER XXXV.

TRIPOLI.

THE district of Tripoli extends from Heri on the one side, to the end of Safita, or the village of Der-Terreen, on the other, its greatest length being a distance of twenty hours' journey. The breadth, from the sea, at the Marina, to the end of Jebel-Nerbeen in the district of Daniyé, is about thirteen hours' journey. It contains a population of 120,000 souls, of whom the greater part are Christians, either Maronites, Greeks, or Greek Catholics; the next, according to number, are the Ansayrians, and then the Mussulmans, Metawâlis, and Jews.

Tripoli is well watered by numerous rivers, and is said to be one of the best cultivated districts in the Turkish Empire. It produces grain, silk, olives, mulberries, oranges, lemons, and almost all the fruit trees of Europe. Oranges alone are exported to other parts of Syria, &c., to the amount of 15,000*l.* a year. The produce of oil amounts to 55,000 kollés, of which 15,000 are consumed in the country itself.* That of silk is about 15,000 okes, the greater part of which is exported, and corn, &c., is produced to the amount of

---
* The kollé is 25 okes and $\frac{448}{}$.

340,000 shumbuls, of which 240,000 shumbuls are shipped to other parts of Syria, or to Europe.

Not including the oranges (before mentioned), Tripoli also produces 1,500,000 piastres worth of fruit, and 1,000,000 piastres worth of other vegetable produce. The former is chiefly exported to other parts of Syria, as also to Greece and Constantinople.

The town of Tripoli is situated on the River Kadisha, which divides it into two parts. That on the left bank is flat, while the right bank is much elevated. It is well built for an eastern town, the streets being generally wider and straighter than is usual in Turkey, and the houses possess the advantage of having always a constant supply of good water, which is found even up to the second floor. There are (including the Marina) about 4,128 houses, 12 mosques, 3 Greek churches, 4 Latin churches, 1 Maronite church, and 1 synagogue. There are also 10 khans, 10 baths, and 13 cafés. The population is estimated at 18,100, viz., 13,000 Mussulmans, 4,700 Greeks, 300 Maronites, and 100 Jews.

The port of Tripoli (Marina, or the Mina, as the natives call it) is the best on the coast of Syria, after Alexandretta. It is sheltered by several islands (the Isle of Palms, &c.) from the south-west winds, and only open to those from the north-west, which, however, very seldom blow. It is the sea-port for the most fertile countries of the Ottoman Empire, namely, the provinces of Hamah, Homs, and the Bekàa, but, unfortunately, the roads communicating with these interior provinces are, as usual throughout Turkey, very indifferent. The road from Tripoli to Homs runs along a broad valley between the northern and southern chains of Lebanon; and were it sufficiently improved to admit of the introduction of wagons, instead of the primitive mode of conveyance at present existing (camels, mules, &c.), the exports, and, as a natural consequence, the imports, would be enormously increased.

The following Tables give the imports and exports for the year 1857 :—

THE RESOURCES OF TURKEY.

Specification and Value of Imports at the Port of Tripoli in the year 1857.

Names of Articles.	From Great Britain.	From Turkey.	From France.	From Egypt.	Total Value in Francs.
	Francs.	Francs.	Francs.	Francs.	Francs.
Cotton manufactures	1,200,000	36,000	. . .	. . .	1,236,000
Cloths	. . .	60,000	50,000	. . .	110,000
Corn, &c.	. . .	45,000	. . .	. . .	45,000
Coffee	. . .	. . .	30,000	15,000	45,000
Fruits	. . .	5,000	. . .	. . .	5,000
Iron	. . .	. . .	50,000	. . .	50,000
Leather	. . .	. . .	. . .	200,000	200,000
Rice	. . .	. . .	. . .	175,000	175,000
Salt	. . .	22,000	. . .	. . .	22,000
Soda	. . .	. . .	50,000	150,000	200,000
Sugar	. . .	. . .	40,000	. . .	40,000
Wood	. . .	96,400	. . .	. . .	96,400
Sundries	. . .	88,000	400,000	50,000	538,000
Total	1,200,000	352,400	620,000	590,000	2,762,400

Specification and Value of Exports at the Port of Tripoli in the year 1857.

Names of Articles.	To Great Britain.	To Turkey.	To France.	To Egypt.	To Greece.	To Italy.	Total Value in Francs.
	Francs.	Francs.	Francs.	Francs.	Francs.	Francs.	Francs.
Corn, &c.	80,000	91,000	80,000	.	.	42,000	293,000
Castor oil nuts	107,000	.	.	.	.	.	107,000
Madder	100,000	100,000	.	.	.	.	200,000
Flour	.	200,000	.	.	.	.	200,000
Fruits	.	120,000	.	.	.	.	120,000
Manufactured goods	.	140,000	.	140,000	.	.	280,000
Sponges	.	10,000	270,000	.	10,000	10,000	300,000
Silk	.	405,000	.	1,800,000	.	.	2,205,000
Soap	.	130,000	.	120,000	.	.	250,000
Soda	.	410,000	.	.	.	.	410,000
Tobacco	.	.	.	130,000	.	.	130,000
Wool	.	100,000	18,000	.	.	16,000	134,000
Sundries	.	109,000	10,000	120,000	.	.	239,000
Total	287,000	1,815,000	378,000	2,310,000	10,000	68,000	4,868,000

CHAPTER XXXVI.

LATAKIA.

LATAKIA is an agricultural district, and, from the richness and fertility of its soil, sustains by its produce not only its own population, but, in favourable years, exports a large quantity of grain. The mode of culture and the implements in use are, however, of the most primitive description, and one-half of the best ground for cereal crops is uncultivated. The present farmers are too poor to provide working cattle, implements, and seed, and are accustomed to look to the richer class for advances with which to provide all these requisites, while they furnish the necessary labour, and give to him who makes the advance one-half or three-fourths in kind of the entire produce.

The chief produce of the mountainous part of the district is tobacco, of which large quantities are exported; that grown in the district of Djebail being considered the best. When this has been hung up in the rooms of the peasants, and there allowed to absorb the smoke of the dwarf oak, it acquires a delightful perfume, and is then called *Abu Richa*, or Father of Scent. The peculiar property which this tobacco derives from being exposed to the smoke was accidentally discovered as follows:—One year, there being no demand for tobacco, the leaves were hung up for the winter in the peasants' huts, exposed to the continual smoke of their fires, and the succeeding year it was sent to Egypt, where it was considered so good, that a large order was sent to Latakia for more of the same quality, which was then called *Abu Richa*.

The produce of the low country consists chiefly of wheat, barley, millet, sesame, silk and cotton, for export; olive-oil and figs, for home use and occasional export; while nut-galls, wax, and cochineal can be had for the gathering. It is almost needless to add, that with the introduction of capital and the use of improved agricultural implements, all the products of the soil could be increased to a considerable extent.

A very profitable branch of industry is the making of earthen jars, both for water, as well as for the stowage of winter family necessaries, such as corn, flour, butter, oil, &c., and large quantities, especially those of very great size, are annually exported.

Another source of considerable gain is to be found in the sponge fishing on the coasts; in which severe but successful commercial pursuit a small fleet of boats, of from fifteen to twenty tons, manned each by six or ten hands, including the divers, are daily occupied.

The port of Latakia was formerly a very large and safe one, capable of containing a thousand galleys, but it now requires considerable clearing and improvement. It could, with a little expense, be made an excellent harbour for both steamers and sailing vessels, as the holding-ground is trustworthy, the entrance favourably situated, and it is well sheltered by closely surrounding hills.

The population of Latakia and its district, in 1856, was as follows:—

Greeks	75,000
Mussulmans	46,000
Ismaïlines	10,000
Maronites	1,000
Armenians	500
	132,500

APPENDICES.

APPENDICES.

APPENDIX I.

Convention of Commerce and Navigation between Her Britannic Majesty and the Sultan of the Ottoman Empire. Signed at Balta-Liman, near Constantinople, August 16, 1838.

During the friendly intercourse which has happily subsisted so long between the Sublime Porte and the Kings of Great Britain, capitulations granted by the Porte, and treaties concluded between the two Powers, have regulated the rates of duties payable on merchandise exported from and imported into the dominions of the Sublime Porte, and have established and declared the rights, privileges, immunities and obligations of British merchants trading to or residing in the Imperial territories. But since the period when the abovementioned stipulations were last revised, changes of various kinds have happened in the internal administration of the Ottoman Empire, and in the external relations of that empire with other powers; and Her Majesty the Queen of the United Kingdom of Great Britain and Ireland, and His Highness the Sultan, have therefore agreed now to regulate again, by a special and additional Act, the commercial intercourse of their subjects, in order to increase the trade between their respective dominions, and to render more easy the exchange of the produce of the one country for that of the other. They have consequently named for their Plenipotentiaries for this purpose, that is to say:

Her Majesty the Queen of the United Kingdom of Great Britain and Ireland, the Right Honourable John Brabazon Lord Ponsonby, Baron of Imokilly, a peer of the United Kingdom of Great Britain and Ireland, Knight Grand Cross of the Most Honourable Order of the Bath, of the *Nishan* of Honour, &c., &c., Her Majesty's Ambassador Extraordinary and Plenipotentiary at the Sublime Porte, &c., &c.;

And His Highness the Sultan, the most Illustrious and most Excellent Vizier Mustapha Reshid Pasha, Minister for Foreign Affairs, bearing the decoration belonging to his high rank, a Knight Grand Cross of the Legion of Honour of France, &c., &c.; the Excellent and most Distinguished Mustapha Kiani Bey, a member of the Supreme Council of State, Assistant to the Prime Minister, President of the Council of Agriculture and Industry, a Minister of State of the First Class, bearing the two decorations belonging to his offices, &c., &c.; and the Excellent and most Distinguished Mehemed Nouri Effendi, a Councillor of State in the department for Foreign Affairs, bearing the *Nishan* of Honour of the First Class, &c., &c.;

Who, after having communicated their respective full powers, found to be in due and proper form, have agreed upon and concluded the following Articles:—

Art. 1. All rights, privileges, and immunities which have been conferred on the subjects and ships of Great Britain by the existing capitulations and treaties, are confirmed now and for ever, except in as far as they may be specifically altered by the present Convention: and it is moreover expressly stipulated, that all rights, privileges, or immunities which the Sublime Porte now grants, or may hereafter grant, to the ships and subjects of any other foreign Power, or which it may suffer the ships and subjects of any other foreign Power to enjoy, shall be equally granted to, and exercised and enjoyed by, the subjects and ships of Great Britain.

Art. 2. The subjects of Her Britannic Majesty, or their agents, shall be permitted to purchase at all places in the Ottoman dominions (whether for the purposes of internal trade or exportation) all articles, without any exception whatsoever, the produce, growth, or manufacture of the said dominions; and the Sublime Porte formally engages to abolish all monopolies of agricultural produce, or of any other articles whatsoever, as well as all *permits* from the local governors, either for the purchase of any article, or for its removal from one place to another when purchased; and any attempt to compel the subjects of Her Britannic Majesty to receive such *permits* from the local governors shall be considered as an infraction of treaties, and the Sublime Porte shall immediately punish with severity any viziers and other officers who shall have been guilty of such misconduct, and render full justice to British subjects for all injuries or losses which they may duly prove themselves to have suffered.

Art. 3. If any article of Turkish produce, growth, or manufacture be purchased by the British merchant or his agent for the purpose of selling the same for internal consumption in Turkey, the British merchant or his agent shall pay, at the purchase and sale of such articles, and in any manner of trade therein, the same duties that are paid, in similar circumstances, by the most favoured class of Turkish subjects engaged in the internal trade of Turkey, whether Mussulmans or Rayahs.

Art. 4. If any article of Turkish produce, growth, or manufacture be purchased for exportation, the same shall be conveyed by the British merchant or his agent, free of any kind of charge or duty whatever, to a convenient place of shipment, on its entry into which it shall be liable to one fixed duty of 9 per cent. *ad valorem*, in lieu of all other interior duties.

Subsequently, on exportation, the duty of 3 per cent., as established and existing at present, shall be paid. But all articles bought in the shipping ports for exportation, and which have already paid the interior duty at entering into the same, will only pay the 3 per cent. export duty.

Art. 5. The regulations under which firmans are issued to British merchant vessels for passing the Dardanelles and the Bosphorus, shall be so framed as to occasion to such vessels the least possible delay.

Art. 6. It is agreed by the Turkish Government, that the regulations established in the present Convention shall be general throughout the Turkish Empire, whether Turkey in Europe or Turkey in Asia, in Egypt, or other African possessions belonging to the Sublime Porte, and shall be applicable to all the subjects, whatever their description, of the Ottoman dominions: and the Turkish Government also agrees not to object to other foreign powers settling their trade upon the basis of this present Convention.

Art. 7. It having been the custom of Great Britain and the Sublime Porte, with a view to prevent all difficulties and delays in estimating the value of articles imported into the Turkish dominions, or exported therefrom, by British subjects, to appoint, at intervals of 14 years, a commission of men well acquainted with the traffic of both countries, who have fixed by a tariff the sum of money in the coin of the Grand Signior which should be paid as duty on each article; and the term of 14 years, during which the last adjustment of the said tariff was to remain in force, having expired, the high contracting parties have agreed to name conjointly fresh Commissioners to fix and determine the amount in money which is to be paid by British subjects, as the duty of 3 per cent. upon the value of all commodities imported and exported by them; and the said Commissioners shall establish an equitable arrangement for estimating the interior duties which, by the present Treaty, are established on Turkish goods to be exported, and shall also determine on the places of shipment where it may be most convenient that such duties should be levied.

The new tariff thus established to be in force for seven years after it has been fixed, at the end of which time it shall be in the power of either of the parties to demand a revision of that tariff; but if no such demand be made on either side within the six months after the end of the first seven years, then the tariff shall remain in force for seven years more, reckoned from the end of the preceding seven years; and so it shall be at the end of each successive period of seven years.

Art. 8. The present Convention shall be ratified, and the ratifications shall be exchanged at Constantinople, within the space of four months.

In witness whereof the respective Plenipotentiaries have signed the same, and have affixed their seals thereunto.

Done at Balta-Liman, near Constantinople, on the 16th day of August, 1838.

(Signed)

(L.S.) PONSONBY.   (L.S.) MUSTAPHA RESHID,
                                  (L.S.) MUSTAPHA KIANI,
                                  (L.S.) MEHEMED NOURI.

APPENDIX II.

Hatti-Humáyoun du 18 *Février* 1856.

À vous, mon grand vizir Méhémed-Emin-A'ali-Pasha; que Dieu vous accorde la grandeur et double votre pouvoir.

Mon désir le plus cher a toujours été d'assurer le bonheur de toutes les classes de mes sujets que la divine Providence a placés sous mon sceptre impérial, et, depuis mon avènement au trône, je n'ai cessé de faire tous mes efforts dans ce sens. Grâces en soient rendues au Tout-Puissant! Ces efforts incessants ont déjà porté des fruits utiles et nombreux. De jour en jour, le bonheur de la nation et la richesse de mes États vont en augmentant. Désirant aujourd'hui renouveler et élargir encore les règlements nouveaux, institués en vue d'arriver à obtenir un état de choses conforme à la dignité de mon empire et à la position qu'il occupe parmi les nations civilisées, et les droits de mon empire ayant aujourd'hui, par la fidélité et les louables efforts de tous mes sujets, et par le concours bienveillant et amical des grandes puissances, mes nobles alliées, reçu de l'extérieur une consécration qui doit être le commencement d'une ère nouvelle, je veux augmenter le bien-être et la prospérité intérieure, rendre heureux tous mes sujets, qui sont tous égaux à mes yeux et me sont également chers, et qui sont unis entre eux par des rapports cordiaux de patriotisme, et assurer les moyens de faire, de jour en jour, croître la prospérité de mon empire.

J'ai donc résolu et j'ordonne la mise à exécution des mesures suivantes:

1. Les garanties promises de notre part à tous les sujets de

mon empire par le *Hatti-Humáyoun* de Gulhané et les lois du Tanzimat, sans distinction de classe ni de culte, pour la sécurité de leurs personnes et de leurs biens, et pour la conservation de leur honneur, sont aujourd'hui confirmées et consolidées, et des mesures efficaces seront prises pour qu'elles reçoivent leur plein et entier effet.

2. Tous les priviléges et immunités spirituels accordés *ab antiquo*, et à des dates postérieures, à toutes les communautés chrétiennes ou à d'autres rites non musulmans dans mon empire, sous mon égide protectrice, sont confirmés et maintenus.

3. Chaque communauté chrétienne ou d'autres rites non musulmans sera tenue, dans un délai fixe, et avec le concours d'une commission formée *ad hoc* dans son sein, de procéder avec ma haute approbation, et sous la surveillance de ma Sublime-Porte, à l'examen de ses immunités et priviléges, et d'y discuter et soumettre à ma Sublime-Porte des réformes exigées par le progrès des lumières et des temps. Les pouvoirs concédés aux patriarches et aux évêques des rites chrétiens, par le sultan Mahomet II et ses successeurs, seront mis en harmonie avec la position nouvelle que mes intentions généreuses et bienveillantes assurent à ces communautés. Le principe de la nomination à vie des patriarches, après la révision des règlements d'élection aujourd'hui en vigueur, sera exactement appliqué, conformément à la teneur de leurs firmans d'investiture. Les patriarches, les métropolitains, archevêques, évêques et rabbins, seront assermentés à leur entrée en fonctions, d'après une formule concertée en commun entre ma Sublime-Porte et les chefs spirituels des diverses communautés. Les redevances ecclésiastiques, de quelque forme et nature qu'elles soient, seront supprimées et remplacées par la fixation des revenus des patriarches et chefs des communautés, et par l'allocation de traitements et de salaires équitablement proportionnés à l'importance, au rang et à la dignité des divers membres du clergé. Il ne sera porté aucune atteinte aux propriétés mobilières et immobilières des divers clergés chrétiens; toutefois, l'administration temporelle des communautés chrétiennes, ou d'autres rites non musulmans, sera placée sous la sauvegarde d'une assemblée choisie dans

le sein de chacune desdites communautés parmi les membres du clergé et les laïques.

4. Dans les villes, bourgades et villages où la population appartiendra en totalité au même culte, il ne sera apportée aucune entrave à la réparation, *d'après les plans primitifs*, des édifices destinés au culte, aux écoles, aux hôpitaux et aux cimetières. Les plans de ces divers édifices, en cas d'érection nouvelle, approuvés par les patriarches ou chefs des communautés, devront être soumis à ma Sublime-Porte, qui les approuvera par mon ordre impérial, ou fera ses observations dans un délai déterminé. Chaque culte, dans les localités où ne se trouveront point d'autres confessions religieuses, ne sera soumis à aucune espèce de restriction dans la manifestation publique de sa religion. Dans les villes, bourgades et villages où les cultes sont mélangés, chaque communauté, habitant un quartier distinct, pourra également, en se conformant aux prescriptions ci-dessus indiquées, réparer et consolider ses églises, ses hôpitaux, ses écoles et ses cimetières. Lorsqu'il s'agira de la construction d'édifices nouveaux, l'autorisation nécessaire sera demandée, par l'organe des patriarches ou chefs des communautés, à ma Sublime-Porte, qui prendra une décision souveraine, en accordant cette autorisation, *à moins d'obstacles administratifs*. L'intervention de l'autorité administrative dans tous les actes de cette nature sera entièrement gratuite. Ma Sublime-Porte prendra des mesures pour assurer à chaque culte, quel que soit le nombre des adhérents, la pleine liberté de son exercice.

5. Toute distinction ou appellation tendant à rendre une classe quelconque des sujets de mon empire inférieure à une autre classe, à raison du culte, de la langue ou de la race, sera à jamais effacée du protocole administratif. Les lois séviront contre l'emploi, entre particuliers ou de la part des autorités, de toute qualification injurieuse ou blessante.

6. Vu que tous les cultes sont et seront librement pratiqués dans mes États, aucun sujet de mon empire ne sera gêné dans l'exercice de la religion qu'il professe, et ne sera d'aucune manière inquiété à cet égard. Personne ne pourra être contraint à changer de religion.

7. La nomination et le choix de tous les fonctionnaires et autres employés de mon empire étant entièrement dépendants

de ma volonté souveraine, tous les sujets de mon empire, sans distinction de nationalité, seront admissibles aux emplois publics et aptes à les occuper selon leurs capacités et leur mérite, et conformément à des règles d'une application générale.

8. Tous les sujets de mon empire seront indistinctement reçus dans les écoles civiles et militaires du Gouvernement, s'ils remplissent d'ailleurs les conditions d'âge et d'examens spécifiées dans les règlements organiques desdites écoles. De plus, chaque communauté est autorisée à établir des écoles publiques de sciences, d'arts et d'industrie. Seulement, le mode d'enseignement et le choix des professeurs dans les écoles de cette catégorie seront sous le contrôle d'un conseil mixte d'instruction publique, dont les membres seront nommés par un ordre souverain de ma part.

9. Toutes les affaires commerciales, correctionnelles et criminelles, entre des musulmans et des sujets chrétiens ou d'autres rites non musulmans, ou entre chrétiens et autres sujets de rites différents, seront déférées à des tribunaux mixtes. L'audience de ces tribunaux sera publique; les parties seront mises en présence et produiront leurs témoins, dont les dépositions seront reçues indistinctement sous un serment prêté selon la loi religieuse de chaque culte. Les procès ayant trait aux affaires civiles continueront d'être jugés publiquement, d'après les lois et les règlements, par-devant les conseils mixtes des provinces, en présence du gouverneur et du juge du lieu.

10. Les procès civils spéciaux, comme ceux de successions ou autres de ce genre, entre les sujets d'un même rite chrétien ou autre non musulman, pourront, à leur demande, être envoyés par-devant les conseils des patriarches ou des communautés.

11. Les lois pénales, correctionnelles et commerciales, et les règles de procédure à appliquer dans les tribunaux mixtes, seront complétées le plus tôt possible et codifiées. Il en sera publié des traductions dans toutes les langues en usage dans mon empire.

12. Il sera procédé, dans le plus bref délai possible, à la réforme du système pénitentiaire dans son application aux maisons de détention, de punition ou de correction et autres

établissements de même nature, afin de concilier les droits de l'humanité avec ceux de la justice. Aucune peine corporelle, même dans les prisons, ne pourra être appliquée que conformément à des règlements disciplinaires émanés de ma Sublime-Porte, et tout ce qui ressemblerait à la torture sera radicalement aboli. Les infractions à ce sujet seront sévèrement réprimées, et entraîneront, en outre, de plein droit, la punition, en conformité du code criminel, des autorités qui les auraient commises.

13. L'organisation de la police dans la capitale, dans les villes de province et dans les campagnes, sera revisée de façon à donner à tous les sujets paisibles de mon empire les garanties désirables de sécurité quant à leurs personnes et à leurs biens.

14. L'égalité des impôts entraînant l'égalité des charges, comme celle des devoirs entraîne celle des droits, les sujets chrétiens et des autres rites non musulmans devront, ainsi qu'il l'a été antérieurement résolu, aussi bien que les musulmans, satisfaire aux obligations de la loi de recrutement. Le principe du remplacement ou du rachat sera admis.

15. Il sera publié, dans le plus bref délai possible, une loi complète sur le mode d'admission et de service des sujets chrétiens et d'autres rites non musulmans dans l'armée.

16. Il sera procédé à une réforme dans la composition des conseils provinciaux et communaux, pour garantir la sincérité des choix des délégués des communautés musulmanes, chrétiennes et autres non musulmanes, ainsi que la liberté des votes dans les conseils. Ma Sublime-Porte avisera à l'emploi des moyens les plus efficaces de connaître exactement et de contrôler le résultat des délibérations et des décisions prises.

17. Comme les lois qui régissent l'achat, la vente et la disposition des propriétés immobilières sont communes à tous les sujets de mon empire, il pourra être permis aux étrangers de posséder des propriétés foncières dans mes États, en se conformant aux lois et aux règlements de police, en acquittant les mêmes charges que les indigènes, et après que des arrangements auront eu lieu avec les puissances étrangères.

18. Les impôts sont exigibles au même titre de tous les sujets de mon empire, sans distinction de classe ni de culte. On avisera aux moyens les plus prompts et les plus énergiques

de corriger les abus dans la perception des impôts, et notamment des dîmes. Le système de la perception directe sera successivement, et aussi-tôt que faire se pourra, substitué au régime des fermes dans toutes les branches des revenus de l'État. Tant que ce système demeurera en vigueur, il sera interdit, sous les peines les plus sévères, à tous les agents de l'autorité et à tous les membres des *medjlis* de se rendre adjudicataires des fermes qui seront annoncées avec publicité et concurrence, ou d'avoir une part quelconque d'intérêt dans l'exploitation de ces fermes. Les impositions locales seront, autant que possible, calculées de façon à ne pas affecter les sources de la production, comme à ne pas entraver le mouvement du commerce intérieur.

19. Les travaux d'utilité publique recevront une dotation convenable, à laquelle concourront les impositions particulières et spéciales des provinces appelées à jouir de l'établissement des voies de communication par terre et par mer.

20. Une loi spéciale ayant déjà été rendue, qui ordonne que le budget des recettes et des dépenses de l'État soit fixé et communiqué chaque année, cette loi sera observée de la manière la plus scrupuleuse. On procédera à la révision des traitements affectés à chaque emploi.

21. Les chefs et un délégué de chaque communauté désignés par ma Sublime-Porte seront appelés à prendre part aux délibérations du conseil suprême de justice dans toutes les circonstances qui intéresseraient la généralité des sujets de mon empire. Ils seront spécialement convoqués à cet effet par mon grand vizir.

22. Le mandat des délégués sera annuel. Ils prêteront serment en entrant en charge. Tous les membres du conseil, dans les réunions ordinaires et extraordinaires, émettront librement leur avis et leur vote, sans qu'on puisse jamais les inquiéter à ce sujet.

23. Les lois contre la corruption, la concussion ou la malversation, seront appliquées, d'après les formes légales, à tous les sujets de mon empire, quelles que soient leur classe et la nature de leurs fonctions.

24. On s'occupera de la création de banques et d'autres institutions semblables, pour arriver à la réforme du système monétaire et financier, ainsi que de la création de fonds

destinés à augmenter les sources de la richesse matérielle de mon empire.

25. On s'occupera également de l'établissement de routes et de canaux, qui rendront les communications plus faciles et augmenteront les sources de la richesse du pays. On abolira tout ce qui peut entraver le commerce et l'agriculture. Pour arriver à ces buts, on recherchera les moyens de mettre à profit les sciences, les arts et les capitaux de l'Europe, et de les mettre ainsi successivement en exécution.

Tels étant mes volontés et mes ordres, vous, qui êtes mon grand vizir, vous ferez, suivant l'usage, publier, soit dans ma capitale, soit dans toutes les parties de mon empire, ce firman impérial, et vous veillerez avec attention et prendrez toutes les mesures nécessaires afin que tous les ordres qu'il contient soient dorénavant exécutés avec la plus rigoureuse ponctualité.

APPENDIX III.

Commercial Treaty between Her Britannic Majesty and the Sultan of the Ottoman Empire. Signed at Kanlidja, near Constantinople, April 29, 1861.

Article 1. All rights, privileges, and immunities which have been conferred on the subjects or ships of Great Britain by the existing capitulations or treaties, are confirmed now and for ever, with the exception of those clauses of the said capitulations which it is the object of the present treaty to modify; and it is, moreover, expressly stipulated that all rights, privileges, and immunities which the Sublime Porte now grants or may hereafter grant to, or suffer to be enjoyed by, the subjects, ships, commerce, or navigation of any other foreign power, shall be equally granted to, and exercised and enjoyed by, the subjects, ships, commerce, and navigation of Great Britain.

Art. 2. The subjects of Her Britannic Majesty, or their agents, shall be permitted to purchase, at all places in the Ottoman dominions and possessions (whether for the purpose of internal trade or of exportation) all articles, without any exception whatsoever, the produce or manufacture of said dominions and possessions; and the Sublime Porte having, in virtue of the second article of the convention of commerce of the 16th of August, 1838, formally engaged to abolish all monopolies of agricultural produce or of any other article whatsoever, as well as all permits (*teskeres*) from the local governors, either for the purchase of any article, or for its removal from one place to another when purchased, any attempt to compel the subjects of Her Britannic Majesty to receive such permits from the local governors shall be considered as an infraction of treaties, and the Sublime Porte shall immediately punish with severity any viziers or other officers who shall have been guilty of such misconduct, and shall render full justice to British subjects for all injuries or losses which they may duly prove themselves to have suffered thereby.

Art. 3. If any article of Turkish produce or manufacture be purchased by British merchants or their agents, for the purpose of selling the same for internal consumption in Turkey, the said British merchants or their agents shall pay, at the purchase and sales of such articles, and in any manner of trade therein, the same duties that are paid in similar circumstances by the most favoured class of Ottoman subjects, or of foreigners engaged in the internal trade of Turkey.

Art. 4. No other or higher duties or charges shall be imposed in the dominions and possessions of either of the contracting parties, on the exportation of any article to the dominions and possessions of the other, than such as are or may be payable on the exportation of the like article to any other foreign country; nor shall any prohibition be imposed on the exportation of any article from the dominions and possessions of either of the two contracting parties to the dominions and possessions of the other, which shall not equally extend to the exportation of the like article to any other country.

No charge or duty whatsoever will be demanded on any article of Turkish produce or manufacture purchased by British subjects or their agents, either at the place where such article is purchased, or in its transit from that place to the place whence it is exported, at which it will be subject to an export duty not exceeding 8 per cent., calculated on the value at the place of shipment, and payable on exportation; and all articles which shall once have paid this duty shall not again be liable to the same duty, however they may have changed hands, within any part of the Ottoman dominions.

It is furthermore agreed that the duty of 8 per cent. above mentioned will be annually reduced by one (1) per cent., until it shall be in this manner finally reduced to a fixed duty of one (1) per cent. *ad valorem*, destined to cover the general expenses of administration and control.

Art. 5. No other or higher duties shall be imposed on the importation, into the dominions and possessions of Her Britannic Majesty, of any article the produce and manufacture of the dominions and possessions of His Imperial Majesty the Sultan, from whatever place arriving, whether by sea or by land, and no other or higher duties shall be imposed on the importation into the dominions and possessions of His Imperial Majesty of any article the produce or manufacture of Her Britannic Majesty's dominions and possessions, from whatever place arriving, than are or may be payable on the like article the produce or manufacture of any other foreign country; nor shall any prohibition be maintained or imposed on the importation of any article the produce or manufacture of the dominions and possessions of either of the contracting parties into the dominions and possessions of the other, which shall not equally extend to the importation of the like articles being the produce or manufacture of any other country.

His Imperial Majesty further engages that, save as hereinafter excepted, he will not prohibit the importation into his dominions and possessions of any article the produce or manufacture of the dominions and possessions of Her Britannic Majesty, from whatever place arriving; and that the duties to be imposed on any article the produce or manufacture of the dominions or possessions of Her Britannic Majesty, imported into the dominions or possessions of His Imperial Majesty, shall in no case exceed one fixed rate of eight (8) per cent. *ad valorem*, or a specific duty, fixed by common assent, equivalent thereto.

Such rate shall be calculated upon the value of such articles at the wharf, and shall be payable at the time of their being landed, if brought by sea, or at the first custom-house they may reach, if brought by land.

If these articles, after having paid the import duty of eight (8) per cent., are sold at the place of their arrival or in the interior of the country, neither the buyer nor the seller shall be charged with any further duty with respect to them; and if such articles should not be sold for consumption in Turkey, but should be re-exported within the space of six months, the same shall be considered as merchandise in transit by land,

and be treated as is stated in Article 12; the administration of the customs being bound to restore at the time of their re-exportation to the merchant, who shall be required to furnish proof that the goods in question have paid the import duty of eight (8) per cent., the difference between that duty and the duty levied on goods in transit by land, as set forth in the article above cited.

Art. 6. It is understood that any article the produce or manufacture of a foreign country, intended for importation into the United Principalities of Moldo-Wallachia, or into the Principality of Servia, which shall pass through any other part of the Ottoman dominions, will not be liable to the payment of customs' duty until it reaches those principalities; and, on the other hand, that any article of foreign produce or manufacture passing through those principalities, but destined for some other part of the Ottoman dominions, will not be liable to the payment of customs' duty until such article reaches the first custom-house under the direct administration of the Sublime Porte.

The same course shall be followed with respect to any article the produce or manufacture of those principalities, as well as with respect to any article the produce or manufacture of any other portion of the Ottoman dominions, intended for exportation: such articles will be liable to the payment of customs' duties, the former to the custom-house of the aforesaid principalities, and the latter to the Ottoman custom-house, the object being, that neither import nor export duties shall in any case be payable more than once.

Art. 7. The subjects of one of the contracting parties shall enjoy, in the dominions and possessions of the other, equality of treatment with native subjects, in regard to warehousing, and also in regard to bounties, facilities, and drawbacks.

Art. 8. All articles which are or may be legally importable into the dominions and possessions of Her Britannic Majesty, in British vessels, may likewise be imported in Ottoman vessels, without being liable to any other or higher duties or charges of whatever denomination than if such articles were imported in British vessels; and reciprocally all articles which are or may be legally importable into the dominions and possessions of His Imperial Majesty the Sultan, in Ottoman vessels, may likewise be imported in British vessels, without being liable to any other or higher duties or charges of whatever denomination than if such articles were imported in Ottoman vessels. Such reciprocal equality of treatment shall take effect without distinction, whether such articles come directly from the place of origin or from any other country.

In the same manner, there shall be perfect equality of treatment in regard to exportation, so that the same export duties shall be paid, and the same bounties and drawbacks allowed, in the dominions and possessions of either of the contracting parties, on the exportation of any article which may be legally exportable therefrom, whether such exportation shall take place in Ottoman or in British vessels, and whatever may be the place of destination, whether a port of either of the contracting parties or of any third Power.

Art. 9. No duties of tonnage, harbour, pilotage, lighthouse, quarantine or other similar or corresponding duties, of whatever nature, or under whatever denomination, levied in the name or for the profit of Government, public functionaries, private individuals, corporations or establishments of any kind, shall be imposed in the ports of the dominions and possessions of either country, upon the vessels of the other country, which shall not equally and under the same conditions be imposed in the like cases on national vessels in general. Such equality of treatment shall apply reciprocally to the respective vessels, from whatever port or place they may arrive, and whatever may be their place of destination.

Art. 10. All vessels which according to British law are to be deemed British vessels, and all vessels which according to Ottoman law are to be deemed Ottoman vessels, shall for the purposes of this treaty be deemed British or Ottoman vessels respectively.

Art. 11. No charge whatsoever shall be made upon British goods being the produce or manufacture of British dominions or possessions, whether in British or other ships, nor upon any goods the produce or manufacture of any other foreign country carried in British ships, when the same shall pass through the Straits of the Dardanelles or the Bosphorus, whether such goods shall pass through the Straits in the ships that brought them, or shall have been transhipped to other vessels; or whether, after having been sold for exportation, they shall, for a certain limited time, be landed in order to be placed in other vessels for the continuance of their voyage. In the latter case the goods in question shall be deposited at Constantinople in the magazines of the custom-house, called *transit* magazines; and in any other places where there is no *entrepôt*, they shall be placed under the charge of the Administration of the Customs.

Art. 12. The Sublime Porte desiring to grant by means of gradual concessions all facilities in its power to transit by land, it is stipulated and agreed that the duty of three (3) per cent. levied up to this time on articles imported into Turkey, in their passage through Turkey to other countries, shall be reduced to two (2) per cent. payable, as the duty of three per cent. has been paid hitherto, on arriving in the Ottoman dominions; and at the end of eight years, to be reckoned from the day of the exchange of the ratifications of the present treaty, to a fixed and definite tax of one (1) per cent., which shall be levied, as is to be the case with respect to Turkish produce exported, to defray the expense of registration.

The Sublime Porte at the same time declares that it reserves to itself the right to establish, by a special enactment, the measures to be adopted for the prevention of fraud.

Art. 13. Her Britannic Majesty's subjects, or their agents, trading in goods the produce or manufacture of foreign countries, shall be subject to the same taxes, and enjoy the same rights, privileges, and immunities as foreign subjects dealing in goods the produce or manufacture of their own country.

Art. 14. An exception to the stipulations laid down in the 5th article shall be made in regard to tobacco, in any shape whatsoever, and also in regard to salt, which two articles shall cease to be included among those which the subjects of Her Britannic Majesty are permitted to import into the Ottoman dominions.

British subjects, however, or their agents, buying or selling tobacco or salt for consumption in Turkey, shall be subject to the same regulations, and shall pay the same duties, as the most favoured Ottoman subjects trading in the two articles aforesaid; and furthermore, as a compensation for the prohibition of the two articles above-mentioned, no duty whatsoever shall in future be levied on those articles when exported from Turkey by the subjects of Her Britannic Majesty.

British subjects shall, nevertheless, be bound to declare the quantity of tobacco and salt thus exported to the proper custom-house authorities, who shall, as heretofore, have the right to watch over the export of these articles, without thereby being entitled to levy any tax thereon on any pretence whatsoever.

Art. 15. It is understood between the two high contracting parties, that the Sublime Porte reserves to itself the faculty and right of issuing a general prohibition against the importation into the Ottoman dominions of gunpowder, cannon, arms of war, or military stores; but such prohibition will not come into operation until it shall have been officially notified, and will apply only to the articles mentioned in the decree enacting the prohibition. Any of these articles which have not been so specifically prohibited shall, on being imported into the Ottoman dominions, be subject to the local regulations, unless Her Britannic Majesty's Embassy shall think fit to apply for a special licence, which licence will in that case be granted provided no valid objection thereto can be alleged.

Gunpowder, in particular, when allowed to be imported, will be liable to the following stipulations:—

1st. It shall not be sold by subjects of Her Britannic Majesty in quantities exceeding the quantities prescribed in the local regulations.

2nd. When a cargo or a large quantity of gunpowder arrives in an Ottoman port on board a British vessel, such vessel shall be anchored at a particular spot to be designated by the local authorities, and the gunpowder shall thence be conveyed, under the inspection of such authorities, to depôts or fitting places designated by the Government, to which the parties interested shall have access under due regulations.

Fowling-pieces, pistols, and ornamental or fancy weapons, as also small quantities of gunpowder for sporting, reserved for private use, shall not be subject to the stipulations of the present article.

Art. 16. The firmans required for British merchant vessels,

passing through the Dardanelles and the Bosphorus, shall always be delivered in such manner as to occasion to such vessels the least possible delay.

Art. 17. The captains of British merchant vessels, with goods on board destined for the Ottoman Empire, shall be obliged, immediately on their arrival at the port to which they are bound, to deposit in the custom-house of the said port a true copy of their manifest.

Art. 18. Contraband goods will be liable to confiscation by the Ottoman treasury, but a report or *procès-verbal* of the alleged act of contraband must, as soon as the said goods are seized by the authorities, be drawn up and communicated to the consular authority of the foreign subject to whom the goods said to be contraband shall belong, and no goods can be confiscated as contraband unless the fraud with regard to them shall be duly and legally proved.

Art. 19. All merchandise the produce or manufacture of the Ottoman dominions and possessions, imported into the dominions and possessions of Her Britannic Majesty, shall be treated in the same manner as the like merchandise the produce or manufacture of the most favoured nation.

All rights, privileges, or immunities which are now or may hereafter be granted to, or suffered to be enjoyed by, the subjects, ships, commerce, or navigation of any foreign power in the British dominions or possessions, shall be equally granted to, and exercised and enjoyed by, the subjects, ships, commerce, and navigation of the Ottoman Porte.

Art. 20. The present treaty, when ratified, shall be substituted for the convention concluded between the two high contracting parties on the 16th August, 1838, and shall remain in force twenty-eight years from the day of the exchange of the ratifications; each of the high contracting parties being, however, at liberty to give to the other, at the end of fourteen years (that time being fixed, as the provisions of the treaty will then have come into full force), notice for its revision or for its determination at the expiration of a year from the date of that notice, and so again at the end of twenty-one years.

The present treaty shall receive its execution in all and every one of the provinces of the Ottoman Empire, that is to say, in all the possessions of His Imperial Majesty the Sultan situated in Europe or in Asia, in Egypt, and in the other parts of Africa belonging to the Sublime Porte, in Servia, and in the United Principalities of Moldavia and Wallachia.

The Sublime Porte declares that she is ready to grant, to other foreign powers who may seek to obtain them, the commercial advantages contained in the stipulations of the present treaty.

Art. 21. It is always understood that Her Britannic Majesty does not pretend, by any article in the present treaty, to stipulate for more than the plain and fair construction of the terms employed, nor to preclude in any manner the Ottoman Government from the exercise of its rights of internal administration, where the exercise of those rights does not evidently infringe upon the privileges accorded by ancient treaties, or by the present treaty, to British subjects or British merchandise.

Art. 22. The high contracting parties have agreed to appoint, jointly, commissioners for the settlement of a tariff of custom-house duties, to be levied in conformity with the stipulations of the present treaty, as well upon merchandise of every description, being the produce or manufacture of the British dominions and possessions imported into the Sultan's dominions and possessions, as upon articles of every description the produce or manufacture of the dominions and possessions of the Sultan, which British subjects, or their agents, are free to purchase in any part of the Ottoman dominions and possessions for exportation to Great Britain or to any other country.

The new tariff to be so concluded shall remain in force during seven years, dating from the 1st of October, 1861.

Each of the contracting parties shall have the right, a year before the expiration of that term, to demand the revision of the tariff. But if, during the seventh year, neither the one nor the other of the contracting parties shall avail itself of this right, the tariff then existing shall continue to have the force of law for seven more years, dating from the day of the expiration of the seven preceding years; and the same shall be the case with respect to every successive period of seven years.

Art. 23. The present treaty shall be ratified, and the ratifications shall be exchanged at Constantinople in two calendar months, or sooner if possible, and shall be carried into execution from the 1st of October, 1861.*

Done at Kanlidja, on the 29th day of April, 1861.

    (L.S.)   Henry L. Bulwer.
    (L.S.)   A'ali.

* By a subsequent convention it was agreed that this treaty should not come into operation until the 13th of March, 1862.

THE END.

www.ingramcontent.com/pod-product-compliance
Lightning Source LLC
Chambersburg PA
CBHW032053220426
43664CB00008B/986